AF754585

Venture Capital, Islamic Finance and SMEs

Venture Capital, Islamic Finance and SMEs

Valuation, Structuring and Monitoring Practices in India

Mansoor Durrani and Grahame Boocock

palgrave
macmillan

© Mansoor Durrani and Grahame Boocock 2006

All rights reserved. No reproduction, copy or transmission of this publication may be made without written permission.

No paragraph of this publication may be reproduced, copied or transmitted save with written permission or in accordance with the provisions of the Copyright, Designs and Patents Act 1988, or under the terms of any licence permitting limited copying issued by the Copyright Licensing Agency, 90 Tottenham Court Road, London W1T 4LP.

Any person who does any unauthorized act in relation to this publication may be liable to criminal prosecution and civil claims for damages.

The authors have asserted their rights to be identified as the authors of this work in accordance with the Copyright, Designs and Patents Act 1988.

First published 2006 by
PALGRAVE MACMILLAN
Houndmills, Basingstoke, Hampshire RG21 6XS and
175 Fifth Avenue, New York, N. Y. 10010
Companies and representatives throughout the world

PALGRAVE MACMILLAN is the global academic imprint of the Palgrave Macmillan division of St. Martin's Press, LLC and of Palgrave Macmillan Ltd. Macmillan® is a registered trademark in the United States, United Kingdom and other countries. Palgrave is a registered trademark in the European Union and other countries.

ISBN-13: 978–1–4039–3638–7 hardback
ISBN-10: 1–4039–3638–2 hardback

This book is printed on paper suitable for recycling and made from fully managed and sustained forest sources.

A catalogue record for this book is available from the British Library.

Library of Congress Cataloging-in-Publication Data
Durrani, Mansoor, 1965–
Venture capital, Islamic finance and SMEs : valuation, structuring and monitoring practices in India / Mansoor Durrani and Grahame Boocock.
p. cm.
Includes bibliographical references and index.
ISBN 1–4039–3638–2 (cloth)
1. Venture capital–India. 2. Small business–Finance–India. 3. Finance–Islamic countries. 4. Finance–Religious aspects–Islam. I. Boocock, Grahame, 1952– II. Title.

HG5738.D87 2006
332′.094154′0954–dc22 2005051548

10 9 8 7 6 5 4 3 2 1
15 14 13 12 11 10 09 08 07 06

Printed and bound in Great Britain by
Antony Rowe Ltd, Chippenham and Eastbourne

Success comes only from Allah, the Mighty, the Wise
(Qur'an, 3: 126)

To those who strive to establish a just and fair economic order.

Mansoor Durrani

To Clare, Chris and Alex for their patience and understanding.

Grahame Boocock

Contents

List of Tables

List of Figures

Preface

This book grew out of the PhD studies of Mansoor Durrani, the first doctoral research ever undertaken on the subject of VC in India. Whilst working on his thesis, Mansoor met Grahame Boocock, an academic with longstanding research interests in the areas of risk capital and the financing of small and medium-sized enterprises (SMEs). Grahame had previously spent a year at University Utara Malaysia. This book represents the fruits of their collaboration at Loughborough University, a highly rated University in the East Midlands of England.

Mansoor Durrani would like to acknowledge the assistance provided by the following individuals. Thanks are due to my PhD supervisor Professor John Presley for his invaluable comments and continued guidance throughout my doctoral studies. For Professor Khurshid Ahmad (Chairman, Markfield Institute of Higher Education, UK), I just do not have words to express my gratitude. May Allah reward him for his support, encouragement and guidance. I am also grateful for the contributions of Drs. Umer Chapra and Tariqullah Khan, both of Islamic Development Bank (Jeddah), in shaping Chapter 9.

Both authors wish to acknowledge the valuable contributions of Professor Mike Wright (Director, Centre for Management Buy-out Research: University of Nottingham), and Drs. Dave Coates and Neil Doherty (both lecturers at Loughborough University Business School).

A final debt of thanks should be expressed to members of the Indian venture capital industry who gave generously of their time, despite operating under the pressures of modern business!

Currency Exchange Rates

As at 31/12	US$/Indian Rupee	As at 31/12	UK£/Indian Rupee
1994	31.37	1994	48.27
1995	31.58	1995	48.62
1996	35.60	1996	55.12
1997	35.75	1997	57.49
1998	43.16	1998	69.82
1999	43.42	1999	69.46
2000	45.90	2000	68.79
2001	47.12	2001	68.04
2002	48.55	2002	74.64
2003	45.87	2003	73.11
2004	46.31	2004	84.67

Source: Datastream

Glossary

ACOST	Advisory Council on Science and Technology
ADB	Asian Development Bank
AMT	Advanced Manufacturing Technology
ARD	American Research and Development
AVCJ	Asian Venture Capital Journal
BPO	Business Process Outsourcing
BVCA	British Venture Capital Association
CAGR	Cumulative annual growth rate
CBDT	Central Board of Direct Taxes
CCPPO	Cumulative convertible participating preferred ordinary share
CEO	Chief Executive Officer
CVC	Corporate venture capital
DCF	Discounted cash flow
DFI	Development finance institution
DTI	Department for Trade and Industry
EBIT	Earnings before interest and taxes
EBITDA	Earnings before interest, taxes and/or before depreciation and amortization
EQ	Emotional Quotient
ESOP	Employee Stock Options Programme
EVCA	European Venture Capital Association
FDI	Foreign Direct Investment
GDP	Gross Domestic Product
GEM	Growth Equity Market
HBS	Harvard Business School
HR	Human resources
HRM	Human resources management
ICICI	Industrial Credit and Investment Corporation of India
IDBI	Industrial Development Bank of India
IFCI	Industrial Finance Corporation of India
IP	Intellectual property
IPO	Initial Public Offering
IQ	Intelligence Quotient
IRR	Internal rate of return
IT	Information Technology

ITMT	IT, media and telecommunications
IVCA	Indian Venture Capital Association
KLSE	Kuala Lumpur Stock Exchange
LGS	(Small Firms') Loan Guarantee Scheme
LP	Limited partnership
MBA	Master of Business Administration
MIT	Massachusetts Institute of Technology
MoI	Multiple of investment
NBFC	Non-banking finance company
NEA	New Enterprise Associates
NPL	Non-performing loan
NPV	Net present value
NRI	Non-Resident Indian
NSE	National Stock Exchange (of India)
OECD	Organization for Economic Co-operation and Development
OTCEI	Over The Counter Exchange of India
P&L	Profit and loss
PBUH	Peace be Upon Him
PLS	profit and loss sharing
R&D	Research and development
RBI	Reserve Bank of India
SBA	Small Business Administration
SBRC	Small Business Research Centre (Cambridge University)
SEBI	Securities and Exchange Board of India
SIDBI	Small Industries Development Bank of India
SMEs	Small and medium-sized enterprises
SOE	State-owned enterprise
SPSS	Statistical Package for Social Sciences
SQ	Spiritual Quotient
SSIs	Small scale industries
STPI	Software Technology Parks of India
SVC	Social venture capital
TDICI	Technology Development and Information Company of India
TPIC	Technology Policy Implementation Committee
TQM	Total quality management
TTMM	Two-Tier *Mudarabah* Model
USM	Unlisted Securities Market
UTI	Unit Trust of India
VC	Venture capital
WIIG	Walden International Investment Group

1
Introduction

The book covers two broad areas, the small and medium-sized enterprises (SMEs) sector and the operation of the venture capital (VC) industry, and a third strand examines the potential role of Islamic VC. These topics are considered in the context of India, a nation of many contrasts and enormous economic potential. The book is underpinned by a major study of the VC sector in India. The survey was conducted in the early part of the new Millennium, and the data were supplemented by ongoing dialogue with the VC community in that country. The authors also draw upon a comprehensive literature review, as well as secondary data and information from specialist research institutions and the financial media. The material should be of interest to finance practitioners, policy makers, entrepreneurs and academics.

The structure of the book is now set out briefly. Chapters 2 and 3 describe the contribution and operations of SMEs. The SME sector provides many economic and social benefits, and its contribution is ever more important in an era of rapid technological change. However, it is a misconception to see smaller firms as scaled down versions of their larger counterparts. The sector is characterized by heterogeneity. SMEs face constraints that stem from their size in relation to other market participants. Within the population of small firms, it is acknowledged that only a minority will be 'star performers'. Firms in this category have usually managed to secure external capital hence the characteristics of the financial markets available to small firms are examined. This encompasses the banking sector, as well as a more general assessment of 'equity gaps' affecting SMEs across the world.

The growth and development of many smaller enterprises is constrained by a lack or resources hence it is no surprise that governments choose to assist SMEs. However, the diversity of growth patterns for SMEs, and the variety of barriers faced by such firms, present problems in providing customized assistance for smaller enterprises within a coherent framework of support.

Chapter 4 introduces the concept of VC and traces its history. In modern times, VC was associated first with equity investments in the high-technology sphere. Nowadays, the VC industry covers a host of institutions, and venture capitalists differ in their approach to deal size and sector focus. The formal VC sector (the most high profile within the industry) has switched focus from start-up deals to larger, later-stage investments. A vibrant VC industry supports firms that contribute significantly to wealth creation; venture capitalists provide 'capital and consultancy'. There has been a massive expansion of VC activity from its US base, and the book outlines how governments across the globe have taken steps to encourage the growth of an indigenous VC industry.

Chapter 5 describes the VC investment process as a series of distinct stages then explores the theoretical foundations of VC financing. The key theme is agency theory, with most VC models examining the relationship between VC firm and entrepreneur(s) from the principal-agent perspective. The principal focus for past research studies has been the appraisal criteria adopted by venture capitalists. We concentrate on the valuation, structuring and monitoring of VC deals. These methods of risk mitigation are under-researched areas, and this book fills a gap in existing knowledge, especially for emerging economies.

Chapter 6 presents an overview of Indian economy to set the research programme in context. This fascinating nation has a population of around one billion people, and a land mass of around 3.3m kilometres (over 13 times the size of the UK). The largest cities are Mumbai (formerly Bombay), with 12.6m inhabitants, Kolkata (Calcutta), 11m, New Delhi, 8.4m, and Chennai (Madras), 5.4m. The urban population has expanded steadily since 1960 but over half of the population still lives in villages with fewer than 5,000 people in them, and they depend upon agriculture for a living. The contrasts between rich and poor, urban and rural, modern and traditional, agriculture and IT, and so on have to be borne in mind when considering the economic and financial systems of the nation.

The banking system in India has been subject to a modest programme of reform but Government ownership and control of the largest banking organizations have exacerbated longstanding market imperfections. The nation's capital markets have achieved global standards in trading infrastructure yet offer few opportunities for SMEs to raise capital. The Indian Government has long valued the contribution of SMEs, and Indians have never lacked the spirit of entrepreneurship. The presence of funding gaps has led the authorities to offer preferential financing for SMEs, and firms are directed to appropriate funding bodies through a large network of business support agencies. However, this official support system is not noted for its effectiveness and there is also a striking anomaly at the heart of the Government's assistance for small firms.

The VC industry has operated since the mid-1980s. Its development and current activity is described. The authors suggest that the VC sector in India will, over time, play an even more prominent role in the financial spectrum, especially if the nation secures its status as a global economic powerhouse. Nevertheless, the authors also highlight areas to be addressed before the VC market can fulfil its maximum potential.

Chapter 7 applies the issues identified in the VC literature to the Indian context to formulate a series of research questions in three under-researched areas. The authors investigate a number of propositions, eight in all, covering the valuation, structuring and monitoring of deals. The conclusions are based on the most comprehensive study ever carried out on the VC industry in India. The main research instrument is a questionnaire-based empirical survey.

In Chapter 8, the research findings are presented. The effort and resources required to gather this data should not be underestimated. Barry (1994) states that: 'Empirical research in venture capital is not easy. There are few tapes to spin. Because of that difficulty, comparatively little has been done, and the opportunity to develop results that are novel and important is great'. These comments are especially apposite in a developing nation like India. The high response rate enabled the authors to conduct basic statistical analysis on the data gathered and then to divide the sample on the basis of demographic factors; this approach allowed the authors to utilize more advanced statistical techniques (including cluster analysis and logistical regression) to present a more detailed picture of the operations of different elements of the VC sector.

In Chapter 9, Durrani discusses how business relationships built on a framework of trust and fairness could reduce agency problems and hence the need for corporate governance. This analysis is set in the context of the principles of the Islamic faith. Durrani demonstrates the striking similarities between contemporary venture capital and Islamic Finance, a funding alternative that is growing rapidly throughout the Muslim world. He argues that it is possible to adapt existing Islamic financing structures to VC, and that practitioners in this new field should be able to apply almost all of the conventional valuation, structuring and monitoring techniques.

The conclusions and implications of the research programme are presented in Chapter 10. Taken as a whole, the findings of our research programme, our analysis of the literature and the experience of other countries have a number of implications for policy makers, SMEs/entrepreneurs, VC practitioners, those involved with Islamic finance and academics. The findings are expected to trigger further interest in academic research on the Indian VC industry. We also put forward a series of recommendations for consideration by the authorities in India; these proposals should have relevance for other developing countries.

2
An Introduction to the Small Business Sector

2.1 Introduction

Small and medium-sized enterprises (SMEs) are considered to be an engine for growth in both developed and developing countries; the benefits of a vibrant SME sector include: the creation of employment opportunities; the strengthening of industrial linkages; the promotion of flexibility and innovation; and the generation of export revenues (Mensah, 1996; Harvie and Lee, 2001; Lerner, 2002).

Academics and policy makers have long recognized the significance of this sector, for example, Clay (1932, p.226) argued that, in the British economy: 'not only are the great majority of firms small, but most of the firms that are now large began as small firms'. More recently, most industrialized countries have experienced substantial restructuring of their economies since the early 1980s. This restructuring has been combined with a decline in the manufacturing sector and a corresponding increase in the service sector. Small firms can operate effectively and efficiently within both traditional and emerging industries and hence they occupy a high public profile.

Smaller enterprises are an essential element in the renewal process that characterizes market economies, notably by introducing innovations that lead to technological change and productivity growth. One of the principal reasons for the increased importance of the SME sector is its ability to respond rapidly to change, especially as the pace of technological change grows ever quicker. There is also growing recognition of the role that SMEs can play in wider social and economic restructuring (Smallbone and Welter, 2001).

Small businesses have given millions of individuals across the world a chance of economic opportunity and upward mobility. In India, for example, SMEs are not only seen as potentially a key engine for economic growth and job creation, but also as playing a crucial role in poverty reduction (www.worldbank.org); likewise, the Government in Pakistan accords high priority to the development of micro, small and medium-sized enterprises because such firms can increase incomes and reduce poverty (www.adb.org). Chinese SMEs have flourished as ideological barriers have fallen; a hostile political atmosphere restricted the growth of entrepreneurial firms up until the early 1990s yet SMEs are now recognized by the authorities as an important element in securing social stability.

In order to capture the economic and social benefits described above, virtually all governments offer soft business support to this sector (Wren and Storey, 2002) and there has also been increasing utilization of more traditional forms of hard support, notably credit guarantee schemes (Levitsky, 1997) and support for venture capital (Lerner, 1999; Karsai et al., 1998).

SMEs are most frequently defined in relation to employment. The latest Department of Trade and Industry (UK) and EU definitions refer to an SME as having fewer than 250 employees, with sub-categories of 'micro' firms (0–9 staff), 'small' firms (10–49) and medium-sized firms (50–249). The vast majority of UK firms, over 99 per cent of a total population of 4.0m, employ fewer than 50 people and nearly 2.9m are sole traders (Small Business Service, 2004). Other quantitative definitions of 'small', 'medium' and 'large' firms can be quite complex, classifying firms in relation to shareholders' funds or turnover bands. Any definitions based on financial indicators obviously need to be updated regularly to take account of inflation.

Some researchers have attempted to classify firms by utilizing qualitative definitions. The Bolton Report (1971), for example, defined small firms as having a relatively small share of the market, and being managed in a relatively personalized way with no formal management structure. The use of the term 'relatively' points to the difficulty of adopting such qualitative definitions in practice. Nonetheless, it is generally accepted that the typical business experience of smaller enterprises is quantitatively and qualitatively different from that of large organizations.

This chapter explores how SMEs can benefit economies in terms of creating employment opportunities, promoting flexibility and innovation, and increasing international activity. It then explores the characteristics of SMEs, especially the differences between large and smaller enterprises in the organization of their operations, and summarizes the features of successful and unsuccessful firms.

2.2 The benefits of SMEs

2.2.1 SMEs: employment opportunities

Across the globe, smaller enterprises dominate the profile of businesses in national economies. In the US, SMEs represent over 99 per cent of all firms, creating two out of every three jobs, and accounting for 39 per cent of GNP (SBA, 1999). Small businesses account for approximately 97 per cent of all private sector businesses and 51 per cent of private sector employment in Australia (Wijewardena and Tibbits, 1999); the corresponding figures for New Zealand are 99 per cent and 60 per cent respectively (McGregor and Gomes, 1999). In Korea, more than 70 per cent of the workforce is employed in small and medium-sized firms (Rho and Whybark, 1990). The statistics are similar for nations that might not be expected to have vibrant SME sectors. In Pakistan, there are over 400,000 SMEs and they employ 80 per cent of the industrial labour force, and are responsible for 40 per cent of GDP. The growing significance of SMEs in the economy of China is hard to ignore; it is estimated that SMEs now account for about 60 per cent of industrial output and employ around 75 per cent of the workforce in cities and towns. In short, the contribution of smaller enterprises to employment and output is both consistent and consistently staggering!

However, the link between SMEs and employment has been the subject of much debate. Birch (1979) claimed that over two-thirds of net new jobs created in the US between 1969 and 1976 were in firms employing fewer than 20 staff. The assumptions and conclusions in this study have been questioned and it has not been possible to replicate the findings elsewhere. There is no doubt that small firms create employment opportunities, but it is not easy to draw any universal conclusions in a sector characterized by such diversity. The SME sector encompasses, for example, a part-time business with no employees in Indonesia and a semiconductor manufacturer employing a significant number of people in China (Hall, 2001).

One striking trend is the prevalence of very small or micro firms in economies across the world. This concentration stems from push factors such as unemployment, as well as structural changes in the global economy, especially growth in the service sector and among knowledge-based firms. The vast majority of very small firms will be engaged solely in a struggle for survival, and the jobs created will often be of low quality and short-lived. Many of these firms will not survive, and they will be gathered up in the huge numbers of start-ups and failures (the 'churn') that characterize the population of micro enterprises.

Others will generate jobs by moving from (say) five to ten employees – this cohort of 'modest' growers can have a marked impact on the employment figures.

At the other extreme, a relatively small group of high-growth firms can generate significant and sustainable employment. It has been suggested that only three or four of every 100 new firm starts will be major job creators (Storey, 1994). In the context of this book, these are the type of firms that venture capitalists aim to support, especially where they are engaged in innovative activity.

2.2.2 SMEs: flexibility and innovation

The cornerstone of a competitive industrial society is the emergence of new ventures. Without new entrants, any economy is destined for long-term decline. Indeed, Hoffman (1972) suggests that a critical determinant for the sustained development of a region is the creation of conditions conducive to new company formation and growth. However, it is innovative companies that raise the threshold of technology, thus creating the potential for increased productivity (Huntsman and Hoban, 1980).

The US Commerce Department found that 95 per cent of all radical innovations since World War II stemmed from new, small companies (Bygrave and Timmons, 1992); smaller enterprises in the US have generally been more effective contributors than large and established players in enhancing innovation and productivity (Wetzel, 1982; Almus and Nerlinger, 1999). Nonetheless, it is important to keep a sense of perspective here; innovation will stem from large firms in industries that are capital-intensive and dominated by a small number of big players. Industries in the earlier stages of the product life cycle leave much more room for innovative activity by smaller enterprises.

The definition of 'innovation' is problematic. According to one study, innovation is viewed as the creation, development and introduction of new products and services, or products and service components, or a new procedure or process for doing things of benefit to one or more of the stakeholders in an organization (Birchall et al., 1996). Other approaches classify high-technology activity quite restrictively within the broader framework of innovation. For example Butchart (1987) defines technology-intensive industries as those comprising a high percentage of knowledge workers in the workforce and/or a high proportion of expenditure on research and development (R&D) as a percentage of sales. Harding (2000) is more inclusive as she distinguishes between firms that adapt existing technologies and genuine high-technology companies; the latter require radical innovations and radical new infrastructures to support them. Firms in the biotechnology sector, for example, require large capital outlays to support their efforts to discover products and processes with high-growth potential and hence the scope to change the market place.

For our purposes, it is probably appropriate to focus on innovation. In most cases, venture capitalists will not restrict investments solely to firms operating in 'high-technology' industries, as defined by (say) Butchart (1987), but would look to back the broader range of firms engaged in innovation. This would imply using the approach put forward by Birchall et al. (1996) or using either of the categories identified above by Harding (2000). In other words, venture capitalists support growth companies in any field, but are especially keen to invest in companies that adapt existing technology or bring radical changes to the economy.

2.2.3 SMEs: internationalization

International business activity is increasingly prominent, even among the smallest and newest organizations (McDougall and Oviatt, 2000). Mainstream trade theories suggest that companies need to offer superior products to overcome the liability of 'foreignness' and to achieve competitive advantage (Caves, 1982). However, examples abound of firms that have adopted an international vision from the earliest stage of their operations, these are termed 'born global firms' or 'instant internationals' (Granitsky, 1989; Oviatt and McDougall, 1994; Preece et al., 1998). In the past, it was mainly large manufacturing companies seeking to exploit technological advantage that captured the benefits of internationalization through economies of scale. Nowadays, the pace of economic and technical change is breaking down established patterns of business and trade, and creating opportunities for SMEs to enter overseas markets.

In discussing internationalization, a universal definition of this concept remains elusive (Coviello and McAuley, 1999), but Beamish (1990, p.77) offers a holistic view as: 'the process by which firms both increase their awareness of the direct and indirect influence of international transactions on their future, and establish and conduct transactions with other countries.' The definition recognizes that exports are only one element of outward/inward international activities.

It is not appropriate to present a detailed examination of the theories of internationalization – for a comprehensive overview of the literature in this field, refer to Westhead et al. (2001) or Bell and

Young (1998). However, a brief summary of the internationalization literature relevant to SMEs is useful for the themes tackled later in this book.

The 'stages' model proposes that internationalization proceed in one direction through a series of stages, with the ultimate goal of foreign direct investment. Johanson and Wiedersheim-Paul (1978) postulated that firms grow organically, committing resources to foreign markets in stages as knowledge and experience increases. The value placed on interactions, relationships and networks is recognized in the network theory of internationalization (Axelsson and Easton, 1992; O'Farrell et al., 1998). Network theory focuses on mutual interdependence between, for example, producers in the same sector, suppliers, customers and governments. The proponents of this school view internationalization as evolving in a more dynamic, less structured manner.

Another line of thinking that acknowledges the complexity of the internationalization process is the contingency approach (Reid, 1983); firms advance into international markets according to prevailing circumstances and existing resource capabilities. This theme is developed with the resources based view of internationalization that has gained prominence over recent years (McDougall et al., 1994; Bloodgood et al., 1996). The essence of this approach is to take explicit account of the resources and capabilities available to, or assembled by, a firm.

The stages theory has an intuitive appeal to describe how new and/or small firms begin with exporting then progress to more complex forms of servicing the needs of overseas customers. However, the reality of decision-making in organizations is that a wide variety of influences come into play (Chi and McGuire, 1996). The evidence of 'irregular patterns' of internationalization (Welch and Luostarinen, 1988; Bell and Young, 1998) points to the importance of a range of factors. The resource-based and contingency approaches emphasize the importance of entrepreneurial choice and managerial attitudes in developing (or resisting) an international presence (Calof and Beamish, 1994). As will be seen below, the majority of owner-managers do not pursue growth strategies. In this context, many SMEs have neither the inclination nor the ability to be involved in international activity. A lack of resources can create a climate of uncertainty and a reluctance to engage in strategic thinking, and a constant battle for scarce resources is not the ideal preparation for entry into global markets.

The network approach suggests that competitive advantage in many industries may have switched from large firms with long experience towards firms that may be smaller but have unique knowledge and swift response capabilities. Factors such as improved global communications mean that sheer physical size is no longer critical and SMEs prepared to seek pragmatic solutions to meet customer needs can compete by operating through alliances or joint ventures. Calof (1993) stressed that size was not necessarily a barrier to internationalization, as small firms find 'unique' ways of overcoming their smallness (Bonaccorsi, 1992; Gomes-Casseres, 1997).

Bloodgood et al. (1996) suggest that a new venture's ability to enter foreign markets hinges upon its accumulated tangible and intangible resource stocks, and a firm with an 'inimitable' combination of resources will be in a powerful position to capture orders, especially in the high-technology sphere. Some entrepreneurs have a unique constellation of skills and knowledge that allows them to see and exploit windows of opportunity unseen by others. Access to information was also found to be a significant determinant of success in international markets (Cooper et al., 1995).

Finally, knowledge is seen as a key resource, and the role of individual and organizational learning is critical in determining a firm's ability to sustain the internationalization process (Anderson and Boocock, 2002). Oviatt and McDougall (1997) contend that, in pursuing their international ambitions, firms have to draw upon multiple knowledge bases in their research and development, manufacturing and marketing operations. It is essential that firms reflect on their experience and integrate new knowledge into their operations.

It should be evident, therefore, that SMEs *can* make a mark in overseas markets, but success is by no means guaranteed. Some of the characteristics of SMEs work in their favour, whereas other features prevent the exploitation of international opportunities. Venture funds are looking to back growth firms that can compete from the outset in international markets. The venture capitalists can help to plug any gaps in the resources available to a firm, whether finance, information or access to networks. A typical intervention might be for the fund managers to identify joint partners for strategic alliances.

Having explored the contribution of SMEs in relation to employment, innovation and international activity, attention now turns to a more general assessment of the characteristics of SMEs.

2.3 Characteristics of SMEs

Small firms pursue a variety of objectives and each firm claims to face unique problems (Storey, 1994). Curran and Blackburn (2001, p.5) stress that: 'a small number of human beings engaged in a common endeavour create very complex, subtle interactions'. Individual freedom, risk-taking, initiative, thrift and hard work are just some of the features associated with this sector (Megginson et al., 1994). These attributes back up frequent assertions that SMEs are characterized by diversity. Motivations, constraints and uncertainties vary not only between SMEs and large firms, but also between small/small and small/medium-sized firms.

With regard to motivation, most small firms concentrate on survival and independence rather than growth (Curran, 1999). There is a general reluctance of entrepreneurs and owner-managers to accept external advice and a strong commitment to autonomy and independence, even in a crisis (Curran and Blackburn, 1999; Vickerstaff and Parker, 1994). The founder(s) can exert a powerful influence on the firm's direction and development, and the desire to retain independence might be dominant.

Despite the fact that the majority of large firms stem from modest beginnings, as Clay (1932) asserted many years ago, very few start-ups evolve to become large (or even medium-sized) firms and there is no single route to growth (Storey, 1994). This failure to grow may stem not from a lack of motivation, but from the variety of constraints faced by SMEs. The principal internal constraints are a lack of resources, including limited capital and fewer sources of information, and pressures on the owner-manager's time (Buckley, 1989; Marlow, 1998). External barriers obviously include competition from entrenched larger firms.

It might be expected that smaller enterprises would always suffer more uncertainty than their larger counterparts. This assumption is questionable. For instance, Burns (1996) argues that small firms are generally price takers, yet a firm offering a differentiated product in a niche market might be able to charge a premium price. More generally, small firms can reduce uncertainty by making connections across a broad spectrum of external structures and social networks within and beyond the supply chain (Down, 1999; Dalley and Hamilton, 2000). Small firms rely on intuitive approaches and 'episodic knowledge' more readily obtained from business network arrangements rather than official sources (Karagozoglu and Lindell, 1998; Coviello and Martin, 1999). The key to success, according to Gibb (1998, p.18), is that of: 'managing and developing the network of interdependency under conditions of (more or less) uncertainty'.

The literature emphasizes, therefore, that smaller firms are not simply scaled down versions of their larger counterparts. The goals of SMEs are likely to be numerous and complex, for example, the motivations of key players might be non-pecuniary. SMEs are subject to various constraints that stem from their smallness in relation to other market participants. They also rely heavily on network relationships to manage uncertainty. These factors typically combine to result in SMEs reducing the scale and scope of their operations compared to their larger counterparts, and adopting more personalized, informal management styles and less rigid (and hence more diverse) forms of organizational structure (Coviello and McAuley, 1999; Churchill, 1997).

It is not surprising that CEOs in smaller enterprises tend to have more power and influence than their counterparts in large firms (Eisenhardt and Schoonhoven, 1990) and this power is evident in the selection and retention of directors and the overall composition of the board (Mace, 1971). Founder-led firms generally have smaller boards and fewer non-executive directors (Daily and Dalton, 1993). The outcome is that such firms might not benefit from the experience and support that 'outside' directors can bring through their experience and/or reputation in business, for example: when initiating and formulating strategies, or facilitating the acquisition of resources critical to the firm's success (Pfeffer, 1973; Daily and Dalton, 1993; Zahra and Pearce, 1989).

Another key role of the board is its responsibility to monitor and discipline top management. These duties include hiring and firing the CEO, determining executive pay and ensuring that the managers act in the best interest of all shareholders (Fama and Jensen, 1983). It is difficult to perform such duties when, as is the case in many small enterprises, shareholding is concentrated in a small group of individuals who also exercise executive powers!

In relation to specific functions, smaller firms differ from their larger counterparts in a number of ways. A number of functional areas are covered in this section, starting with marketing.

Start-ups have very little choice but to adopt guerrilla warfare tactics in their marketing activities. They cannot compete head-on against larger and more established rivals. Instead, smaller firms have to conserve scarce resources for crucial battles, while using speed and stealth to outwit competitors. Adopting this approach can give first-mover advantages by allowing small firms to build up market share and increase brand equity in niche markets. For example, Optimus Computer (a Polish firm) was founded in 1988, yet had captured 35 per cent of the

Polish PC market by 1995. While competitors imported models approaching the end of their life cycle, Optimus provided locally assembled, low cost PCs equipped with the latest Intel chips, Samsung monitors and Microsoft operating systems (Peng and Shekshnia, 2001). Such strategies enable a small firm to position its products in niches where price is not a key factor in the buying decision, thus creating a unique advantage based on (say) an extensive dealer network (Ruekert and Walker, 1987).

Turning to a more general consideration of strategy, the convergence of personal and firm income frequently forces small businesses to focus on survival, especially in a recession. It is rare that SMEs will be concerned with (say) divesting a business unit or seeking short-term funding from a parent company hence it is imperative for smaller enterprises to come to terms with the responses required in the face of tough macroeconomic conditions. In particular, strategic planning demands that managers must appreciate which resources are at the heart of the firm's competitive advantage. They should maintain their core assets and cut only those factors that can be easily rehired or repurchased (Michael and Robbins, 1998).

Strategic alliances can offer a route by which small firms with innovative ideas and/or products but lacking resources and experience can capitalize on their expertise. Technology-based firms have utilized alliances in the early stages to overcome inherent problems in accessing markets, achieve economies of scale and/or develop innovative technologies; alliances have also allowed small firms to gain access to complementary skills (Johanson and Mattsson, 1987). It must be realized, however, that alliances are not a 'cure-all'. If a firm does not develop as a viable independent entity, it might not benefit fully from an alliance. On the same theme, Miles et al. (1999) argue that firms that rely unduly on alliances may put themselves in a position from which they cannot capture fully their share of the gains stemming from the relationship.

The use of technology to satisfy demanding customers is increasingly a feature of the operations of SMEs, and there is empirical evidence linking the use of technology and enhanced performance. Many small businesses have adopted a policy of total quality management (TQM). Lee (1996) suggested that TQM carries a heavy investment upfront, but the cost is more than recovered by greater sales (especially in export markets) from high-precision products. Likewise, smaller companies can compete in the global market place by utilizing Advanced Manufacturing Technologies – AMT (Millen and Sohal, 1998; Mechling et al., 1995). Maintaining the consistent quality of products and reducing human content are major factors affecting a firm's decision to upgrade technology. Small firms using computerized AMT systems for forecasting and planning perform better than firms without such facilities. Such firms improved the manufacturing process in areas such as material handling, inventory control and production planning, resulting in reduced lead-time in fulfilling orders and greater profitability (Ariss et al., 2000).

It is apparent, therefore, that computer-based information systems (IS) provide an opportunity for SMEs to improve their efficiency and to gain competitive advantage. With ever more powerful personal computers and versatile software packages, such benefits are accessible to smaller enterprises at a modest cost. The rate of adoption of IS depends on the commitment of the founder to utilizing new technology and, critically, the information intensity of the product or service provided (Yap et al., 1994). In the wider context, governments can play an important role in encouraging SMEs to upgrade their technological capability (King et al., 1994). Singapore, the tiny city-nation, is a classic example of government support to develop an IS culture through its National Computer Board (Thong, 1999).

The analysis of marketing, strategic and IT/technological issues should not divert attention from human resource management (HRM) within the smaller enterprise. A number of studies have demonstrated that the need for HRM emerges at the early stages of a firm's development (Flamholtz, 1990). Initially, the founders assume responsibility for all the major business functions. However, as the organization grows and develops, the founders are likely to need assistance in, for example, strategic planning, systems design and business law (Ardichvili et al., 1998).

The recruitment, retention, training and compensation of staff assume much greater importance after achieving a certain level of growth. Small business owners consider the successful recruitment of employees to be one of the most important factors influencing organizational success (Mehta, 1996). While it seems evident that hiring a diverse workforce offers clear advantages for any firm that wants to compete globally, such diversity entails significant costs (Gudmundson and Hartenian, 2000). It can be difficult to identify then attract the right person from many applicants, especially when the net is cast wide. Thereafter, SMEs face difficulties in retaining (say) IS specialists because limited career paths might be available. The overall benefits of working for a smaller enterprise have to be emphasized. Nelson (1994) points out that smaller organizations are more likely to view compensation from a 'total rewards' perspective than their larger counterparts, encompassing psychological rewards, learning opportunities and recognition as well as monetary rewards.

One area where strategic issues and HRM concerns overlap to a great extent is in family-owned SMEs. In such firms, managerial decisions tend to be based upon family as well as business considerations (Dyer, 1986). Family and business interests may not always be congruent hence (say) estate planning and/or tax issues may drive decisions rather than purely economic considerations (Kleiman et al., 1995). In addition to the normal business concerns, family businesses must deal with generational disputes, sibling rivalries and other family conflicts, all of which may absorb precious business resources (Lansberg, 1983).

2.4 Profiles of successful/unsuccessful SMEs

This section takes a somewhat eclectic view of the characteristics of successful and unsuccessful firms. Over 20 per cent of new ventures fail within one year, and 66 per cent fail within six years (Timmons, 1994). In relation to the main thrust of this book, venture capitalists seek out the former and try to avoid the latter! They have been relatively successful in this ambition, and the failure rate of VC-backed enterprises is substantially lower than 'conventional' SMEs.

Dorsey (1979) claims that 85 per cent and Sahlman (1990) suggests that 65 per cent of VC investee companies survive for seven years, compared to a corresponding figure of just 25 per cent for conventional firms. However, many VC-backed firms fail to provide the desired return, and a prominent US venture capitalist (cited in Zacharakis and Meyer, 2000) hopes to hit one 'home run' in every ten investments to salvage the portfolio's return. In broad terms, the key concern is to recognize and support the 'home run' enterprises that will be of greatest value to both venture funds and national economies.

Many owner-managers aspire to maintain a reasonable lifestyle, offering an adequate income and more independence than salaried employment. In these 'lifestyle' firms, Beaver (2002) suggests that little thought is given to strategic management hence the status quo is preserved until the market changes without the founder realizing it. Our attention, by contrast, is on growth-oriented, entrepreneurial firms; these businesses have a different agenda, rooted in a desire to achieve rapid growth in sales and profits, a determination to innovate rather than stagnate, and so on.

Success usually stems from a combination of factors. By way of illustration, a flourishing technology company in Australia, LasaTech, was based on longstanding respect and trust between the two founding members (Warren and Hutchison, 2000). Successful entrepreneurs are more likely to have broader business and prior start-up experience; they also work long hours and are good communicators (Wijewardena and Tibbits, 1999). Nonetheless, the key driver behind growth-oriented firms is, almost invariably, the desire to create wealth by meeting genuine needs in the market place, thus adopting an opportunity-driven and aggressive approach to securing customers (Becherer and Maurer, 1999).

Certain factors characterize successful SMEs wherever they are located, for example: the most successful Singaporean SMEs had the ability to satisfy customers, to find a market niche, to put together a sound management team and to exploit networks (Ghosh et al., 1993). Beaver (2002, p.74, Example 5.4.) draws upon Shepherd and Shanley (1998) and Hofer and Sandberg (1987) to suggest that the principal strategic imperatives to achieve growth include:

- concentrate on industries facing substantial technological or regulatory changes, especially those in the early, high-growth stages of evolution
- differentiate your products from those of your competitors in ways that are meaningful to your customers, particularly in relation to product quality and customer service
- seek to dominate the market segments in which you compete
- emphasize innovation – this covers both product and process
- try to secure organic growth through flexibility and opportunism that builds on existing organizational strengths.

Beaver (2002, p.131) then refers to an unpublished study by the consulting firm, McKinsey, to identify three key factors behind 'hypergrowth' companies. The first factor is fast and effective decision-making by giving key individuals and groups relevant information in a timely fashion. The second is maintaining flexibility by employing experienced personnel in cross-functional teams that are given autonomy to achieve the goals set. Finally (p.132): 'the glue that holds hypergrowth companies together is an incentive-based compensation system ... with tangible links between business objectives, individual roles and incentives'.

These themes are developed and expanded by Taylor (2000), in his summary of the lessons to be learned from 'supergrowth' companies.

Based on a 15-year study of firms in the UK, US and Germany, Taylor (p.281) provides examples of best practice: find a market niche that the firm can defend – this might involve opening up new market segments then creating barriers to entry with (say) patents or exclusive distribution agreements; compete in areas that require speed, flexibility and customer service; diversify into related products and adjacent markets – this avoids over-dependence on key customers; exit the industry before the window of opportunity closes – at some point the firm has to decide whether to grow to become one of the few major players in a consolidated industry or to sell to a competitor.

Taylor (2000) emphasizes that these high-growth companies, irrespective of their country of origin, are a powerful force for innovation and the creation of new wealth. However, he stresses (p.283) that: 'US super-growth companies grow bigger than their UK counterparts and they stay independent longer'. This stems from a number of factors, including greater access to risk capital, a much larger domestic market and the availability of 'spin-out' opportunities, especially in the technology field, from the major universities.

Turning now to the reasons for failure, these usually relate to the quality of the original business idea, a lack of resources to compete successfully, or management shortcomings. For example, Zacharakis et al. (1999) suggest that prominent reasons for failure include: lack of experience in the field; small market size; slow market growth; no product differentiation; poor management strategy; and, the inability to assemble an adequate management team. Barley and Kleiner (1990) add the following reasons: an inadequate business plan; ambiguous goals; over-dependence on one customer; and under-capitalization.

The strategic reasons for business collapse are usually concerned with the absence of a clear strategy and direction, or an inability to respond to change and recognize new competition. Entrepreneurs tend to reach an 'executive limit' (Meyer and Dean, 1990) where inability to manage the firm becomes detrimental. At this point, firms that do not replace the entrepreneur with a professional manager are more apt to fail, suffering from a lack of coordination and control.

A number of studies point to financial expertise and planning as being a critical factor in a firm's chance of survival. For example, Pech and Mathew (1993) highlighted the importance of cash flow, debtor and inventory management. Pousson (1996) highlighted financial weakness as a good predictor of failure, with firms failing to secure sufficient finance at the outset, or taking on too much debt and not enough equity in the initial financial package.

2.5 Summary

This chapter has assessed the SME sector in relation to the creation of employment opportunities, the promotion of innovation and involvement in international activity. Some of the key characteristics of SMEs were identified, and there was consideration of the differences between successful and unsuccessful firms. Chapter 3 continues to explore the SME sector, starting with the barriers to growth faced by SMEs and concentrating on finance-related constraints. The final section summarizes the reasons why governments choose to assist SMEs.

3
Barriers to Growth in SMEs

3.1 Introduction

This chapter deals with the barriers to growth faced by SMEs. The focus here is on financing issues because access to credit, especially for new investment, has been a recurring constraint on the growth and development of smaller enterprises across the globe (Levy, 1993; Parker et al., 1995). The chapter then discusses other barriers affecting the SME sector, for example: the issues of critical concern for UK SMEs over recent years have been not only the cost and availability of finance but also market-related factors, namely the threat of competition and/or lack of demand (Burns, 2001). Finally, the chapter draws together the arguments as to why governments choose to intervene to assist SMEs.

3.2 Barriers to growth: finance-related

According to the well-established 'pecking order' theory of fund raising, entrepreneurs prefer to use internal sources, wherever possible, to finance investment opportunities. The problem is that smaller enterprises have a limited capacity to generate cash from excess liquid assets yet they might have to fund relatively large amounts of expenditure. Faced with a shortfall in the finance available to satisfy their expansion plans, the founders of a business are reluctant to cede control to outside investors. As a result, SMEs, wherever they are located in the world, look to raise bank finance.

New equity will be issued only as a last resort, even where a local venture capital (VC) industry is well developed, for example: the dependence on bank finance is apparent in both the UK and US, where venture funds have operated for decades. However, the reliance on bank debt is even more marked in countries where VC is less well-established; this trend is prevalent in developed nations such as Germany, as well as in emerging nations like China (Binks and Ennew, 2000). Despite consistent recourse to bank financing, SMEs often face inequalities in raising relatively small amounts of funds from these institutions. Finance theory offers insights into the reasons why this might be the case.

High transaction costs are a serious disincentive for both lenders and borrowers. Vogel and Adams (1997) argue that higher transaction costs, and hence higher interest margins, are a reflection of commercial reality in the operation of financial markets; they contend that market *imperfections* are more likely to be associated with information externalities and asymmetries. Stiglitz and others (Stiglitz and Weiss, 1981; Greenwald, Weiss and Stiglitz, 1984) first demonstrated how information asymmetries could result in credit rationing. Under conditions of perfect information, each borrower would be charged an interest rate that reflects the risk involved in the proposition and this rate would be adjusted in the light of changing circumstances affecting the firm.

Nevertheless, experience has led bankers to perceive new ventures as more prone to failure compared with established firms. Banks thus raise interest rates for all SME borrowers to a point where excess demand still exists; the lenders then create the potential for further problems by failing to monitor their advances effectively. Such actions lead to adverse selection (good borrowers with viable low-risk projects will scale back their plans or delay them until internal resources are available, leaving the lender with a higher risk portfolio) and moral hazard (funds are diverted by borrowers to more risky projects).

If the individual adjustment of interest rates cannot be used as a mechanism to bring supply and demand into equilibrium, the most common alternative is for banks to take collateral from SME borrowers. Collateral acts as a substitute for information, limits the downside risk for the lender and signals that the entrepreneur believes the project is likely to succeed (Stiglitz and Weiss, 1981). However, some good quality borrowers will not be able to provide collateral (KPMG, 1999); credit rationing means that worthwhile proposals are turned away and adverse selection is again the consequence.

These theoretical issues affecting the funding of SMEs are set to one side – to be considered further in Chapter 5 – and the discussion now explores the extent of any financing gaps experienced by SMEs in practice. The analysis focuses on the longstanding debate in the UK on the adequacy of SME funding, taking into account all sources of finance available to smaller enterprises. The situation in the UK is then compared to that prevailing in a number of other countries.

In 1931, the MacMillan Committee found a gap in the market for firms seeking to raise 'long-dated capital' (equity and/or long-term loans) of less than £200,000, around £7m at current prices. This structural failure within the financial system became known as the 'MacMillan' or 'Equity Gap'. The onset of the Great Depression of the 1930s then the Second World War meant that there was a delayed response to the MacMillan Report; the outcome was the formation in 1945 of what is now known as the 3i Group, Europe's biggest VC firm.

For many years, 3i retained the reputation of making relatively small investments and being a patient investor in small companies. This approach was thought to stem from the fact that the Bank of England (which held 15 per cent of its shares) and the major clearing banks owned 3i's share capital. There was perhaps less pressure to return dividends to the shareholders. The approach may have changed after the privatization of 3i in the 1990s.

The first major enquiry into the activities of UK small firms was published in 1971 (Bolton, 1971). This Report concluded that SMEs still faced genuine disabilities in seeking funds (stemming from the information asymmetries and so on discussed above). Despite the significant contribution of 3i in providing equity capital to SMEs, Bolton confirmed the existence of an equity gap affecting firms trying to find 'sums below £250,000', a considerable reduction in real terms over the period since MacMillan. Nonetheless, Bolton argued that a more significant problem was a lack of awareness of funding opportunities among SMEs; this was termed the 'information gap' and a network of official agencies was established to increase awareness of the funding sources that could be tapped.

The Wilson Committee (1979, 1980) came to broadly the same conclusions as Bolton regarding the existence of the equity gap, but was prepared to take a proactive approach to intervene in the financial market. The Government adopted Wilson's recommendations, and implemented a series of measures to increase the supply of equity capital and bank loans to SMEs. A junior stock market (the forerunner of the present Alternative Investment Market) was introduced in 1981, to provide a route for established firms to issue publicly quoted securities. Various forms of tax relief were also granted to individuals prepared to invest in unquoted companies.

Wilson considered that the main clearing banks were sometimes taking an excessively cautious view of viable lending propositions; the

Government introduced the Loan Guarantee Scheme (henceforth LGS) in 1981. Banks and other lenders were encouraged to make loans available to smaller enterprises, on the understanding that the government would reimburse a percentage of the loan should the firm default. Despite a number of changes to the parameters of the Scheme, the LGS still plays an important role today in supplying bank loans to firms without collateral.

Over the 1980s, there were major changes in the lending ethos of the UK clearing banks. Loans became longer-term and more flexible, and banking groups started to encompass asset finance (especially leasing), factoring and export finance within their activities. At this time, VC was emerging to complement the growth in bank finance, although the bulk of VC investments moved quickly from start-up/seed funding to larger deals. The impact of these developments was assessed in three reports published in the early 1990s.

The Advisory Council on Science and Technology (ACOST, 1990) found that an inadequate supply of external risk capital was still the main barrier to growth for innovative firms looking to expand. Although high-technology firms were prominent among a small minority of disadvantaged firms, a DTI/Aston Business School Report (1991) found very few cases of market failure, namely where firms are refused funding for reasons other than genuine concerns about the commercial viability of project. Finally, a questionnaire survey (Cambridge University SBRC, 1992) revealed that the most serious constraint affecting SMEs, especially fast growth firms, was the availability and cost of finance. Nevertheless, a series of follow-up interviews with selected respondents brought to light the fact that only a small number of firms had, in fact, failed to obtain external finance. There was also evidence that firms had moved from bank finance to alternative sources, notably leasing and the factoring of debts.

The third report cited above (Cambridge University SBRC, 1992) exposes the differences in perspective between funding bodies (especially the banks) and smaller enterprises. Burns (2001) argues that SMEs will almost inevitably cite a lack of appropriately priced finance as a major constraint on their progress, but it is clearly unrealistic to expect the banks to provide virtually all the funds required for a new venture or to enable an established firm to expand its operations. While lenders can develop profitable relationships from young firms that grow into successful businesses, there are risk/return asymmetries that cause bankers to pose the question: 'If you become successful, we cannot share in your success, so why should we lose if you lose?' (Levie, 2000, p.99).

The overall thrust of official and academic studies nowadays is that any funding gaps are reducing in importance (Cruickshank Report, 2000) and that, in general, the UK debt market functions efficiently and effectively in channelling funds to SMEs. Where problems do persist, they relate mainly to a lack of relatively small amounts of equity capital to support growth-oriented, innovative firms. The Bank of England (2001), for example, found that opportunities to raise formal VC under £500,000 were fairly limited; due diligence and transaction costs are high per unit of funds invested.

As an aside, the UK Government has responded to this perceived gap by setting up a network of regional VC funds operated through official bodies (Regional Development Agencies) and supported from the public purse; these funds utilize a mix of private and public capital, and they operate at the lower end of the financing spectrum. The maximum investment is restricted to £250,000. In an efficient financial system, one would anticipate that the private sector would move to fill any gaps in the financing spectrum, provided this could be done at a profit. It will be interesting to monitor the success of this initiative to provide relatively small sums of risk capital.

How does the situation in the UK compare to other countries?

The US is an obvious starting point for comparison because the role of the US financial markets in meeting the needs of SMEs has also been subject to frequent review. Studies carried out in the US between 1935 and 1940 arrived at an identical conclusion to MacMillan (1931); they pointed to the existence of a gap in the market for relatively small amounts of long-term risk capital (Dominguez, 1974). However, this inequality appears to have been reduced over the intervening years, in the light of improvements in the provision of both bank finance and risk capital.

The existence of credit rationing in the market for SME debt in the US does not appear to be widespread. Thakor (1989) suggested that the balance of evidence pointed to the existence of this phenomenon, whereas Berger and Udell (1990) argued that it was prevalent only where collateral was a prime concern of lenders. While SMEs might face difficulties in raising bank finance in certain sectors or regions, therefore, the problem is relatively limited in scale and scope.

Access to bank lending in the US (and other developed countries) has sometimes been affected by the possibility of a 'credit crunch' for SMEs in the wake of mergers among financial organizations (see, for example: Keeton, 1995, 1997; Peek and Rosengreen, 1998; and, Strahan and Weston, 1998). A wave of consolidation among US banks and financial institutions in the second half of the 1990s does seem to have reduced the availability of credit to small business (Berger and Udell, 1998).

An authoritative recent study by Levenson and Willard (2000) broadened the scope from bank lending to a more general consideration of the external finance available to small firms. A mere two per cent of US firms could not access the funding for which they had applied, while a similar figure experienced temporary constraints before they obtained the required funding; a further four per cent were estimated to have been discouraged from applying for credit as they expected a refusal from the credit providers. Levenson and Willard (2000, p.92) concluded that: 'the total number of credit constrained firms seems quite small'.

Harding (2002) confirmed that there was no general evidence of any funding gaps in US financial markets; she found financial support to be especially strong in the high-technology hotspots of Silicon Valley and the Boston corridor. Regional variations existed, but areas of peak demand for risk capital were well serviced. Harding also suggested that the equity gap was not an issue for SMEs in key European nations (Germany, the Netherlands and France) or Singapore. In these countries, and the US, the respective governments had already taken steps to fill the sort of gaps identified in the UK studies. The establishment of the regional VC funds in the UK was described above, and more examples of similar initiatives are given in the following chapter.

In the developing world, Collier and Mayer (1989) confirmed that banks are the principal source of finance for smaller enterprises, although much of the funding is short-term. Government involvement in the banking system is often considerable. Lenders are inexperienced and they tend to rely upon collateral hence credit rationing might be expected to be more prevalent (Berger and Udell, 1990). The banking systems of three emerging economies (India, China and Malaysia) all display these characteristics.

The banking system in India is largely government-dominated and it is effectively an instrument of social policy (Dossani and Kenney, 2001). The sector has been remarkably successful in penetrating rural areas and in providing stability to depositors yet it has also been viewed as being both expensive and inept (Banerjee, Cole and Duflo, 2003). Banerjee and his colleagues argue that there has been 'definite evidence of very substantial underlending'. Non-performing loans (NPLs) are prevalent, and bankers are reluctant to make new loans to SMEs (even those showing healthy profit forecasts), for fear of being accused of corruption. The development of credit appraisal skills is not helped by the existence of targeted lending programmes that force banks to commit 40 per cent of net credit to priority sectors (including SMEs) at a maximum interest rate of four per cent over prime lending rate (ADB, 1990). Bhattacharya and Patel (2003) accuse the Government of 'political meddling' that distorts the efficient allocation of credit and fails to impose market discipline. Bhattacharya and Patel confirm that high levels of NPLs restrict the actions of bankers and point out that lending to priority sectors has been associated with higher than average NPLs. This implies a degree of moral hazard. The banking and VC sectors in India are considered further in Chapter 6; attention now turns to China.

Four state-owned banks dominate the banking market in China and the level of NPLs is approaching 20 per cent, despite an improvement in asset quality in recent years (Ping, 2003). This weak asset quality has contributed to low levels of capital adequacy. In addition (Ping, p.4): '... banks in China also suffer from poor corporate governance and internal controls, and a lack of adequate risk management skills'. The lending portfolios of the four main banks are dominated by state-owned enterprises (SOEs), and many of the current NPLs are found in the SOE sector.

As a result, SMEs will continue to face difficulties in gaining access to conventional bank finance until the SOEs are put on a firmer financial footing or restructured to some degree. It is somewhat ironic that the Chinese Government has introduced numerous schemes that provide finance for smaller enterprises, in an effort to remedy a problem caused by its own policy of condoning NPLs among SOEs.

The influence of official directives is also apparent in Malaysia, where SMEs rely heavily upon the banking sector for their external funding requirements at both the initial and expansion stages of development. Once again, the banking sector is dominated by a small number of domestic institutions controlled by Government or quasi-governmental entities. These dominant banks have imposed a substantial risk premium on the cost of borrowing to this sector, typically 3–5 per cent over prime lending rate, and they continue to place heavy reliance upon collateral to support SME lending (Lin See Yan, 1994). For many years, therefore, Bank Negara (the Central Bank) has published lending guidelines (effectively quotas) that force the banks to assist smaller enterprises; interest margins are also restricted. Penalties are imposed for non-compliance with these guidelines. Yet again, the imposition of such targets appears to have had the unintended consequence of restricting the development of credit appraisal techniques in the private sector (Boocock and Wahab, 2001).

The principal alternatives to bank finance in Malaysia are loans from finance companies or Government-sponsored bodies. The formal VC market is emerging and the Government supplies a large part of its investment pool. Informal risk capital has a long history within the Chinese community in Malaysia, although the operation of this market, as elsewhere, tends to be somewhat opaque. Despite this apparent progress, there is a lack of knowledge among SMEs about the funding opportunities available (Boocock and Wahab, 2001).

In the global context, it might be expected that SMEs would secure more equal access to funding alternatives as financial markets develop, but this does not appear to be the case. Demirguc-Kunt and Maksimovic (1999) examined 30 countries over the period 1980–1991 and discovered that large firms have more long-term debt in countries with active stock markets. The existence of well-functioning stock markets does not seem to influence the debt levels of SMEs to any significant extent.

On the same theme, a number of studies have investigated whether financial liberalization has eased the financing constraints of SMEs; the findings in lower income economies have generally not been encouraging (Steel, 1994). Kariuki (1995) concluded that credit to SMEs in Kenya declined after liberalization, as relaxing controls on the financial market resulted in higher nominal interest rates. In Bangladesh, Nepal and the Philippines, Meier and Pilgrim (1994) found that only larger enterprises had access to formal sector finance, even where schemes had been designed specifically for small firms. Credit through formal channels was also out of reach of SMEs in Ghana and Tanzania (Dawson, 1993). Despite changes to financial markets in Eastern Europe, Hungarian entrepreneurs claimed that access to finance was one of their major problems, especially when seeking to invest in new technology (Roman, 1991), a message that was reinforced by entrepreneurs in Slovakia (Ivy, 1997).

3.3 Non-financial barriers to growth

The two principal barriers to growth cited at the start of this chapter were finance and market related factors. Having explored possible finance constraints, we now discuss briefly a variety of other factors that might constitute obstacles to growth.

Small enterprises can rarely, if ever, compete in mass markets where price is a key factor in the buying decision (Ruekert and Walker, 1987).

However, there are strategies that can be adopted to penetrate new markets and hence to overcome the market power of entrenched competitors. The internationalization activity of SMEs (refer to Section 2.2.3.) illustrates how the early exploitation of export markets can have positive effects on both profitability and growth (Roper, 1999). Likewise, Lautanen (2000) concluded that export-oriented Finnish small firms could achieve high levels of competitiveness from the outset, and this pattern has been repeated by clusters of small enterprises across the globe, notably in Pakistan, Italy and Brazil (Cook and Nixon, 2000).

Burns (2001, p.295) offers general advice to firms attempting to overcome market-related barriers and secure competitive advantage; the key message is to understand your customers and ensure that your product/service provides more benefits than those offered by competitors. In addition, the firm should be able to answer the following questions: 'What are our core competencies? How do we add value to customers? Which strategies have worked in the past? Future strategy should build upon these strengths.' This approach represents sound common sense, although it is underpinned by a number of classic academic concepts.

A few basic tools can inform strategy formulation, but the strategy process does not have to be very formal. Most small business text books advocate an awareness of the Porter 'Five Forces' and 'Value Chain' (Porter, 1980) as a good starting point, along with the ability to conduct a SWOT analysis and an understanding of how to assess pertinent changes in the external environment, especially legal, political, economic, social and technological factors.

As confirmation that strategy creation does not have to follow rigid lines, Beaver (2002) argues that rapid expansion and growth in SMEs is often characterized by bold moves and intuitive decisions. The crucial factor is that the owner-managers and/or entrepreneurs adopt a positive attitude towards growth and change. This is not always the case. Many founders guard their autonomy and independence; they may be reluctant to grow beyond a certain size because, for example, they are reluctant to expose potential managerial shortcomings (Marlow, 1998). Young firms might therefore grow quickly but stop when they reach the minimum efficient scale of operations that enables the firm to survive (Storey, 1994). These comments might seem self evident, but it has to be emphasized that SMEs are characterized by their heterogeneity, and goals and motivations differ widely. The critical brake on growth is often self-imposed – a lack of ambition to expand.

As a firm grows, it changes in character. It has often been suggested that businesses move through a number of stages of development, and a number of 'stage theories' have been put forward to explain this progression (including: Greiner, 1972; Churchill, 1997). Greiner, for example, proposes that firms evolve through five phases, with the end of each phase being marked by a crisis; this approach has been described as evolution and revolution. While stage theories have claimed a modest degree of empirical support, they have been criticized on a number of counts. It is evident that SMEs develop in unpredictable, idiosyncratic ways that do not conform to 'standard' patterns; very few firms progress in a linear fashion and a significant number fail to negotiate the early phases. However, the stage models do give insights into the changes in organizational structure, strategy and behaviour that need to be implemented if firms are to grow and develop. It is vital for SMEs to manage the transitions between phases by making appropriate changes in, for example, organizational structures and the management of human resources.

The stage models emphasize the need to strike a balance between retaining the flexibility to cope with unprecedented levels of change in global markets and creating an orderly structure to meet other business needs. At some point, smaller enterprises have to recognize the need to introduce 'formal structures, systems, procedures and controls' (Gorman and Doran, 1999, p.60); likewise, McMohan (1999) concluded that regular financial reporting was an important factor in realizing the growth aspirations among manufacturing SMEs in Australia. An inability to handle information can also pose a severe barrier to a firm that aspires to growth. It is no surprise that, when investigating the performance of 150 small firms in Scotland, Smith (1999) found that investment in IT had a very positive association with performance, even for micro firms in the early stages of their existence. Firms that do not wish to grow can retain much simpler organizational structures and avoid the time and expense of creating formal financial reporting systems or investing in IT.

Another means of managing transitions, especially where resources are limited, relates to a key characteristic of SMEs outlined in the previous chapter – those firms that do not develop vibrant networks will generally fail to manage uncertainty (Gibb, 1998). The utilization of networks can also compensate for weaknesses in business planning (Storey and Westhead, 1996). This failure to plan often extends to the management of human resources.

It was noted earlier that SMEs face barriers in recruiting staff of sufficient calibre. When recruiting new members of staff, attention can be drawn to the flexibility of working in a dynamic environment, but the payment of market-based salary levels and associated financial benefits is beyond the reach of many small firms. The training and development of existing staff becomes a necessity in such circumstances yet SMEs rarely offer formal training programmes (Scott et al., 1996; Vickerstaff, 1992). This does not imply that no training takes place; the extent of informal training within SMEs is often underestimated (Curran et al., 1997). Employees have to be multi-skilled. Firms have to react quickly and provide appropriate training when, for example, up-to-date equipment is installed or the firm is planning a move into new markets.

This brief look at the barriers faced by SMEs illustrates some of the problems that smaller enterprises will encounter either at the outset or when looking to develop and expand their operations. However, it is acknowledged that many factors contribute to growth, including the characteristics of the entrepreneur, the firm, the strategy adopted and the external environment (Storey, 1994). There is no single route to growth. Bridge et al. (2003, p.292) sum up the current state of knowledge as follows: 'Growth is likely to occur when a number of key factors in each category combine, although it is most unlikely that there is only one or a few combinations, and the combinations for success could change as the business develops and market circumstances alter'.

The previous statement highlights the difficulties confronting policy makers in framing proposals to assist smaller enterprises, an issue that is taken up in the following section.

3.4 SMEs: a case for government support?

The evidence presented thus far suggests that the SME sector is a major driver of sustainable economic growth. As the level of entrepreneurial activity increases, economic performance improves, along with the rate of innovation, technological change and exports. A vibrant SME sector can lead to an increasingly resilient and adaptable economy. Smaller enterprises also enhance social inclusion and create opportunities for many more members of society to participate in productive economic activity. In a broader context, this inclusion extends to the desire of transition economies to catch up with the developed world and attain the perceived affluence of Western nations. The level of entrepreneurial activity (along with the level of education) has been found to contribute significantly to a nation's long-term prosperity (Peng and Shekshnia, 2001).

The job creation capacity of the sector was discussed in Section 2.2.1, and some of the more extravagant claims made by some academics for SME job creation (notably: Birch, 1979) were called into question. Despite this scepticism, there can be no doubt that self-employment and micro/small firms are an important source of new jobs, especially with reduced opportunities for employment in many larger companies and (often newly-privatized) public sector bodies. In Canada, for example, a significant proportion of employment growth in the early years of the 1990s came from self-employment and micro-enterprises (Ernst and Whinney, 1994). In the US, the very smallest firms – those with between one and four employees – created 450,000 jobs in 1995, or 35 per cent of the jobs created in that year (Fassin, 1998). A similar situation has occurred in England and, to a lesser extent, in Europe (Arzeni, 1998). The potential for job creation in India (Dutt and Sundharam, 2000) and the countries of East Asia remains immense.

Employment generation and the other benefits stemming from SMEs mean that the sector is becoming more important economically and politically. Across the globe, policy makers are seeking to create an attractive business environment that will favour smaller enterprises, and allow such firms to be established and then fulfil their potential. The creation of the 'right' macroeconomic conditions is part of this approach, but it has proved much more difficult for governments to fund the SME sector efficiently and effectively. The aim of SME policy is usually to generate additional economic activity over and above what would have occurred in the absence of government intervention, but Bryce (1965, p.77) cautions policy makers that:

> Properly defined and realistically approached, the small-industry field is important and can contribute much to the whole process of industrialization. If confused by sentimentalism and approached emotionally with little regard to the costs and benefits involved, small industry development can easily become a missionary movement which accomplishes little but which diverts scarce resources of development funds and people away from other activities.

Indeed, there are some commentators who argue that government incentives and/or protection for smaller enterprises prevent the development of some critical attributes required for success, principally self-reliance and determination. With very few, if any, exceptions, governments have not followed this line of thinking!

Having decided to support this sector, a key decision is whether to attempt to increase the number of small firms or to target assistance at growth firms. Bridge et al. (2003, p.292/3) summarize the pros and cons of these approaches. Targeting should, in theory, concentrate resources where they are most needed and produce the 'best' return on government funds (especially if job creation is the main objective). However, opponents would argue that: it is not easy to target the small proportion of 'winners'; start-ups often face greater obstacles in the financial markets; and, new firms are the seedbed of future medium-sized and large firms. Moreover, job creation results not only from the small number of high-growth firms, but also from the sheer volume of new micro firms. The outcome of this debate is that most governments seek to assist firms across the spectrum from potential start-ups to well-established medium-sized companies.

In view of the constraints outlined in Section 3.1, it is no surprise that governments offer financial help to SMEs, especially those engaged in innovation. Improved access to subsidized finance should reduce the cost of capital of smaller enterprises relative to their large counterparts and enable SMEs to increase their share of GDP (Cook and Nixon, 2000). This, of course, assumes that the firms currently affected by funding gaps have a genuine need for finance in support of a commercially viable project.

Harding (2002) details the financial assistance offered in a number of developed economies; this ranges from loan guarantees and soft loans, to grants and R&D assistance. It is noteworthy that many governments have worked with private sector VC funds to support high-technology start-ups, or offered stand alone seed funds to plug any funding gaps as they emerge – this theme is taken up in the following chapter. There have also been considerable efforts to encourage coordination between funding sources. The UK has lagged behind other countries in offering such measures; this omission might help to account for the fact that the equity gap seems more prominent in the UK than in other developed nations.

Market related issues were cited as another major constraint facing the SME sector. Official support to tackle this problem can lead to unwanted distortions in the economy. In India, for example, there is a well-defined policy of product reservation for small-scale firms (described in more detail in Chapter 6). Companies that grow above a certain size are deprived access to cheap capital and other subsidies hence the policy penalizes those that are successful; there is no incentive for small firms to move into global markets or become more competitive.

Even if deserving cases for funding could be identified, and appropriate market-related measures put in place to avoid the sort of anomalies that occur in India, this might not be sufficient to ensure a thriving SME sector. The diversity of growth patterns among SMEs, and the variety of barriers faced by smaller enterprises, make it difficult to provide worthwhile assistance. In relation to management training and development, for example, Curran (1999) argues that the vast majority of UK firms reject help from the Government because the advice given will conflict with their intuitive and informal approach. Moreover, training providers tend to offer generic programmes for the SME sector, whereas small firms are seeking the answers to their 'unique' problems (Bennett et al., 1994).

Governments across the globe, and especially in the developing world, do not have the resources to provide customized assistance that meets the requirements of individual firms. In such circumstances, the private sector can play a critical role in supplementing public support. This is where the VC industry can offer tremendous assistance to the SME sector. Apart from their obvious capacity to provide risk capital: 'venture capitalists take a very close interest in their investee companies and provide management with advice, hands on support and industry connections' (O'Shea, 1996, p.16). This role is very much in line with the networking ethos that forms the lifeblood of so many SMEs.

Finally, individual initiatives (whether public or public/private) have to form part of an integrated framework of support if the potential benefits of the SME sector are to be realized. For example, government schemes might be instrumental in motivating entrepreneurs to set up enterprises, but decisions to expand and invest often depend upon access to technological opportunities (Pandit and Siddharthan, 1998). Likewise, the willingness of SMEs to respond to structural adjustment reforms is influenced by a wide range of factors, including the degree of infrastructure development and the prevailing institutional and political framework (Cook and Nixon, 2000).

3.5 Summary

The brief survey of possible funding gaps affecting smaller enterprises suggested that SMEs in the developed world could generally expect to receive funding if they have a commercially viable proposition. The banks are the principal source of funding and a lack of collateral might result in credit rationing in some cases. Innovative firms seeking to grow might be disadvantaged, but gaps in the market for risk capital are being filled by the VC sector or government-linked schemes. In the developing world, SMEs face more problems in accessing bank finance, whether short-term advances, long-term loans or equity finance (as the following chapter will confirm).

Having examined the constraints on growth in SMEs and summarized the case for government support for this sector, it is clear why so many governments intervene to assist SMEs. However, private sector support can complement official assistance and the role of VC was highlighted above. This mode of financing is well developed in some regions and at the embryonic stage in many parts of the world. It is now time to turn to a detailed examination of the VC sector. This forms the basis of Chapters 4 and 5.

4
An Introduction to Venture Capital

4.1 Introduction

As discussed in the preceding chapter, SMEs are playing an increasingly important role in the evolution of both developed and developing countries. Most governments support the creation and development of smaller enterprises, based on the presumption of job creation and other benefits from the SME sector. It was noted that small firms have made a significant contribution to GDP by introducing innovative products, generating employment, contributing taxes to the Exchequer and so forth. The role of SMEs as an engine of economic growth was emphasized by Berger and Udell (1998, p.614), when they argued that public attention on smaller enterprises in the 1990s stemmed: 'from the belief that innovation – particularly in the high-technology, information and bio-technology areas – was vitally dependent on a flourishing entrepreneurial sector'.

The advantages associated with SMEs will be captured only if they have access to financial and other resources. The funding available to both start-up ventures and expansion-oriented firms has been a source of debate (summarized in Section 3.1). Governments have stepped in to fill perceived gaps in the funding of SMEs, but it is acknowledged that smaller enterprises still rely principally on personal funding, or private sector financial institutions (especially the banks).

If expansion-minded firms take on higher levels of borrowing, this increases their exposure to risk and it may create vulnerability to debt-servicing crises. Moreover, the owners effectively give full control of a firm's prospects to its bank from the start (Diamond, 1991). Many firms face collateral-related constraints and they will not have to deal with such dilemmas; young firms and/or firms based on intangible assets have little or no collateral hence they cannot secure bank funds.

The emphasis placed by commercial banks and other lending institutions on an established track record and collateral leaves a funding gap for potentially viable ventures. An alternative approach is for the founder(s) to relinquish part ownership of the company to venture capitalists in exchange for equity-based financing; the returns to the VC firm usually come from capital gains achieved through a public listing or trade sale.

VC has been described as a remarkable feat of financial engineering (Barry, 1994). Firms avoid the interest and capital repayments on loans and can achieve profitability more quickly. Amit et al. (1990, p.106) contend that: 'risk sharing and lack of funds drive entrepreneurs to seek venture financing'. Zider (1998) argues that VC exploits a niche created because of the structure and rules of capital markets. Someone with an idea or a new technology cannot obtain funding from the banks because the interest margin on a loan would be prohibitively high. Without significant sales and assets, and a reasonable profit history, that proposal cannot access the public equity markets. VC thus fills the void between the two extremes of bank lending and flotation on public equity markets.

Once investments have been made, venture capitalists contribute their business experience and industry knowledge gained from helping other young companies. Entrepreneurs with a technical orientation but little or no general management experience often require assistance in establishing appropriate managerial systems and controls (Ehrlich et al., 1994). This expertise and guidance across a whole range of issues has added value to many projects in the US and Western Europe (Fenn and Liang, 1998), and there is great potential for repeating this process in the emerging market economies.

This chapter offers an introduction to venture capital; theoretical issues are left to later chapters. It opens with a definition of VC then presents a brief history of this concept. The main types of investor are discussed, before the global spread of VC is considered. The final section draws together these themes by summarizing the macroeconomic impact of VC and exploring how and why governments have supported the development of national VC industries.

4.2 Definition of venture capital

Shilson (1984, p.208) defines VC as: 'an activity by which investors support entrepreneurial talent with finance and business skills to exploit market opportunities and thus obtain long term capital gains'.

The original ethos of VC was support for high-growth, high-risk ventures (typically new companies and/or technologies). The following characteristics emerged as the bedrock of this form of finance:

- Equity-based financing;
- Funding linked to managerial assistance;
- Rewards through capital gains rather than running (dividend) yields;
- Investment in young and start-up companies hence ...
- Long-term, patient investment.

VC still comprises longer-term finance in unquoted companies where the primary reward is an eventual capital gain. However, as we shall see later, the bulk of global venture funds are now directed to larger deals in later stage investments.

4.3 History of venture capital

The broad concept of 'venture capital' dates back for centuries, and evidence of the VC industry can be found in the 15th Century activities of the merchant venturers in the Far and Middle East. These individuals were active traders who also set up commercial enterprises. It is also thought that primitive VC was practised on the Arabian Peninsula in the pre-Islamic era. There are certainly similarities between the operation of VC and the basic beliefs held in the Islamic world; the Italians are said to have borrowed the Islamic concept of *Mudaraba* (see Chapter 9) in the 10th Century and this type of financial instrument then spread throughout Europe (Cizacka, 1995).

More recently, the phenomenal growth of the German economy over much of the last century is attributed to its banking system adopting a venture-capital approach to the financing of business enterprises. As Foxwell noted (1917, p.512): 'German banks are partners, often controlling partners, in many of the largest and most successful enterprises. Many of them have been nursed from their earliest beginnings by the banks, and largely owe their success to guidance received from them'.

The German banks were in close touch with the iron and coal industries, manufacturing and trading companies, and the ocean steamlines. The banks provided not only conventional bank finance, but also held share capital in many companies and played an active role at board level (Economist, 1911). The German banks were definitely not mere lenders or passive capital providers, and it was this: 'close union between the financial experts and the captains of industry that gave German industry its remarkable efficiency' (Foxwell, 1917, p.521).

4.4 Evolution of contemporary venture capital

The origins of the term venture capital are reputed to lie with the American financier, John Whitney. After the Second World War, Whitney set up a US$10m fund for the purpose of making investments in risky projects. 'His partner, Benno Schmidt, suggested the term "venture capital" over lunch, as best combining the sense of both risk and adventure, and Whitney approved it on the spot' (Reid, 1998, p.17). The unprecedented success of J.H. Whitney and Company, as well as another early fund, Payson and Trask, provided a major incentive for other individuals and firms to enter the industry (Dominguez, 1974).

In its institutional form, VC came into existence in the US in 1946 when MIT President (Karl Compton), Harvard Business School Professor (Georges F. Doriot) and local business leaders formed American Research and Development – ARD (Gompers et al., 1998). ARD provided risk capital for new and rapidly growing small firms, primarily in the manufacturing and high-technology sectors (Bygrave and Timmons, 1992).

In the UK, Scottish investment trusts were leaders in providing private funds for companies engaged in high-risk ventures like railways and canals during the 19th Century. Modern VC emerged in the UK, not with the formation of the 3i Group in 1945 but when Charterhouse launched a specialist fund to provide equity finance for fast-growing, new small businesses in the 1930s (Reid, 1993).

These trends across the globe led to radical changes in the mobilization of long-term risk capital for SMEs and brought this new funding opportunity to the attention of smaller enterprises. The VC sector now forms an indispensable part of the financial markets in many economies.

4.5 The spectrum of venture capital

Encouraged by early successes of venture funds, and bolstered by government support, VC is now available through individuals (either singly or collectively) and a variety of fund structures. This section describes the principal institutional forms of venture fund then outlines four broad categories of investors. The complexities associated with the management of venture funds are beyond the scope of this book, but the analysis below gives a flavour of how venture funds are structured.

4.5.1 The venture capital institutions

Venture funds can be divided into two main categories: independent and captive. The former are the most common, and they are typically structured as self-liquidating funds that have a definite lifespan and a specified investment policy. The ability to adopt the 'limited partnership' legal form has been a key driver in the growth of independent funds (although this route is not possible in many countries, including India).

The venture capitalist acts as a general partner, takes all investment decisions and conducts all dealings with investee companies. The institutional investors are limited partners who commit funds during the lifetime of the fund. When investments are sold, the proceeds are redistributed to the limited partners. The limited partnership format offers significant tax advantages to the investors. The general partner receives an annual fee for managing the fund, and also has the incentive of 'carried interest'. In other words, the investment managers are entitled to a share of the profit generated by the fund, provided that a specified minimum rate of return has been achieved.

Captive funds tended to be subsidiaries of major financial organizations, typically banks or insurance companies. However, a range of organizations now operates captive funds, from technology-oriented firms to major conglomerates with interests across many sectors. These VC funds are usually open-ended and they draw monies from the parent for investment, as and when required.

Between these two extremes, there are many 'hybrid' venture funds that combine (say) funds from a parent organization and money raised from other sources. For further detail on the operation of the VC market, the reader is directed to a succinct overview of the situation in Europe (Deville, 2002.)

At the top end of the financing spectrum, some rather secretive bodies have had a powerful impact over recent years, especially in the US and the UK. These are the 'private equity' providers who supply capital for transactions outside normal public markets. This group encompasses a wide range of investors, from major investment banks to specialist funds and financial 'boutiques'. The term 'private equity' has started to replace 'venture capital' in the popular and financial press. Private equity can be used to develop new products and technology, to expand working capital, to make acquisitions, or to strengthen a company's balance sheet. It can also resolve ownership and management issues, for example, succession in family-owned firms.

VC is thus included within the broader remit of private equity. The two terms are often taken to be synonymous, and it is certainly difficult to separate the two concepts when compiling statistics on VC/private equity deals. For the purposes of this book, the focus is on VC as defined above by Shilson (1984), whereby the venture fund makes an injection of cash in exchange for equity (or equity-linked financial instruments). VC also includes buy-outs where the incumbent management retains a substantial stake in the post-investment entity. However, the use of private equity to fund acquisitions or high value leveraged buy-outs is beyond the scope of this book.

Within the VC market as a whole, there are four broad categories of investor, although any distinction is bound to be rather artificial and the boundaries are very blurred. There are also syndicated deals where financial packages are put together from one or more of these sources; for example, social VC might be combined with funding from an independent private sector fund.

4.5.2 Formal venture capital

Formal VC is the dominant and the most widely recognized (and researched) segment of this asset class. It comprises a wide range of independent, captive and hybrid funds, and usually refers to venture funds operated by the private sector alone.

As discussed above, talented entrepreneurs with novel ideas often find it tough to raise the requisite finance. They do not have a proven track record, or collateral to secure bank debt, and they are not in a position to tap the public equity markets. VC fills the void between these two extremes (Zider, 1998). Some VC firms invest in companies of all sizes and sectors, but many venture capitalists will invest only in companies at a particular stage and/or sector.

Formal VC was traditionally associated with seed capital for start-up firms engaged in research and development, product and/or market development and so on, and the industry's role in funding such companies is acknowledged. Venture funds have also been described as the dominant source of post start-up finance for growth-oriented technology-based companies (Freear and Wetzel, 1990). However, the risk of an investment tends to increase in line with the length of time before the investment is realized; moreover, smaller and/or early stage investments incur greater appraisal and monitoring costs in relation to the amount invested. Across the globe, therefore, the focus of investments in established VC markets has tended to shift from the early stage of the firm's existence to relatively late stage investments, notably expansion capital or buy-out funding (Wright and Robbie, 1998).

The private equity market has been among the fastest growing markets for corporate finance in the US. In the 15 years between 1980–1995, the organized private equity market grew from around US$4.7bn to US$100bn while the corresponding figures for VC were US$3bn to US$90bn (O'Shea, 1996). The phenomenal growth patterns in these similar but overlapping forms of finance have resulted in fierce competition among investors for good quality investment opportunities. At the top end of the VC market (later stage funding and larger deals), private equity firms compete with traditional VC firms to invest in companies in financial distress or those seeking buy-out financing. This competition for deals has been fuelled by the emergence of sophisticated hybrid products that have elements of debt and equity, notably cumulative redeemable preference shares. In these circumstances, classic VC skills that add value in company formation, building and harvesting, have sometimes been superseded by financial engineering know-how that generates short-term gains (Bygrave and Timmons, 1992).

4.5.3 Corporate venture capital

Corporate venture capital (CVC) is very common across the developed world, notably in the US, Europe and Japan. Cash-rich companies, typically multinational corporations, make equity investments in unlisted, privately held companies for financial reward and to fulfil strategic objectives (Siegel et al., 1988). The first corporate venture capitalist was probably Du Pont when that Company took a 38 per cent stake in General Motors in 1919 – General Motors was one of its principal customers at the time.

CVC investments are made directly or indirectly. Direct investments occur when companies spot an investment opportunity, carry out their own due diligence process and then take a minority stake in the target. This is often through the mechanism of a captive fund. Many investments in high potential young ventures are driven by purely financial motives, with the aim of securing a specified rate of return; others are tailored to the long-term goals of the investor (Gibson and Blake, 1992). These goals could include the expansion of markets, tying up raw material sources, reducing competition, gaining access to new technologies and assisting with product development (Reid, 1998;

Elango et al., 1995). It should be apparent that achieving these 'non-financial' goals can also have a significant impact on the investor's profitability.

Indirect CVC usually refers to situations where large organizations contribute to an independent venture fund. More than 100 US corporations have been involved in indirect CVC for many years (Winters and Murfin, 1988), and they are still substantial investors. Even though the investments are through a third party, funding the desired industries can create future synergies for corporate investors.

4.5.4 Social venture capital

There has been increasing recognition that certain sections of the community have been neglected by the private VC industry. This neglect has led to the growth of what has been called social venture capital (SVC). Funds whose primary aims are not high economic returns may now be responsible for around 40 per cent of venture or venture-like disbursements in the US, and more than half of early stage investments (HBS, 2000). Governments in Europe and Asia have also undertaken similar initiatives.

Waddell (1995) surveyed nine US venture funds that pursue social as well as financial goals, for example: by investing in environmentally sensitive enterprises or those owned by employees or members of ethnic-minority communities. He found clear differences between social and conventional venture funds; the former: 'have developed explicit missions, different investments profiles and have different associational networks' (Waddell, 1995, p.337).

Across the globe, such funds operate in a variety of ways. It might be a fund operated solely by the government, or an independent fund that combines public and private monies. Whatever the structure of the fund, the need for official efforts to supplement the private sector is predicated on two shared assumptions: that the private sector provides insufficient capital to new firms, at least in certain regions and industries; and that governments can identify firms where investments will ultimately yield high social returns (HBS, 2000).

A number of studies have explored the extent to which SVC has led to SME growth. Cooke and Wills (1999) associated this form of finance with civic engagement involving a high degree of trust, reliability and reciprocity among social networks; in a sizeable proportion of investee firms in Denmark, Ireland and Wales, social capital has resulted in enhanced business performance. Likewise, businesses offering support to their local communities will be recognized and rewarded by residents who act as customers, employees, professional service providers, suppliers and so on (Besser, 1999).

Such achievements are laudable, but it has proved very difficult for fund managers to balance conflicting objectives (Lerner, 1996). The key question is whether social objectives can be achieved without sacrificing financial returns. Private investors frequently fail to appreciate the long-run nature of investments with a social dimension. Another important problem identified by Lerner is the design of appropriate compensation schemes for both investors and fund managers, especially where private and public sector money is combined in a single investment pool. This issue is considered further in Section 4.8 below.

4.5.5 Business angels

The market for VC is not just institutional. Many individuals ('angels') invest relatively small amounts of equity (seed capital) in a venture in which they have had no prior connection. Angel investors seek financial gain and also the opportunity to contribute to the growth of a firm; they are often entrepreneurs who have sold their own business at a substantial profit. These individuals are able to provide seed capital and share their know-how and expertise, to the benefit of their investee companies. The involvement of angel investors might be less formal than the requirements of venture funds, but can be equally effective, and frequently more so (Mason and Harrison, 2000).

The role of angels used to decline sharply in the later stages of firm development, where the sums involved are too large for a single investor (Freear and Wetzel, 1990). This situation has changed as groups of individuals now invest through syndicates hence the investment size can obviously be considerably higher; recent evidence from the UK suggests that around 40 per cent of angel investments were in established companies or to fund later stage deals (Mason and Harrison, 2002). Most informal investors in US have a preference for investing in high-technology enterprises (Haar et al., 1988), whereas UK business angels invest across a broader spectrum of sectors, both manufacturing and services (Mason and Harrison, 2002).

The informal VC market in the US is over twice as large as the private placement market, and eight times larger than the formal VC sector in terms of the amount invested (Gatson, 1989). In the UK, Mason and Harrison (2000) estimate that angels invest around £500 million per annum. This figure is acknowledged to be based on some questionable assumptions yet it is probably the most accurate available. The size of the UK angel market is therefore around 10–12 times smaller than the formal VC market, almost the reverse of position in the US. This may offer another explanation as to why the 'equity gap' still prevails in the UK but not the US.

4.6 Venture capital in established markets

Until the late 1970s, VC had been primarily a US phenomenon. After World War II, individuals such as John Whitney established a reputation for profitable investment in emerging industries. The efforts of these pioneers caught the attention of wealthy American families like the Rockefellers, and institutional investors were soon attracted into the flourishing VC industry.

Venture funds backed high-technology firms such as Cisco Systems, Microsoft, Netscape and Sun Microsystems, as well as a number of prominent service firms including Federal Express, Staples and Starbucks (Gompers et al., 1998). Apple Computers, Data General, Intel, Prime, Tandem and Digital Equipment also figured among the spectacular success stories of VC investments. On the other hand, the industry has also been involved in some astonishing failures, including Ovation Technology, Osborne Computers, Ztel and Gavilan, where venture capitalists were left with worthless investments (Sahlman, 1990). While such failures may have brought temporary halts to the growth of this sector, the upward trend in the volume of funds available for VC investment has been remorseless.

Despite the modest activity in the UK in the 1930s, the global proliferation of the VC industry stemmed largely from the high profile US activity described earlier: Venture capital quickly crossed the Atlantic, spreading first to the UK then throughout Europe (Wright et al., 1991).

The most prominent UK VC firms in the early days were Charterhouse (formed in 1934) and the institution now known as the 3i Group (formed in 1945). The 3i Group backed some outstanding performers, including Rodime, Xenotron, and Spring Ram (Clark, 1987), but it is fair to say that the VC industry in the UK did not achieve immediate success on the scale of the US fund managers. There was a flurry of activity in the mid-1970s, but the UK VC community declined in the face of big losses from backing high-technology companies. A small core of VC firms survived until the UK market started to revive from around 1984.

Between 1985 and 1990, British venture capitalists invested over £5.4bn in the UK (BVCA, Report on Investment Activity, various). The UK VC community was, and remains, the largest in Europe. Investment levels in the UK rose steadily over the 1990s, from just over £1bn per annum in 1991 to £6.4bn in 2000. This proved to be a high point. Investments in high-technology companies were thought to be driving the country to levels of prosperity unimaginable 30 years ago (Christensen et al., 2001). However, this perception changed markedly in the aftermath of a worldwide 'meltdown' in confidence and share prices in the technology sector in the early part of the new millennium.

The VC industry in Western Europe during the early 1980s (excluding the UK) was in its infancy and investment activity was 'relatively small' (Tyebjee and Vickery, 1988). As with the UK, this situation changed quickly. By 1988, more capital was committed to the combined VC pools of the UK and continental Europe than the US market (Bygrave and Timmons, 1992). This dramatic increase in the scale of VC activity continued over the 1990s and into the new millennium. In 1989, there were 93 VC companies registered with the European Venture Capital Association (EVCA), managing a total of £1.15bn. In 2003, EVCA registered VC companies had invested an aggregate of €29bn in 7,446 companies, while the outstanding portfolio of investments (at cost) was estimated at €139bn (www.evca.com).

The Government of Japan established three Small Business Investment Companies in 1969, but their impact was minimal. A few private VC firms were formed in the early 1970s. However, the 'Oil Crises' of that period led to economic strains that, combined with stock market volatility, resulted in a dearth of exit opportunities and brought Japan's initial VC boom to an end (O'Shea, 1996). The slower than expected growth in VC since then stems from the fact that: 'the Japanese industrial and social context is so different from the American' (Clark 1987, p.27). VC investment in Japan totalled approximately US$90m in 1982, a figure that had risen to US$6bn by 1989 (Leinbach, 1991). Despite severe economic pressures in Japan, the money available for VC investment grew from US$17.8bn in 1995 to US$25bn in 1999 (Christensen et al., 2001).

4.7 The dissemination of venture capital

It is estimated that nearly 80 per cent of the world's population lives in developing countries. It is therefore logical that there should have been a massive expansion of VC activity from its US base into Europe, Asia and Australia. According to one estimate, global VC had invested in assets valued at over US$90bn by 1994 (O'Shea, 1996), and more than half of the venture funds under management worldwide was held outside the United States. Over the last five years of the last century, cross-border private equity flows rose sharply from US$268bn to US$1.1trillion in 2000 (Persaud, 2001).

VC is becoming a major factor in the creation and development of businesses in Asia. In Korea, the Government has been supporting VC firms since the 1980s, as part of its programme to develop high-technology industries. The number of VC companies increased exponentially from four in 1986 to 56 in 1991, by which time they were managing aggregate funds of US$1.15bn (Rah et al., 1994). In Taiwan, there were 29 VC firms in 1994; the largest fund was US$44.5m and the total investment pool across the 29 funds was US$150m (Pandey and Jang, 1996). At the end of 1987, there were only four active VC firms in Singapore, but 80 were in operation by 1991 (Economic Development Board, 1991); US$100m was under management in 1985, a sum that had increased to US$1.2bn by 1991 (AVCJ, 1993).

Growth in VC investment across the region has been spectacular since the early 1990s. Investment increased from US$1.2bn in 1992 to US$12.3bn in 2000 – refer to Table 4.1. A significant milestone was passed in 1995, when global VC investments by private sector funds grew by a greater dollar amount in Asia than anywhere else. This growth was more dramatic in the developing nations than in Japan (HBS, 2000). At present, some 70 per cent of funds for investment in these emerging nations are sourced from the US and UK (Karsai et al., 1998). However, East Asian nations have very high saving rates, often about 30 per cent of GDP, hence pension funds in those countries are likely to become an increasingly important source of investment funds for the VC community.

Table 4.1 shows that Asian VC volumes more than doubled between 1998 and 2000, and that there has been a strong recovery in 2003 after the worldwide volatility in stock markets in the early part of the new millennium. The growth of VC is not confined to the established economic powers in Asia. After launching its first venture fund in 1984, with an amount equivalent to US$5.5m, Malaysia had 17 funds managing an aggregate amount of US$175m by 1994; these figures had increased to 40 funds and over US$500m respectively by 2002 (Bank Negara, Annual Reports).

Elsewhere, Biekpe (2001, p.10) states that: 'African governments are increasingly aware that VC investing is critical to the growth of their economies'. The emerging market economies of Central and Eastern Europe represent a further environment in which VC has a role to play. Hungary, Poland and Slovakia were thought to be prime candidates in

Table 4.1 Annual VC Investment in Asia

Year	Total (US$m)
1992	1,162
1993	1,587
1994	2,486
1995	5,534
1996	5,561
1997	4,611
1998	4,914
1999	9,071
2000	12,329
2001	11,225
2002	9,112
2003	17,486

need of finance to support enterprise growth. It is estimated that VC investment in Hungary totalled US$400–500m in 350–400 investee firms by the mid-1990s. At the same time, venture funds under management in Poland totalled over US$750m; Slovakia was the most underdeveloped of the three countries with only US$96m available for investment in 1996 (Karsai et al., 1998).

4.8 The macroeconomic impact of venture capital

In the global context, market failure in entrepreneurial financing means that many viable projects to remain unfunded (Amit et al., 1998). The VC industry plays a relatively modest role in new business formation, but venture-backed firms have a significantly lower failure rate than conventional firms (Bygrave and Timmons, 1986), as well as a multiplier effect that gives rise to the formation of other firms and even whole industries (Bygrave and Timmons, 1992). This generates a virtuous circle whereby a vibrant economy creates attractive opportunities for entrepreneurs to start new firms that eventually increase the demand for VC (Gompers, 1998).

Hoffman (1972) contended that an efficient and effective VC sector was a necessary precondition for growth and development, especially at a time of unprecedented advances in technology and science. There is increasing global awareness that a modern economy cannot reach its full potential without encouraging its entrepreneurs to innovate, and this realization enhances the prospects for VC (Schwartz, 1994; Patricof, 1989).

Venture capital backed start-ups are an important source of innovation and technological development and serve as a major source of new wealth creation in the US. Investee firms that achieve IPOs typically account for one-third of the market value of all IPOs in each year (Sahlman, 1990). Likewise, venture-backed firms have created approximately 230,000 jobs every year and have spent over US$5bn on research and development (Bygrave and Timmons, 1992). Between 1991–1995, firms supported by VC increased employment and revenues at a far higher rate than the Fortune 500 companies (Biekpe, 2001). Moreover, venture-backed firms employ more highly skilled professionals (53 per cent) than the workforce as a whole (13 per cent), as well as far fewer administrators (10 per cent) compared to the Fortune 500 companies (25 per cent).

The benefits have not been confined to the recipients or the wider economy. Investors have been very satisfied, as the returns on VC have beaten all other investment opportunities in the US – see Figure 4.1 below.

The US studies described above provide sufficient evidence to suggest that the VC sector has enhanced national wealth, even though there are some dissenting voices, for example: Manigart and Sapienza (2000) point out that there has been very little analysis of failures or low-growth investee companies.

However, studies outside the US have confirmed that VC has had a positive impact. Venture-backed firms in France and the Netherlands produce substantial numbers of jobs and export sales per unit of equity

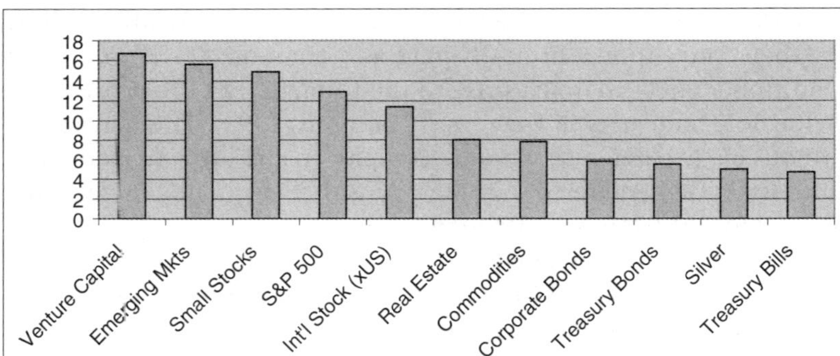

Figure 4.1 Average Annual Returns on US Assets, 1945–1997 (%)
Sources: Morgan Stanley Research; Dimensional Fund Advisors; Hobotson Associates; National Association of Retailers; FactSet Research Systems and Venture Economics.

investment (Coopers and Lybrand, 1993; VNO, 1994). This form of finance has also contributed significantly to the economic growth and global competitiveness of the UK economy; enterprises selected for VC funding outperformed leading UK companies in relation to annual growth rates in sales revenue, pre-tax profits, total net assets and job creation (BVCA, 1996).

Another area where VC has contributed to economic restructuring has been in supporting spin-out ventures from both private and public sectors. In the global economic downturns of the late 1980s and early 1990s, large corporations sought to increase profit margins by selling off parts of the organization. At the same time, governments were offloading public sector enterprises at a rapid rate. It is estimated that, across 80 countries, more than 7,000 privatizations were undertaken in the early 1990s (Megginson et al., 1994). In such circumstances, the VC sector often supported the incumbent management or employees to purchase the entity being divested in the private sector or privatized by government.

The returns to investors obviously depend on the skill of the fund managers in selecting and managing the investment portfolio. However, the availability of investment opportunities at a reasonable price and the rate of economic growth also contribute to the returns achieved. The VC markets in the UK and US are reaching maturity, and there is a perception of diminishing investment opportunities in those nations, particularly the US. It is no surprise, therefore, that investment funds mobilized in the US are invested by VC firms outside that nation's borders.

It was noted above that around 70 per cent of funds for investment in the emerging nations of Asia are sourced from the US and UK (Karsai et al., 1998). Funds have been attracted to these developing nations because of their economic strength, for example: developed economies grew at an inflation adjusted annual rate of 1.9 per cent between 1990 and 1995, whereas emerging market economies grew at 5.2 per cent per annum over the same period (Deirdre, 1995).

Despite the prospect of high returns, threats accompany every opportunity. Some private equity investors are not keen to enter developing markets. Even when they are prepared to conduct deals in such countries, venture funds have tended to target established firms in traditional industries (Lerner and Pacanins, 1997). Investments have typically been associated with privatizations, strategic alliances with foreign partners, or infrastructure projects (such as bridges and highways). Fund managers are reluctant to invest in the kind of early-stage, technology-intensive deals that bring the benefits described above. This reluctance might stem from (say) a scarcity of trained technologists or an inadequate infrastructure; sometimes, intellectual property (IP) protection is weak and the enforcement of IP rights is questionable (HBS, 2000).

Many governments in developing countries across Eastern Europe and Asia have encouraged the growth of VC by laying the groundwork for this sector and removing major hurdles in its development. They are aware of the benefits that the SME sector can bring and that firms in receipt of VC funding are generally more successful than the 'average' small firm. An investment portfolio that excludes innovative firms is therefore a source of frustration to policy makers. However, it has to be accepted that many fund managers feel that it is imprudent to take on the additional risks of investing abroad, unless the 'home country' government provides some form of risk mitigation.

Official assistance to reduce the risks faced by venture capitalists can take many forms, summarized in Jeng and Wells (2000). In Portugal, for example, the Government granted significant tax exemptions to venture funds and it also contributed to private equity funds; likewise, the Norwegian Government committed significant funds for VC investment after the nation's banking crises of the late 1980s. The authorities in Holland covered venture fund losses of up to 50 per cent from 1990–1995, although this scheme has now been withdrawn, and the Irish Government permitted equity investments by pension funds that led to a big increase in the supply of funds to the VC industry.

The most successful official attempt to recreate the 'Silicon Valley' funding environment is acknowledged to be Israel from 1992 onwards (Autler, 2000). With its Yozma initiative, the Israeli Government provided pump-priming finance to venture funds. This initiative also encouraged foreign and local corporations to invest directly in high-technology start-ups, notably data communications, software and multimedia. Scientists and engineers left secure jobs to start their own companies that received generous government support for R&D programmes; VC funding then made further growth possible (Jeng and Wells, 2000). A record number of firms went public, either in Israel or on the US equity markets. In total, ten Yozma funds were created between 1993 and 1996; they thrived by combining domestic and foreign expertise, and exploiting economies of scale in the appraisal of high-technology investments located in a cluster (Teubal, 2002).

After the Yozma programme was withdrawn, the Israeli Government continued to foster growth in VC by allowing tax advantages to foreign venture funds and individual investors (home and foreign). This culture allowed investors to benefit financially from their investments (Dossani and Kenney, 2002), and it was a key factor in maintaining healthy VC investment after direct Government support ended. The original Yozma funds spawned follow-up funds and the group of investors associated with the Yozma initiative now have funds under management of approximately $5bn, a large share of the total VC funds managed in Israel (Teubal, 2002).

Government VC schemes can therefore play a vital role in stimulating the supply of private capital, through co-investing with the private sector or lowering the risks of VC through (say) the provision of guarantees (O'Shea and Stevens, 1998). The most successful VC programmes have been those funded by governments but managed by professionals in the private sector. Conflict between public policy objectives and the private sector philosophy of venture fund management has led to problems in the past (Lerner, 1996). In essence, fund managers should be given investment guidance that is not too restrictive, but it is sometimes very difficult for governments to stand aside when there is a history of state allocation of national capital (Dossani and Kenney, 2002).

4.9 Summary

Having defined VC and described its main institutional forms, the chapter also offered a brief overview of its development and global impact. It is no surprise that governments across the globe have tried, through a variety of mechanisms, to develop an indigenous VC industry. Attention now turns from describing the operations of the sector to consideration of the theoretical issues associated with VC investing.

5 Venture Capital: Theoretical Foundations for Research

5.1 Introduction

Academic interest in this field was raised by the early success stories of venture-backed companies. However, it took practitioners some time to be convinced that empirical research in this field was worthwhile; Barry (1994, p.11) suggests that research: 'on VC was virtually non-existent before the decade of the 1990s ... mainly because of lack of data, but some good examples do now exist, and unanswered questions are available in abundance.' Over recent years, the importance of VC backed companies in employment generation, exports and new product development has led to an explosion of academic activity to tackle these 'unanswered questions' (Wright et al., 1999). In this upsurge of research activity, a host of topics have been investigated and this introduction gives the reader a flavour of the breadth of study in this field.

Despite the sheer volume of studies conducted on this topic, a number of key themes have emerged. The unifying theme is undoubtedly agency theory. Most VC models view the relationship between venture capitalist and entrepreneur(s) from the principal-agent perspective (Manigart and Sapienza, 2000). Although attention in the literature centres on the relationship between venture fund and investee companies, it will be appreciated that venture capitalists are also acting as agents of their capital suppliers.

The role of venture funds is to reduce information asymmetries by seeking out and assessing valuable investment proposals that uninformed 'outsiders' would reject (Amit et al., 1998). Adamati and Pflederer (1994) stress that venture capitalists act as inside investors by gaining private information on investment projects during pre-investment screening. It is no surprise, therefore, that many studies concentrate on the appraisal criteria used in the investment decision. Prominent work in this area has been conducted by MacMillan (1985), Fried and Hisrich (1994), Zacharakis and Meyer (2000) and Riquelme and Watson (2002). There is also increasing interest in the investment cycle adopted by VC firms (Hall and Hofer, 1993) and the way in which appraisal criteria might change throughout that cycle (Boocock and Woods, 1997).

Other aspects of VC activity that have caught the attention of academic researchers include: the composition of the investment portfolio of VC funds (Bygrave and Timmons, 1986); the information sources utilized by venture capitalists (Bergemann and Hege, 1998); the role of VC in promoting leveraged buy-outs, especially those led by the incumbent management (Wright et al., 1999); and the factors that affect the ability of venture funds to raise finance for investment purposes (Gompers et al., 1998).

Research on the US venture capital industry has been supplemented by studies in other developed regions or countries. Important studies have been conducted in: Europe (Wright and Robbie, 1998); Korea (Rah et al., 1994); Japan (Choy, 1990); Canada (McNaughton, 1991); New Zealand (Norman, 1989); Australia (Ryan, 1991); Israel (Autler, 2000); and Singapore (Scheela, 1994). Studies in the emerging markets have demonstrated that VC has now grown into a truly global industry, for example: China (Choy, 1990); Malaysia (Boocock, 1996); Taiwan (Pandey and Jang, 1996); Hungary, Poland and Slovakia (Karsai et al., 1998); and South Africa (Biekpe, 2001). To complete the picture, cross-country studies have been carried out for: 20 OECD countries (O'Shea, 1996); Eastern European economies (Manigart et al., 2000); and Canada, Europe and the Asia Pacific Region (Knight, 1998).

A good proportion of the studies above deal with the appraisal criteria and sources of information used by venture capitalists in deciding whether to invest. However, even if the selection process can reduce the risk of subsequent failure, robust post-investment monitoring is essential to ensure that investments realize their full potential. This has been a relatively neglected area for study (Steier and Greenwood, 1995), although research in the US has started to address monitoring and control issues (for example: Gompers, 1995; Manigart and Sapienza, 2000). Wright et al. (2002) stress the need for further research on the structuring and monitoring of investments in emerging VC markets like India.

The research programme that underpins this book concentrates on the valuation, structuring and monitoring of VC deals in India. These three issues are firmly rooted in the unifying theme of agency relationships that, in turn, stem from fundamental concepts in finance theory (covered in Section 5.2 below). The remainder of the chapter deals with the VC investment process or cycle, to place the valuation, structuring and monitoring of deals in the context of how venture capitalists operate, from raising the funds for investment purposes through to the final exit from the deal.

5.2 Theoretical foundations of research into venture capital

The theory of the firm relates to every business organization, including venture funds. Theoretical work on the principal-agent relationship also has particular relevance for research into the VC industry. Within the principal-agent framework, adverse selection underpins the valuation process and influences the techniques employed by venture capitalists to accept or reject investment proposals. The theory of contracts is also examined, as this has a critical impact on the structuring of VC deals. Finally, corporate governance and moral hazard will be discussed in the context of monitoring VC investments.

5.2.1 Theory of the firm

With the separation of ownership from control within the firm, many of the checks that operated to limit the power of the (controlling) managers began to disappear (Berle and Means, 1932). The interests of the owner(s) and manager(s) of a firm may and often do diverge. This issue retains a central position in the economic theory of the firm (Demsetz, 1983, p.387) and thus: 'there would seem to be a demand for an ongoing supervision of management or for a linking of the interests of management to those of shareholders'. The split between ownership and control creates a number of challenges for venture fund managers.

5.2.2 The principal-agent relationship

The principal-agent relationship is concerned with situations in which one party, the agent, acts on behalf of another party, the principal. If both parties seek to maximize utility then there is a strong possibility that the agent might not fulfil the contract in the best interests of the principal. This situation can occur in all organizations and at every level of management (Jensen and Meckling, 1978). Theoretical analysis based on the principal-agent view has been widely adopted in the field of economics. Its acceptance within disciplines such as accounting and finance was slower (Sahlman, 1990), although it is now acknowledged that few financial settings contain as many potential agency problems as VC (Amit et al., 1990).

Most studies have treated the venture fund as principal and the entrepreneur or owner-manager as agent. The venture capitalists provide the bulk of funding but have no involvement in the day-to-day operations of the firm. It is expensive for the venture fund to verify progress: 'when an agent has private information about the projected future performance of a project, the principal is unable to completely monitor the agent's actions, and information asymmetry prevails' (Harrison and Harrell, 1993, p.636). There is clearly the potential for goal conflict between the principal and agent, especially where the agent overstates his/her capability to deliver certain results; this could happen when a capital-starved entrepreneur receives funding for a start-up project that relies upon untested technology. On the same theme, principal and agent often have different attitudes towards risk hence they might pursue different actions to achieve their objectives.

5.2.3 Adverse selection

Kanodia et al. (1989) argued that entrepreneurs or managers have more information about the viability of projects than either owners or investors. Those directly involved with the firm are in an advantageous position when deciding whether (and how) to proceed with a project. In dealing with a lender or investor, entrepreneurs might conceal certain aspects of their character and it is difficult to judge integrity in the appraisal process; entrepreneurs usually (although perhaps not always) have more idea than the financiers about the value of collateral offered and/or the prospects for their business. In other words, they possess inside information about the enterprise. Without effective mechanisms to transfer bankable information, the market for funds may not function properly; an average price will be offered to all proposals, and good quality projects will be driven away (Akerlof, 1970). In these circumstances, adverse selection is the almost inevitable outcome.

It was noted above that venture funds have expertise in backing proposals that uninformed outsiders would reject (Amit et al., 1998; Adamati and Pflederer, 1994). Fund managers develop 'more complete information systems, thus eliminating private information' (Harrison and Harrell, 1993, p.636). It is therefore essential to identify the most valuable sources of information used by venture capitalists in ascertaining the true characteristics of entrepreneurs and the value of their proposed ventures (Jensen and Meckling, 1978).

The correct valuation of a business (especially in the start-up or early stages) is a crucial first step in allowing venture capitalists to earn the desired rate of return on their investments, yet venture capitalists can rarely (if ever) rely totally on established benchmarks for valuation and risk assessment (Manigart et al., 1997). The standard valuation techniques will have to be tailored to the specific circumstances of the project under consideration. For example, venture capitalists using discounted cash flow (DCF) techniques will apply different rates of discount to counter possible optimism on the part of the entrepreneur in relation to his/her capabilities, market size and so on.

Investments might be discouraged if high discount rates are applied to uncertain, long-term projects, but setting appropriate rates is an integral part of the complex process of reducing adverse selection and wider agency problems (Sahlman, 1990). Prudent investors will invest in those projects offering the highest return for an equivalent level of risk. It is accepted, however, that: 'the nature of the adverse selection problem may not be constant for all entrepreneurial ventures, but may vary with the stage and sector of an investment' (Wright and Robbie, 1998, p.538).

A key aim of the research programme conducted for this book was to investigate the sources of information used by Fund Managers in India in valuing potential investments and hence in determining the entry price for the deal. Another important element was to explore whether different discount rates are applied to firms in different sectors and/or at different stages in their development.

5.2.4 Theory of contracts

An organization comprises a connected series of contracts, written and unwritten, between the owners of factors of production and their customers. These contracts specify the rights of each agent in the organization, the performance criteria on which agents are evaluated, and the payoff functions they face (Fama and Jensen, 1983). The theory of optimal contracts under conditions of uncertainty has received considerable attention in recent times; a deeper understanding of the nature of contracts has emerged as an emphasis on the legalities associated with individual contracts has given way to a more general concern with the contractual purposes to be served (Wright and Robbie, 1998).

Previous studies suggest that contracts are a good deal more varied and complex than is commonly realized and that governance structures vary with the nature of the transaction. Williamson (1979) proposed that three elements underpin the value of transactions: the level of uncertainty associated with a transaction (the critical attribute); the degree to which durable transaction-specific investment is incurred; and, the frequency with which a transaction recurs. The VC deal is characterized by considerable uncertainty, it demands a substantial, non-refundable ('durable') investment in appraising the deal, and follow on financing is often required. The VC contract therefore has high value and it has to be structured with great care and attention.

The literature has identified two primary approaches to establishing the optimal contract between principal and agent, namely 'complete' and 'incomplete' contracts (Spier, 1992). Complete contracts are almost invariably preferred by venture capitalists, and such contracts can be based on either behaviour or outcomes. The former specify that agents should behave in accordance with what was contractually agreed (Sappington, 1991; Jensen and Meckling, 1978). In the VC context, the terms of agreement might include restrictions on further fund raising without prior approval, or place limits on board representation and the appointment of auditors and/or key employees. Likewise, fund managers will generally impose anti-dilution clauses, to ensure that additional shares are not sold to new investors without the consent of the initial investor(s). An outcome-based contract influences behaviour indirectly by aligning the interests of agent and principal (Eisenhardt, 1989); VC funding will usually be advanced in stages, as certain milestones are achieved.

The basic objective of structuring contracts in this way is to minimize the risk involved in VC investments. This risk falls into two broad categories, market risk and agency risk. Market risk depends on factors such as the size, growth and accessibility of the market, the existence of a market need and the reaction of competitors (Scherer, 1980). Venture capitalists devote considerable attention to market factors in investment appraisal, as well as the character and track record of the entrepreneur seeking funds. However comprehensive the appraisal process, there is a danger that the entrepreneur will pursue his own interests once the funds have been advanced. Venture capitalists have learned how to combat such agency risks by utilizing stringent contractual provisions in complete contracts (Fiet, 1995). These provisions allow fund managers, for example, to replace underperforming managers or to increase their shareholding without any further cash injection (Amihud and Lev, 1981).

One of the most challenging problems in venture financing is to determine when to release funds for continued development (Bergemann and Hege, 1998). The achievement of milestones is not always easy to ascertain, especially where high-technology projects are concerned. The use of 'ratchets' in financial instruments is also widespread; ratchets allow the management team to retain more equity as the performance of the firm improves. In general, however, the way in which venture capitalists utilize certain financial instruments to reduce the risk associated with a deal has received little attention in the literature (Wright and Robbie, 1998).

Our research investigates how venture capitalists in India alleviate agency risk by the use of covenants, the setting of milestones in the staging of investments and the selection of different financial instruments.

5.2.5 Corporate governance

Continuing the theme of agency theory, corporate governance is an umbrella term to cover the mechanisms by which owners of a firm exercise control over management to protect their interests (John and Senbet, 1998). In a market economy, it is apparent that governance structures become more elaborate as agency and market risks are perceived to increase. The governance system should ideally reflect the circumstances affecting a particular firm, and it should be sufficiently robust to ensure that the directors operate in the interests of the shareholders as a whole. In the VC context, a venture fund typically has the right to board representation and its representative might also have the power to replace the CEO of the company in certain circumstances.

As an aside, venture funds also act as agents of their suppliers of finance (Manigart and Sapienza, 2000). The latter exercise power through governance mechanisms imposed on the venture fund; this has been a neglected area in VC research and more detailed reporting requirements are likely to become the norm (Karsai et al., 1995).

The provision of financial information is a crucial aspect of corporate governance; it bridges the information asymmetry between entrepreneurs and external fund providers, and provides a check on the stewardship of the company by the entrepreneur and his/her management team. A key role of the non-executive directors is to monitor the provision and accuracy of financial information, thereby reducing the incidence of fraud, whether deliberate or caused by incompetence.

Our research programme investigates the rights of venture capitalists to board representation and the extent of the power afforded to the representatives appointed by venture fund. In addition, we examine the frequency and extent of monitoring reports that investee companies have to provide at the insistence of the venture funds.

5.2.6 Moral hazard

The problem of moral hazard stems from information asymmetry and constitutes a prime concern of corporate governance. Moral hazard refers to 'hidden' action motivated by self-interest. At the post-investment stage, the venture capitalist has to ensure that the entrepreneur does not pursue objectives that bring the firm into conflict with the venture fund. This problem is especially prevalent in early stage investments in sectors where assets are largely intangible and the firm faces a number of growth options (Amit et al., 1998).

In such circumstances, accounting information is frequently required on a more detailed basis than is statutorily required for quoted companies (Sweeting, 1991; Mitchell et al., 1995). This is not unexpected. Quoted companies will have a proven track record of sales and earnings, whereas venture-backed investments are much less established. Likewise, the venture capitalist requires increased frequency of reporting in the post-investment regime: '... this attenuates moral hazard, and further promotes contractual efficiency by more precise control of the investee firm' (Reid, 1998, p.143). There is evidence that the monitoring process enables venture funds to cut-off new financing in the light of negative information about future returns, and that venture capitalists provide more financing and a greater number of rounds of financing in the more successful transactions (Gompers, 1995).

As stated above, our research programme explores the frequency, nature and breakdown of information gathered by venture capitalists in India.

5.3 The venture capital investment process

It is clear that theoretical concepts from the field of finance underpin the study of VC. Some key research questions have been identified in the previous section. However, before setting out the scope of the research programme, it is necessary to describe the typical cycle of VC investments – see Figure 5.1.

The investment process comprises a number of distinct stages. The precise number of phases is open to debate (Boocock and Woods, 1997) yet most fund managers appear to operate on broadly similar lines. This holistic view of the VC investment process sets our three key research topics in context. The valuation, structuring and monitoring of VC deals represent stages five to seven of the investment cycle.

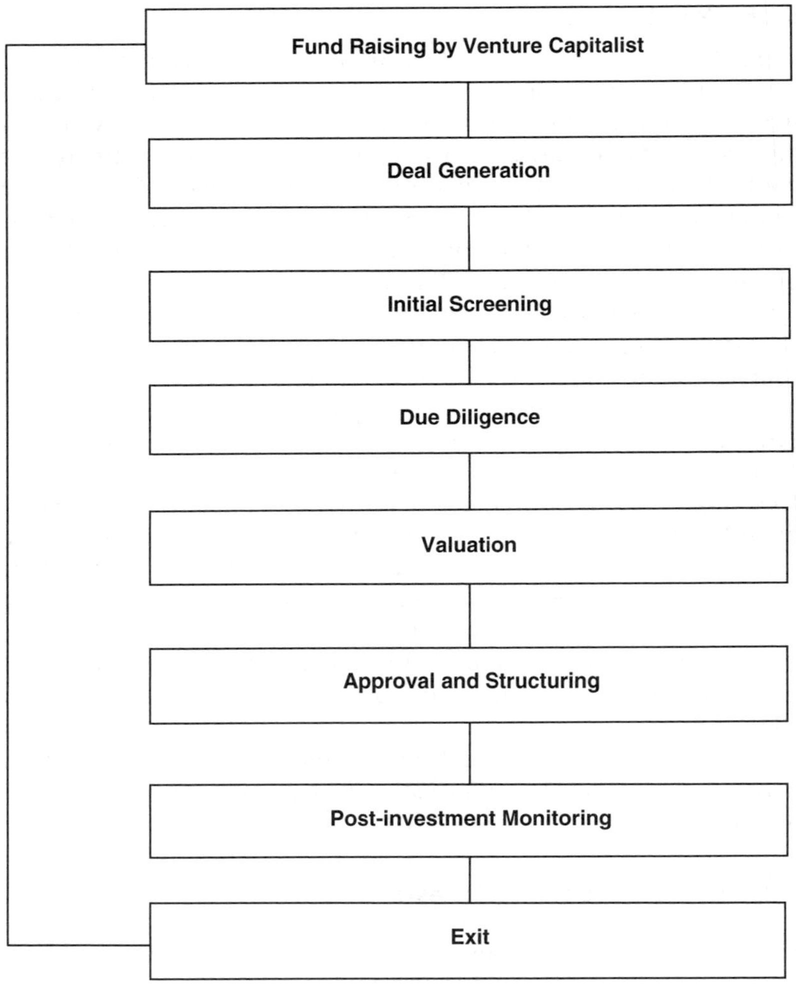

Figure 5.1 The Venture Capital Investment Process
Source: Based on Wright and Robbie (1998, p.535)

5.3.1 Fund raising

Most research on VC has focussed on the investment process. However, the fund management team has first to raise capital from investors. For independent venture funds, the process begins when the team develops its business plan and investment strategy; the fund managers then approach long-term fund providers (typically insurance companies or pension funds). By contrast, a captive fund is supported by a bank or financial institution or sponsored as part of a CVC programme. The parent company or sponsors set aside funds for this purpose. Captive funds spend less time and effort on fund raising activities although some internal lobbying might be required to push their case through (Fassin, 1998). Other types of venture fund (as described in Section 4.5) raise their finance from a variety of official and private sources, ranging from individuals to multinational and/or multilateral finance institutions.

5.3.2 Deal generation

It is crucial to generate a stream of high potential deals. The proposals received must have the promise of generating the target rates of return. Each venture fund develops its own distinct strategy for sourcing potential deals; the long-term investment goals might lead a fund to stipulate the sector, size of the project, location, stage of investment and so on. The deal generation strategy has to take account of the entrepreneurs' search and decision process, as well as increased competition between venture capitalists (Wright and Robbie, 1998).

Venture capital is an intangible service that is often a once in a lifetime deal for a client. The generation of deal flow is not to be taken lightly. Many deals stem from networks within the financial community, such as accountants, investment bankers and stockbrokers. Business school alumni can also form an effective introduction route. In other instances, governments have acted as intermediaries, most notably by establishing systems to match business angels and/or venture funds with entrepreneurs.

Some venture funds are prepared to receive 'cold calls' by post or phone, but these seldom lead to investments (Fried and Hisrich, 1994). Nonetheless, a number of VC firms have experimented with direct marketing campaigns. An alternative strategy is to recruit executives who possess the specific skills required to seek out transactions (Murray, 1995). Fund managers also use a variety of marketing tools (including public relations, advertising and market research) in an attempt to secure ongoing deal flow (Fassin, 1998).

Across the western world, management and/or leveraged buy-outs have emerged as a major source of VC deals. For instance, buy-outs consistently account for over half of UK VC investments in terms of value, and in some years the figure has been over 70 per cent of value (BVCA, various). Investment patterns vary as competitive pressures lead to diminishing returns for this type of deal. However, the VC community remains committed to identifying management and/or investor-led buy-outs, and divestment candidates resulting from corporate refocussing programmes (Thompson et al., 1997).

5.3.3 Initial screening

Venture capitalists obviously seek to attract desirable propositions yet many unwanted proposals are received; these have to be weeded out as quickly as possible. The preliminary screening process should enable fund managers to form an initial view about the project. When handling as many as a thousand proposals a year (Fiet, 1995), venture capitalists need an effective screening system to save time and money, and also to prevent agency problems associated with information asymmetry and adverse selection.

There is broad agreement that proposals are assessed first in relation to the quality of their business plans and the basic concept of the project (Dixon, 1991). The specific factors taken into account in this initial stage are more debatable. MacMillan et al. (1985) suggested that the personality and track record of the entrepreneur and/or management team was vital, while Fried and Polonchek (1993) argued that venture capitalists were more concerned with market acceptance. The appraisal criteria are considered in some depth below, but it has to be appreciated that a full appraisal is conducted for only the ten per cent of proposals that pass from initial screening through to the due diligence stage.

5.3.4 Due diligence

The aim of this part of the investment cycle is to minimize investment risk by conducting a thorough investigation of the information presented in the business plan, with special attention usually paid to the qualities of the entrepreneur or management team, the product and market potential, and the scalability of the business model. The financial projections are also crucial, as they demonstrate the likelihood of an exit route for the venture fund via a trade sale or Initial Public Offering (normally referred to as an IPO or flotation).

The academic literature on the evaluation criteria used by venture capitalists was highlighted in the introduction to this chapter, including notable studies by MacMillan et al. (1985), Fried and Hisrich (1994), Zacharakis and Meyer (2000), and Riquelme and Watson (2002). MacMillan et al. (1985) argued that the evaluation criteria could be grouped in five broad categories: the entrepreneur's personality and experience; product and market characteristics; and financial aspects of the proposition. (The composition of the management team was considered separately.) By asking venture capitalists to rate, on a scale of 1–5, the importance of various factors, MacMillan and his colleagues used a horse racing analogy to conclude that the 'jockey' (the entrepreneur) was the key concern, followed by the product and market characteristics, then the financial aspects (including the exit strategy for the venture fund). Many subsequent studies have attempted to confirm or deny the importance of these factors, and Zacharakis and Meyer (2000) summarize how researchers have classified the information sought by venture capitalists – see Figure 5.2.

Since the early studies by Wells (1974), Tybejee and Bruno (1984) and so on, the complexities of the investment decision have been explored in a variety of ways. The research methodologies have been

Study	Wells (1974)	Poindexter (1976)	Tyebjee & Bruno (1984)	MacMillan et al. (1985)	MacMillan et al. (1987)	Robinson (1987)	Timmons et al. (1987)	Hall & Hofer (1993)
Method	Personal interviews	questionnaire	Phone survey & questionnaire	questionnaire	questionnaire	questionnaire	Unstructured interviews	Verbal protocol
Sample Size	8.97	46 (Study 1) 41 (Study 2)		100	67	53	47	16
Entrepreneur/team characteristics								
Mgmt skills and experience	X	X	X	X	X	X	X	X
Venture team				X	X	X		X
Mgmt stake in firm		X	X					
Personal motivation	X					X		
Entr personality				X				
Product/service characteristics								
Product attributes	X		X	X	X			
Product differentiation			X				X	
Proprietary	X			X	X			
Growth potential			X					
Market acceptance				X			X	
Prototype				X				
Market characteristics								
Market size	X		X				X	X
Market growth	X		X	X		X	X	
Barriers to entry			X				X	
Competitive threat				X	X		X	
Venture creates new market				X				
Financial characteristics								
Cash-out method	X		X					X
Expected ROR		X	X	X			X	
Expected risk		X						
Percentage of equity		X						
Investor provisions		X						
Size of investment	X		X					
Liquidity				X	X	X		
Other								
References	X					X		
Venture development stage		X	X					
VC investment criteria								X

Figure 5.2 Information Factors used in VC Decision

drawn from a variety of disciplines; these include construct analysis (Fried and Hisrich, 1994), verbal protocols (Hall and Hofer, 1993; Sandberg et al., 1988) and social judgement theory (Zacharakis and Mayer, 2000). Whatever the methodology employed, recent studies have tended to confirm the weightings given, and the rankings assigned, to the evaluation criteria put forward by MacMillan et al. in 1985.

However, Riquelme and Watson (2002) point out that the relative importance of these selection criteria may vary as the application progresses through the investment cycle or according to the type of investment being considered.

Fried and Hisrich (1994) were among the first researchers to assess how the criteria changed through the different phases of the investment process. They concluded that venture capitalists use three generic screening criteria: the viability and novelty of the project; the integrity, track record and leadership skills of management; and, the possibility of high returns and a viable exit route for the venture fund. The key contribution of this research was to highlight the fact that the progression of an application depends on a positive shift in the perception of potential investors. It is only after the information in the business plan submitted by the entrepreneur has been verified that venture capitalists develop 'emotional attachment' to a proposal; at this point, emphasis switches from finding reasons to reject the proposal to exploring ways in which these can be overcome. A similar process was apparent in a study conducted by one of the joint authors of this book (Boocock and Woods, 1997).

The investment criteria may also change according to the type of investment. Venture fund managers will place emphasis on different factors as they appraise, for example, a small 'seed corn' investment, a proposal to fit out a factory prior to production or a buy-out of an established business (Wright and Robbie, 1998).

While the evaluation criteria appear to be consistent over time, venture capitalists are not infallible in their selection of investments. The best fund managers should be able to exploit market opportunities and achieve above average returns by capitalizing on their expertise. However, very few studies have examined the relationship between the appraisal criteria discussed above and the subsequent success or failure of investments. The best known attempt to address this issue was a follow-up study conducted by MacMillan et al. (1987); the 'jockey' was critical for securing the finance, yet 'demonstrated market acceptance' and 'proprietary protection' were necessary for investee firms to prosper. These two factors had not been prominent in their initial study (MacMillan et al., 1985).

The small number of studies that have attempted to confirm whether the selection criteria employed have resulted in successful investments have all suffered from methodological shortcomings. Information gathered from venture capitalists has usually been self-reported and collected some time after the event (Hall and Hofer, 1993); this can lead to bias because investors are unable or unwilling to identify (and differentiate between) those criteria that led to success or failure. These studies cannot, therefore, offer conclusive evidence of an association between venture capitalists' appraisal criteria and performance. However: 'there is general agreement on the importance of a number of key variables, namely: characteristics of the managerial team; product superiority; the market; and business strategy' (Riquelme and Watson, 2002, p.401).

It should be apparent that a serious appraisal of these factors takes considerable time and resources on the part of the venture fund. Time restrictions, cost constraints and situational factors may thus impact directly on the level of due diligence carried out (Harvey and Lusch, 1995). In order to exploit their technical and product expertise, and thereby reduce due diligence costs, venture capitalists often specialize in certain types of transactions, industries and/or financing stages (Bygrave, 1987).

5.3.5 Valuation

Valuation is often considered the final phase of due diligence, and it will be required only for that small percentage of proposals still 'in play'. Any valuation is primarily a function of the investors' perception of the risk associated with a project in relation to their target rates of return.

There are a number of valuation techniques that venture capitalists can apply to the financial information contained in business plans submitted to them. Valuation methods are usually linked to the investment culture of a particular country. The most widely used valuation technique in the UK is the multiplication of past or projected future earnings by an appropriate price-earnings ratio; in the Netherlands and Belgium, by contrast, venture capitalists tend to rely upon DCF techniques, while the book value of net worth is used frequently in France (Manigart et al., 1997).

In practice, most venture capitalists (wherever they are located) utilize more than one method to determine the value of a potential investment, and this can lead to prolonged negotiations with entrepreneurs before it is possible to strike a deal. It will be appreciated that setting an incorrect price for a security does not affect the underlying value of the firm; rather it transfers value from one security-holder to another (Myers and Majluf, 1984). The venture capitalists want to strike the deal at the lowest possible price; this maximises the proportion of shares received for their investment and obviously increases their ultimate return when the firm is subsequently floated or sold via a trade sale. The entrepreneur(s) will suffer excessive dilution if the valuation is too low and thus receive a lower proportion of the proceeds when the value of the firm is realized in future.

The consequences of an incorrect valuation can be severe hence this issue is often a stumbling block in putting a deal together. Whatever valuation method is adopted, sensitivity analysis is essential to explore different possible scenarios, especially in the highly uncertain environment of a start-up (Wright and Robbie, 1998). This process will produce a range of valuations around which negotiations can take place.

Having raised the funds for the investment pool, appraised investment opportunities and completed due diligence, the next stage is to structure and execute deals with entrepreneurial teams (Sahlman, 1990).

5.3.6 Approval and structuring

The venture capitalists are now in a position to approve the proposal, but the fund manager and potential investee company still have to negotiate the deal. The former has to achieve the venture fund's required rate of return, while the entrepreneur does not want to give up too much ownership or be subject to excessive constraint in running the firm. The fundamental objective is to ensure that all parties are: '... comfortable with their positions' (Gibson and Blake, 1992, p.41)

This stage of the investment cycle involves consideration of three broad areas: the types of financial instruments used (equity, preferred stock or debt); the specific covenants included in the term sheet or the subscription agreement; and, the release of funds in stages to limit the downside risk of an investment.

The choice of financial instruments used in a deal is a complex decision and these initial comments are expanded in Chapter 7 (Section 7.5.2). Norton and Tenenbaum (1992) found that preferred stock was the most frequently used financing choice of venture capitalists, irrespective of the degree of risk perceived in the proposal (Norton and Tenenbaum, 1993). Adamati and Pfleiderer (1994) argue that venture funds should exercise control through taking equity yet giving the entrepreneur robust incentives to perform. Debt financing can be used in deals where income is generated from the outset, collateral is available and products are recession proof. These are comparatively rare in venture financing and Berglof (1994) recommends convertible debt as the most appropriate way to transfer control rights to the value-maximizing party.

There are a number of key concerns where the use of covenants can protect the venture fund. Venture capitalists, as described above, combat agency risks by stringent contractual provisions (Fiet, 1995). Most contracts protect investors against the dilution of the venture fund's stake and give preferential rights in the event of liquidation. The contract might also stipulate situations where prior approval has to be sought from the venture capitalists, such as amendments to the Articles of Association (Sahlman, 1990).

The release of funds against milestones reduces risk for the venture fund. These milestones can cover everything from the achievement of technical progress to the appointment of a marketing specialist. On the same theme, there are a variety of mechanisms to encourage entrepreneurs to perform well; ratchets allow the entrepreneurs to retain more of the equity if (say) profit targets are achieved or exceeded.

It is worth considering syndication at this point. Syndication is commonly (although not exclusively) associated with larger deals, and it involves the participation of different venture funds in the same deal, under the direction of a lead investor. Syndication is widely practised across the developed world, and it can involve some complex structuring issues.

There are two primary reasons why venture capitalists resort to syndication: diversification of risk; and, the ability to transfer equity to co-investors. First, venture funds can reduce the risk of investee failure by capitalizing upon the expertise of informed co-investors in evaluating, structuring and monitoring investments. (Investors tend to develop a peer group that refers deals to each other.) Syndicate members may also be able to share information, thus reducing uncertainty. However, it is not enough simply to share information and to generate deals; there have to be positive outcomes for syndicate members (Manigart et al., 1997; Murray, 1991). Second, syndicated deals may provide a straightforward exit route for an investment that is not yet ripe for public listing or trade sale. For example, if a venture fund with a finite life is seeking to redeem existing investments, co-investors can transfer shareholdings to each other.

Syndicated deals also spread control among several investors. This dilution of control can result in disputes over the timing and method of realizing investments (Norton and Tenenbaum, 1992). The popularity of syndicates also tends to vary in line with market conditions; the extent of syndication reduces when economic prosperity leads to an increasingly competitive VC market (Ravid and Spiegel, 1997).

Lerner (1994) conducted landmark research on syndication; he concluded (p.1) that experienced venture capitalists: 'primarily syndicate first-round investments to venture investors with similar levels of experience. In later rounds, established venture capitalists syndicate investment to both their peers and to less experienced capital providers'. Syndication can thus facilitate shared learning between venture funds and ensure that the ownership stake of the venture capitalists is maintained throughout different rounds of investment. Over time, venture capitalists might search: '... for syndicate partners with whom they are able both to complete transactions and to undertake effective monitoring' (Wright and Robbie, 1998, p.543).

5.3.7 Monitoring

After investing, the venture capitalists are reliant upon the efforts of the entrepreneur(s); all parties to the deal have been described as being in the same lifeboat! According to one venture capitalist (cited in Sapienza, 1989, p.93): 'Once we've cut the mooring, written the cheque and are rowing out to sea, we can either pull in the same direction or we can hit each other over the head with the oars'.

The experience of New Enterprise Associates (NEA), a US venture firm founded in June 1978, illustrates the value of effective monitoring (Gupta, 1986). The Fund grew from three partners, two offices, US$16.5m investment funds and six portfolio companies in 1978, to ten partners, five offices, US$126m capital under control and 90 portfolio companies in 1984. NEA was neither the largest venture fund in existence, nor did it give the highest returns to investors. However, it had earned a reputation for strong, steady performance because of its hands-on involvement in the management of investments, especially in the monitoring phase. The ten partners sat on 75 boards of directors and brought a whole range of commercial expertise (including operations, technology, banking and retailing) to the benefit of their investee companies. Their efforts had ensured a rewarding relationship over the term of the investment (Gupta, 1986).

Investee companies should not view directors installed by the venture capitalists as necessary evils, rather as valuable new resources. There are three distinct, yet overlapping, roles played by non-executive directors in venture-backed firms: carrying out duties undertaken by all non-executive directors, including protecting the reputation of the company; monitoring the activities of the company on behalf of all investors, by ensuring the regular provision of high quality information on performance; and, most pertinent in this context, performing special duties to protect the interests of the venture fund(s).

The 'protection of interests' function can lead to significant changes in the relationship between venture fund and investee company. The VC firm's representative could, for example, be in a position to advise the firm on how to market its product more effectively through networks known to the venture fund. Alternatively, the representative could draw the investors' attention to indicators that set alarm bells ringing, notably decreases in the ratio of tangible assets to total assets, higher market-to-book ratios and greater R&D intensities (Gompers, 1995). These indicators might cause the fund managers to call for more frequent monitoring or they might, in extreme cases, exercise an option to discontinue funding projects where there is (say) little probability of an IPO.

In a US survey, Rosenstein et al. (1993) examined the composition and activities of boards of directors in 162 venture-funded high-technology companies in California, Boston and Texas. The boards increased in size as the company progressed. The venture capitalists or their representatives were mainly concerned with recruiting the CEO and assessing his/her performance, serving as a sounding board to the management and paying particular attention to financial performance. There was some concern expressed that the board members appointed by venture funds tended to dominate proceedings, at the expense of the executive management team.

Apart from board representation, other forms of communication are recognized as effective monitoring tools. Sahlman (1990, p.508) noted that: 'venture investors visit each portfolio company an average of 19 times per year and spend 100 hours in direct contact (on site or by phone) with the company. Since each venture capitalist is responsible for almost nine investments and sits on five boards of directors, the allocation of time to each portfolio company is considerable'. The more frequent and open communications between entrepreneurs and venture capitalists, the greater the incidence of mutual strategy choices (Bygrave and Timmons, 1992), and the easier it is to resolve problems encountered in establishing or maintaining relationships (Sapienza, 1989).

The financial information sought by the venture fund (and the board) is a key concern. The requirements in this respect were investigated in a UK study involving 20 major venture funds, responsible for managing over 75 per cent of the nation's investment pool (Mitchell et al., 1995). Venture capitalists put binding mechanisms in place to ensure the regular provision of accounting information, in order to prevent information asymmetry and hence moral hazard. In a later study, Mitchell et al. (1997) explored when (and why) venture capitalists call for improvements in the accounting information systems adopted by their investee companies. Such systems are evaluated during due diligence, and any upgrading thought to be necessary is made a pre-disbursement condition. The financial reporting requirements are reviewed in the event of an unexpected call for additional funds or the re-financing of an existing deal.

5.3.8 Exit

Venture capitalists typically seek to multiply their initial investment by a factor of 5–10 times on exit (MacMillan et al., 1985). The existence of a range of exit mechanisms is crucial for a healthy VC industry. The timing and availability of an appropriate exit route is essential for securing the venture capitalists' desired rate of return, especially as most money is earned on firms that eventually go public (Gompers et al., 1998). Traditionally, flotation on the public markets has resulted in a higher premium than a sale to corporate buyers (Fassin and Lewis, 1994). However, an undue reliance on the IPO route can lead to the delayed realization of investments if capital markets are volatile or lacklustre.

In the past, acquisitions (normally termed 'trade sales') tended to increase in popularity as the market for IPOs weakened. However, trade sales have increasingly become the norm as exit routes for venture capitalists. BVCA statistics (various) suggest that divestments from trade sales exceeded flotations, sometimes by a factor of ten in number, over the period from 1997–2000 in the UK. Most of the companies being acquired were healthy, successful businesses, unlike earlier times when most acquisitions occurred because the company could not go public.

Over time, a range of exit routes has been utilized by venture funds; apart from IPOs and trade sales, another growth area has been the sale of shareholdings to other institutional or portfolio investors. Bleackley et al. (1995) found that purchases of shares by portfolio investors were the most common exit route in the US and Canada. By contrast, trade sales, buy-ins and buy-outs were the most frequent routes to realize VC investments throughout Europe. Despite this trend, Bleackley and his colleagues stressed that venture capitalists in the UK and France still preferred IPOs as an exit route. At the other extreme, the most common form of exit for smaller and/or more troubled companies appears to be liquidation or the sale of the venture capitalists' shares back to the original owners of the business (Karsai et al., 1995).

5.4 Summary

This chapter introduced research in this field and highlighted three relatively neglected areas in the literature: the valuation, structuring and monitoring of VC deals. To set our research programme in context, the foundations of research in the field of VC were explored, starting with fundamental concepts from finance theory. These concepts include theoretical work on the firm, the principal-agent relationship and contracts. Within these frameworks, issues of particular interest for the study of the VC industry are information asymmetry, adverse selection, corporate governance and moral hazard.

The second half of the chapter dealt with the investment process or cycle, to place the valuation, structuring and monitoring of deals in the context of how venture capitalists operate, from raising the funds for investment purposes through to the final exit from the deal.

The objective of the research programme that underpins this book is to build on our existing knowledge base, especially in India. The analysis in Chapter 7 returns to the VC literature. It identifies critical elements for further study and develops a series of propositions for investigation.

Before then, it is necessary to provide a brief introduction to the Indian economy and financial system, to discuss the role of SMEs within that country, and to give the reader some background on the VC/private equity industry in India. This forms the basis of Chapter 6.

6

An Introduction to India: The Economy, Financial System, SMEs and Venture Capital

6.1 Introduction

We do not attempt to offer a comprehensive social and economic history of one of the most complex nations on earth. The aim is to give a flavour of key economic and social developments, in order that the reader can place our research findings in context. This chapter starts with a brief introduction to the Indian economy, and it highlights current strengths and weaknesses that influence the nation's ambitions to become a fully-fledged industrial power. Attention then turns to the financial system, with explicit focus on the financial institutions that support SMEs, before considering the role and development of the SME sector within the economy; Government support for smaller enterprises is identified as an area of concern. The chapter concludes with an assessment of the history, current status and prospects of the VC and private equity industry in India.

6.2 The Indian economy

India is one of the oldest civilizations in the world, and it has long been (and remains) one of the most populous nations on earth. For many generations, the outside world tended to associate India with famine, disease, the 'untouchables' of the caste system, and myriads of strange gods (Desai, 2003). As late as the mid-1960s, the Indian economy was crippled by a double harvest catastrophe after successive monsoon failures, and the people were dependent upon food aid from abroad. Within 40 years, however, the country was being spoken of as one of the 'BRIC Four' (Brazil, Russia, India and China) – four dynamic economies expected to make a global mark over the next half-century.

Going back to the early days, there has never been an authority that has ruled over all of India. The *Mughal* dynasty held power over the majority of the country between 1570 and 1707 then lost control in most territories. British rule spanned nearly two centuries from 1757 until 1947, but nearly a third of the country was nominally under the control of native princes. Over the period of the British administration, India experienced roller-coaster eco-political developments. However, the era since the nation became an independent sovereign state in 1947 has seen a transformation in its economic fortunes.

India adopted a centralized framework of planning soon after independence and set up a Planning Commission in March 1950. The Commission has formulated a series of Five-year Plans (ten in all, with the latest covering the period from 2002–2007) with the 'basic objectives of growth, employment, self-reliance and social justice' (Dutt and Sundharam, 2000, p.241). While India advocates the concept of the mixed economy (Balasubramanyam, 1984), a number of commentators suggest that official intervention has held back progress in key areas. For example, Desai (2003) contends that India's world-class textile industry has been stifled by policies that preserve employment in small scale, low technology firms.

Despite concerns over the excessive influence of Government, India has registered consistently positive growth rates in the years since 1947 – often over six per cent per annum (Government of India, 1999–2000). Growth has been affected by monsoon failures, and also two short periods of extreme social volatility: 1965–66, during the India–Pakistan hostilities; and 1979–80, a time of domestic unrest following the imposition of emergency rule. At other times, high growth has been responsible for economic problems, notably trade deficits; broad-ranging fiscal and structural reforms were instituted following a balance of payments crisis in 1991 (Towe, 2001).

India was historically an agrarian-based economy; the share of agricultural output in GDP has now stabilized at around 30 per cent (around half of the 1950 level), although over 60 per cent of the workforce is still engaged in agriculture (Dutt and Sundharam, 2000). The manufacturing and services sectors make up the balance of GDP. Strong advances in the services sector have led economic growth, and the Information Technology (IT) sector is now globally renowned. This move to services is a clear indication of a maturing economy.

Prior to 1984, protectionism was rife in the early stages of the Indian IT industry (Dossani and Kenney, 2002); Indian engineers then had the opportunity to learn about the latest software techniques and developments from the West. In addition, this sector has benefited from the activity of the Software Technology Parks of India (STPI). Founded in 1991, the STPI is an exception to the general rule that official agencies in India are rather cumbersome and bureaucratic. The STPI has operated mainly as a licensing agency, but it has also ensured that a modern IT infrastructure is in place (notably the availability of broadband) and that appropriate fiscal incentives are offered to firms engaged in IT activity.

The growth in services has been principally in business process outsourcing (BPO). This all-embracing term is most visibly associated with the proliferation in call-centres, but it also encompasses (say) support for the complex back office operations of investment banks and major healthcare delivery systems. Much of the IT activity is based on low value added services. The nation's plentiful supply of software engineers and its vast pool of English speakers work on projects that are delivered to clients in the US and elsewhere; this represents a classic reworking of the supply chain to reduce costs yet maintain quality.

While Indian software firms have an assured market for contract programming work, there is little incentive to develop 'hard' high-technology products for the global market. The development of such products carries a much greater degree of risk. The developer has to conduct speculative R&D, and trust that this investment will result in a viable product that meets the needs of demanding customers, in global as well as domestic markets.

Nevertheless, by continuing to focus on basic software development and support, firms such as Wipro and Infosys Technologies have developed rapidly and enjoy a global reputation. Both of these companies are quoted on US stock markets and were trading at high earnings multiples in 2004. Rather than moving into the development of 'hard' technologies, they (and other companies) are now competing vigorously to win contracts in management consultancy. For example, Infosys had launched a technology consultancy division and increased its total headcount from 5,500 to around 33,000 over the period 2000–2004.

Some commentators have questioned whether India will be able to maintain its global dominance of offshore BPO. However, Luce and Merchant (Luce, E. and Merchant, K., Financial Times [FT], 28 January 2004) suggest reasons why India is well placed to survive any protectionist moves from the western world:

- The size of cost savings are significant, and they will remain so because India has the youngest demographic profile of any big country in the world; the supply of good quality, English-speaking graduates keeps wage inflation down and ensures that a flexible workforce is available, many of whom have degrees in engineering or telecommunications

- India has established a world lead in BPO yet the proportion of its workforce employed in this sector is relatively low and growth can only continue as, for example, US venture capitalists insist that investee companies outsource some of their IT requirements to India
- India's service sector productivity is improving rapidly and, in some cases, it is outstripping western levels.

India has other successful firms stories apart from the IT companies cited above. For example, Ranbaxy and Dr. Reddy's Lab are world-class pharmaceutical companies that benefit from a plentiful supply of graduates in chemistry and mathematics. Reliance Industries and the Tata Group are conglomerates that are rated among the world's most respected companies, and there are a host of businesses that compete globally in the 'old' industries, including cars, motorcycles, cement and steel.

Signs of affluence are evident. There are 200m middle class Indians and increasing levels of disposable income have led to a consumer boom. Over 2003/4, for example, India's housing mortgage market was growing at 30 per cent per year, the country was adding 2.2m new subscribers every month to its 40m pool of mobile phone users, and internet usage was growing at a compound annual rate of 70 per cent plus. Shopping malls, multiplex cinemas and luxury car showrooms are commonplace in the booming metropolises of New Delhi, Mumbai (formerly Bombay), Chennai (formerly Madras) and elsewhere (Luce, E., FT, 9 December 2003 and 13 July 2004; Wolf, M. and Luce, E., FT, 4 April 2003).

However, India is a country of contrasts. The luxury goods cited above are the preserve of a minority in a population of around one billion people. India's human development indicators are unimpressive compared to China or other countries in SE Asia, despite some improvement over the past decade. Almost half of India's children remain chronically malnourished by United Nations measures, and the literacy level remains around 65 per cent, a figure that is low even by the standards of developing nations. More than 60 per cent of the workforce of over 400m survives in near subsistence levels in the countryside. The rural poor would welcome investment in the infrastructure (notably, irrigation and roads) that would reduce dependency on weather conditions.

One of the foundations of the nation's industrial policy has been a drive to create a congenial environment for foreign investors and accelerate Foreign Direct Investment (FDI) flow into the economy. FDI can play a very valuable role in transferring skills and technologies. Large sums have been attracted for infrastructure development, and investment in the consumer and capital goods sectors. However, there has been an alarming discrepancy between FDI approvals and funds received – over the 1990s, the actual inflow was a mere 20 per cent of the total amount approved (Reserve Bank of India, Annual Report 1999). It is significant that India has never attracted more than two per cent of the total FDI flow into developing countries; the nation has not been as successful as its regional rivals in garnering FDI.

The position in the early part of the new millennium is one of unfulfilled potential. The reforms of 1991 included changes to the tax system, substantial cuts in budget deficits, liberalization and deregulation in the industrial sector, and a series of measures to modernize the banking system. There was also a willingness to allow market forces the freedom to work and this enhanced the degree of entrepreneurial activity. Nonetheless, according to Acharya (quoted in Wolf, M. and Luce, E., FT, 4 April 2003): '... either the government [still] owns things it shouldn't own or it interferes with things it shouldn't interfere with'. A privatization programme has been modest in scale and met with limited success (Gouri, 1996).

The services sector, the least regulated in the economy, continues to be the strongest performer, while manufacturing, the most regulated sector, is the weakest. The momentum for reform slowed over the late 1990s and some difficult issues are still to be resolved. The outcome is that economic performance falls short of India's potential and its needs, even though recent moves suggest a change in the Government's attitude towards this process. Wolf and Luce (Wolf, M. and Luce, E., FT, 4 April 2003) summarize the principal problems as follows:

- a system of laws and regulations that deters the private sector from investing, especially the statute that prevents companies from dismissing workers without the express permission of the state government – this permission is almost invariably denied; the consequence is that less than 10 per cent of the labour force is employed in the formal economy and there is a spiralling black economy

- the poor infrastructure holding back industry, for example the frequent power cuts and the lack of modern port facilities; some progress has been made in this respect with the building programme for four-lane highways to link the four main cities
- the high cost of capital resulting from an underdeveloped securities market, an inefficient banking sector (covered in more detail below), and the need to finance massive government borrowing that continues to create inflationary pressures
- the increasingly dismal state of the nation's public finances, stemming from a large and growing fiscal deficit, a weak system for collecting tax revenues, and poorly targeted government spending; wasteful expenditure (such as subsidizing wealthy farmers and fertiliser producers) should be eliminated and the government should focus on those areas where it alone should be the provider, such as primary education and health.

The implementation of the 1991 reforms demonstrated that India has enormous capacity for embracing structural change and that sound policies can yield significant benefits in terms of productivity and competitiveness. However, the process of reform is unfinished and much of the fiscal adjustment that was achieved in the early 1990s has been reversed. Towe (2001) maintains that sustained growth henceforth will require a deep commitment to fiscal deficit reduction and wide ranging structural reforms; he goes on to argue that a critical success factor will be less government rather than more, thereby releasing the entrepreneurial talent within India. This theme is revisited in Section 6.4.

6.3 Financial system

In recent years, financial system development has gained increasing attention in both academic and policy circles. It is now acknowledged that a well-functioning financial system can play a crucial role in economic development (Levine, 1997; Pagano, 1993). Financial institutions provide important services such as diversifying and pooling risk, and also allocate funds to the most efficient investment projects by the effective screening and monitoring of borrowers.

In 1955, the Imperial Bank of India, the largest Indian commercial bank, was nationalized as the State Bank of India and charged with the task of expanding into rural areas. The 14 next largest commercial banks were nationalized in 1969, and the banking system effectively became an instrument of social policy. There was a long established system of consortium lending, with the 'lead banks' taking responsibility for assembling adequate long-term funding for sound industrial projects; this approach proved to be a catalyst for achieving post-independence industrial growth (Singh and Weisse, 1998). Nevertheless, prior to the 1991 reforms, the operation of the banking system was characterized by distortions. Depositors were reluctant to place their cash with banks, as the returns were set below the rate of inflation. Bank managers were risk averse civil servants who lent low cost funds to large, safe conglomerates.

SMEs were thus denied access to funding (Dossani and Kenney, 2002). Priya Basu, a senior economist at the World Bank, confirmed that the problems of asymmetric risk/return and information highlighted in Chapter 3 continue to affect SMEs in India (www.worldbank.org):

> SMEs in India have been unable to achieve the competitiveness that would allow them to drive manufacturing sector and overall economic growth, employment and poverty reduction. In large part, this is because of the problems SMEs face in accessing adequate funding ... Bankers are reluctant to lend to SMEs because of the high transactions costs and perceived risks of SME lending in the face of insufficient credit information, inadequate credit appraisal and risk management skills, poor repayment records and low market credibility of SMEs.

Banerjee et al. (2003) suggested earlier (Section 3.2) that the banking sector in India is widely perceived as 'expensive and inept', and characterized by a substantial degree of under-lending, often rejecting projects that might yield very high marginal returns on capital. Much bank lending is short-term, and subject to annual review. Lenders seek a quiet life, especially when past lending decisions have resulted in a substantial burden of non-performing and non-enforceable loans. (India introduced a new law in 2002 that allows the banks to foreclose on borrowers who default, yet this statute is currently, as at 2005, being tested in the courts.) Moreover, there is little incentive to improve credit appraisal skills in the face of a series of politically motivated 'rescues' of ailing financial intermediaries. This is just one example of how the Indian Government exerts a powerful influence on most segments of the financial sector.

Another source of Government influence is setting targets for bank advances to priority sectors, including smaller enterprises. The calculation and enforcement of these targets (effectively quotas) is somewhat opaque. Banerjee et al. (2003) maintain that the targets have, on balance, increased the finance available to SMEs. Unfortunately, non-performing loans represent about 20 per cent of the public sector banks' loans to small firms hence such lending may often be viewed as a social obligation (not a carefully considered lending decision).

Most of the 295 commercial banks are publicly owned. The latter control around 75 per cent of banking system assets and account for about 90 per cent of lending to small firms (www.ADB.org, ref: 36345). Apart from direct ownership, all banks are encouraged to invest substantial amounts in government securities that pay generous rates of interest. In many cases, around 40 per cent of the banks' assets are held in the form of government bonds issued to fund the fiscal deficit (Bhattatacharya and Patel, 2003). The profitability of public sector banks is modest because they are obliged to carry high staff costs (redundancies are out of the question) and they have failed to invest in new technology. The number of bank offices has increased enormously since the early 1990s, mainly in the public sector. A small number of private sector banks have committed funds to modern technology and superior human capital, but these private banks have a relatively modest role within the banking system. There are also stringent rules governing the expansion of the 44 foreign-owned banks; the playing field between domestic and foreign banks is not level.

Overall, the growth in bank lending to small firms has been moderate compared to the amounts advanced to their larger counterparts. Non-performing loans are an ongoing problem. Lenders suffer from the lack of fixed collateral within Indian small firms and the difficulty of registering a claim against property (even where it is available); there is also no provision for taking security over moveable objects. The outcome is that India's largest companies can raise capital at reasonable rates at home or abroad, but smaller enterprises face a cost of capital that is around twice the level faced by similar firms in neighbouring countries, including China (Wolf, M. and Luce, E., FT, 4 April 2003). It is difficult to identify disadvantaged firms, but the implication of high cost finance and credit rationing must be that some SMEs have been denied the opportunity to make a greater contribution to national wealth.

Apart from the banks, the Government has created a whole array of financial institutions to perform specialized lending functions, popularly known as Non-Bank Finance Companies (NBFCs); deposit/lending rates and credit allocation policies are again the subject of detailed control. For example, the Small Industries Development Bank of India (SIDBI) was established in April 1990. A number of development finance institutions (DFIs), for example, the Industrial Development Bank of India (IDBI), provide medium and long-term credit to industry, but their focus of attention is rarely the SME sector. Some of these institutions operate mainly at the national level, lending to large industries, while others cater for the financing needs of regional industry.

Non-bank financial intermediaries in India conduct transactions such as leasing, hire purchase, bill discounting, factoring, and foreign exchange transactions for individuals and the corporate sector. There are about 40,000 such bodies and their number continues to grow (Dutt and Sundharam, 2000). They compete with commercial banks in taking deposits and advancing loans, but a series of financial scandals has deprived thousands of depositors of their savings. The systemic vulnerability of the mutual fund industry in India was illustrated in 1998 when the nation's largest fund, the government-sponsored Unit Trust of India, faced major financial difficulties after mishandling its customers' investments.

It should be noted that a former DFI, the Industrial Credit and Investment Corporation of India (ICICI), has now converted into a private sector commercial bank hence there is evidence that the financial system is evolving over time.

Changes have also taken place in investment banking. A surge in activity over recent years has been sparked by an improving economy and corporate prospects, as well as moves by the Government to revive its privatization programme by selling off shares in a number of public companies. Merger and acquisition activity is also picking up, moving from the sole preserve of large conglomerates such as Tata to encompass smaller enterprises in the IT and pharmaceutical sectors. The three main domestic institutions operating in this field (DSP Merrill Lynch, JM Morgan Stanley and Kotak Goldman Sachs) all have links to foreign partners. These three institutions are being challenged by international groups that can offer a complete investment banking service, for example: Citigroup, HSBC and Deutsche Bank. The domestic groups have managed to stave off competition to date by the ruthless undercutting of fees, but the 'outsiders' have been gaining ground in deals such as Reliance's purchase of the UK's Flag Telecom for US$211m and Infosys' US equity offering (Merchant, K., FT, 20 February 2004).

The Islamic banking and finance industry manages assets worth over US$200bn globally. The primary forms of Islamic finance – *Musharakah* and *Mudarabah* – have many of the characteristics of VC (these instruments are described more fully in Chapter 9). India is home to the second largest Muslim population in the world, and there are estimated to be more than 150 million followers of Islam in the country, yet only a handful of institutions currently offer Islamic finance. These institutions have invested heavily in volatile sectors rather than (say) commercial leasing or Islamically structured mortgage financing. There have also been accusations of financial impropriety, and many small investors have lost their savings when they could ill afford to do so.

Attention now turns to the key features of the Indian stock markets. The proponents of the positive role of stock market development in promoting economic growth include Atje and Jovanovic (1993) and Murinde (1996). Stock markets have the potential to allocate funds to the most deserving projects by addressing the problems of asymmetric information, moral hazard and adverse selection described earlier. They can also decrease the scope for systemic failure within a financial system by reducing reliance upon the banking system. Other researchers insist stock markets encourage investment in short-term projects (Stein, 1989) or operate as 'casinos' that create excessively volatile share prices (Herms and Lensink, 2000; Scholtens, 2000). Singh (1997, p.774) argues that: 'even in developed economies, stock markets do not perform the monitoring, screening and disciplinary role very well'.

The first Indian stock markets were established during British rule in the 19th Century (Schrader, 1997), and a network of exchanges was in place by the 1960s. Despite its socialist leanings, the post-independence Government was keen to encourage individuals to invest in shares, in order to spread the ownership of organizations more widely. One consequence of this philosophy is that the capital structures of smaller enterprises in India are very similar to those in large corporations. The Government also imposed a 40 per cent limit on the ownership of firms (domestic and foreign) wishing to borrow from the banks; this encouraged firms to sell the remaining 60 per cent of shares on the stock markets (Dossani and Kenney, 2002).

The value of shares on the equity markets grew rapidly during the early 1990s, as the markets witnessed a frenzy of activity. Many companies secured a quotation on the back of over-optimistic or fraudulent claims, fetching far higher values than could be justified by the intrinsic value of the business. This volatility caused great problems, and the number of IPOs almost halved from around 1,400 in 1995–96 to 750 in 1996/7. Since that time, the number of IPOs has declined markedly. Over the period 1997–2004, the 'high' point was 124 IPOs in 2000/2001 and the low point an almost negligible 14 IPOs in 2002/3. However, market capitalization rose quickly after the global collapse in share prices following the 'technology meltdown' in the early 2000s. Share values had almost trebled in value by 2004 but the number of IPOs has not risen at the same rate.

Indian bourses have definitely made much progress in improving their trading and settlement practices, backed by a tougher regulatory regime. Trading is now automated and the open outcry system has been abolished. For many years, quoted companies tended to be manufacturing companies that relied upon assets to boost shareholder confidence and to secure additional bank funding. Despite the domestic problems of the mid-1990s and the global depression in technology stocks thereafter, high-technology firms in India are now encouraged to seek a listing; the requirement for an existing profit record has been relaxed and the procedure for new share issues has been simplified.

India is among the top ten stock markets in the world by market capitalization and the largest in relation to the number of listed companies, over 8,000. The investor base is a massive 40–50 million individuals; even so, according to a prominent fund manager, retail participation in quoted equities remains 'staggeringly low' relative to other Asian markets (Milind Barve, cited in Merchant, K., FT, 9 December 2003). This situation will change only when individuals perceive that the return on equities exceeds that available on other securities (mainly Government-issued) carrying less risk. In the meantime, foreign investors are increasingly prepared to invest in medium-sized companies quoted on Indian exchanges; such companies have a market capitalization of less than $US2bn, and they operate across a range of sectors, from consumer goods and energy to banking and commodities.

Overall, the top tier stock markets in India have offered only limited opportunities for established businesses to raise long-term capital and follow-on funding. The number of IPOs has been low for some years (1997–2004) and fund raising remains largely confined to public sector bodies or large corporates. It will be interesting to see whether recent changes will open up the stock markets for smaller enterprises or, more pertinently, provide a route whereby venture capitalists can exit their investments profitably and efficiently.

'Second tier' stock markets in other countries have widened the fund raising options of SMEs and provided an exit route for venture capitalists. Such markets give smaller enterprises the opportunity to qualify for a listing and current profitability is usually not a prerequisite. The Over The Counter Exchange of India (OTCEI) was established in 1994, modelled on the lines of the NASDAQ market in the US. Similar markets have existed in Europe and elsewhere, although their survival rate has been precarious.[1] This experience has been repeated in India.

The timing of OCTEI's launch (1994) was inauspicious and several of the initial entrants proved to be high-profile failures. The market was effectively moribund for a number of years after its launch. The position has slowly improved. Listings stand at 115 (as at 2005) and some of these enterprises are successful local brands, for example Sonora Tiles. The OTCEI has recently allowed early stage companies to trade unlisted securities through its Growth Equity Market (GEM) initiative. It is too early to gauge whether this initiative will be a success, but it is specifically aimed at boosting VC activity by providing an exit opportunity for investors.

Apart from the formal stock markets, private investors in India have a long tradition of equity investment in smaller enterprises. Indeed, Cobham and Subramanium (1998) suggested that Indian small firms make as much or more use of equity finance than large firms; this is not the case across the globe (Berger and Udell, 1998). These equity investors are primarily informal networks of family, friends and contacts. However, the entrepreneurs and their 'angel' investors do not have the capacity to fund potential fast growth businesses that carry high levels of risk. This is where VC can play such an important role – discussed further in Section 6.5.

6.4 SMEs in India

SMEs have long been acknowledged as an important element of the Indian economy, and there is a vibrant SME sector. The leaders of the independence movement were strong supporters of this sector, seeing SMEs as an alternative to 'exploitation' by multinational firms. The perceived value of SMEs was summed up by the Government-appointed Planning Commission of 1956 (p.47): 'they provide immediate large-scale employment, offer a method of ensuring a more equitable distribution of the national income, and facilitate an effective mobilization of resources of capital and skill which might otherwise remain unutilized'. These sentiments still hold currency today.

The definition of what constitutes a 'small' firm in India has evolved over time. In line with some other countries in Asia, the Government refers to SSIs (small scale *industries*) rather than the more widely used term of SMEs (small and medium-sized *enterprises*). However, the authorities adopt a novel approach as they classify smaller enterprises in relation to capital investment; these definitions apply to manufacturing firms or industry-related service enterprises. The categorization of a firm as 'small' or 'medium' is critical because SSIs alone qualify for government assistance (www.ADB.com, ref: 36345).

In 1950, an SSI could invest a maximum of Rs0.5m in plant and machinery. This limit was raised to Rs0.75m in 1966, and subsequent revisions saw the figure climb to Rs6m by 1990. The Government decided that a low capital base was holding back the competitiveness of small firms and the limit for the majority of SSIs was raised to Rs10m (approximately US$220,000) in 1997; for certain products and industries, the investment limit was increased to Rs50m. The Ganguly Committee has recently (2004) recommended that the threshold for an SSI be raised to Rs200m (around US$4.4m).

The SSI subset of the SME sector comprises around 12m firms; for every registered firm, another four firms fail to register with the authorities. The SSI sector contributes 40 per cent to India's industrial manufacturing output, employing 16.7m workers and accounting for 35 per cent of the nation's exports. These firms have achieved impressive cumulative annual growth rates (CAGRs) in the key areas of output, employment and exports – refer to Table 6.1.

Table 6.1 Production, Employment and Exports in the Small Scale Sector

Selected Years	Production (RsBn)	Employment (Ms)	Exports (RsBn)
1973–74	0.7	3.97	0.03
1980–81	2.9	7.10	0.16
1985–86	6.1	9.60	0.28
1990–91	15.5	12.53	0.91
1991–92	17.9	13.00	1.39
1992–93	20.9	13.40	1.78
1993–94	24.2	13.94	2.53
1994–95	29.4	14.66	2.91
1995–96	35.6	15.26	3.95
1996–97	41.3	16.00	3.92
1997–98	46.5	16.72	4.39
1999–2000	52.1	17.16	4.90
2000–01	57.3	17.85	5.42
2001–02	63.9	18.56	6.98
CAGR (%)			
1973–81	21.4	8.7	22.6
1981–91	18.6	5.8	18.6
1991–2002	15.2	4.0	22.7

Source: Seventh Five-year Plan, Volume II; Census.

The main areas of activity are food (processing and production), cotton, clothing, leather/jewellery, wood products and sports goods. There are also a host of firms operating in the service sector (especially retail shops and food outlets) that are not captured in the official statistics. Small firms in India have traditionally been characterized by operations involving high labour absorption and low capital intensity. This trend is still evident, even though smaller enterprises are moving into new areas such as IT.

As we have seen in Chapter 3 (Section 3.3), SMEs across the globe face a number of constraints. The reasons for 'sickness' (failure or impending failure) among SSIs in India were identified in the 2002 census – see Table 6.2.

The lack of demand (affecting 66 per cent of respondents) may reflect the global economic problems prevalent in 2002. However, the vast majority of these firms provide just enough income for the owner and his family by servicing local niche markets, and their fortunes would not be transformed if resources were available to fund additional marketing activity (36 per cent of the sample claimed this was a problem). The funding problems are not unexpected, given the issues discussed in the previous section and the fact that SMEs across the globe almost inevitably cite a lack of appropriately priced finance as a major constraint on progress (Burns, 2001; Levie, 2000). It does seem somewhat contradictory that SSIs cite a lack of demand as the principal problem facing their business yet almost half of the respondents (46 per cent) wanted funds for working capital – presumably to increase output to meet demand! This apparent paradox illustrates that, in India as

Table 6.2 Reasons for Closure of Small Businesses (2002 survey)

No.	Reasons	Per cent
1.	Lack of demand	66
2.	Financing working capital	46
3.	Marketing problems	36
4.	Power shortages	13
5.	Lack of access to raw materials	12
6.	Equipment problems	11
7.	Labour problems	5
8.	Management problems	4

The total exceeds 100 per cent because some units reported more than one reason for 'sickness'.

Source: Compiled from Third All India Census of SSI Units (2002).

elsewhere, it is very difficult to identify genuine cases of market failure where the banks or other funding bodies turn down deserving proposals.

Since independence, the Indian Government has favoured the SSI sector with financial support (targets for priority lending, specialist financial institutions and so on) and a host of policies to promote this sector. A key element of this strategy has been to grant SSIs exclusive production rights in certain sectors since 1967. At the peak of protection in the 1980s, about 900 items were reserved solely for SSIs (www.ADB.com, ref: 36345). This figure has been reducing steadily and it stood at 675 as at January 2005. The aim of this approach was (and remains) to protect SSIs that operate in the domestic market, rather than to encourage small firms to compete globally. This policy is misguided – Chapter 2 stressed the role that even small firms can play in international markets.

The Government has also established a large network of business support agencies, both at central and state government levels, that seeks to promote entrepreneurship in general and offer specific assistance with, for example, marketing, technology transfer and exports. The penetration of this official support network among the SSI population is currently around one per cent, low by international standards. It is expensive and bureaucratic to register a firm with the authorities and thereby qualify for Government assistance. The 'form filling' mentality is anathema to many people of an entrepreneurial disposition, and they choose to remain outside the official support framework.

More generally, the support system is piecemeal in nature and any attempt to provide an integrated framework of assistance (from creating an enterprise culture through to support for medium-sized businesses) has been frustrated by a crucial flaw in the Government's SME strategy. Companies not classed as an SSI are denied access to assistance, especially affordable finance from the banks and/or specialist financial institutions. There is thus no incentive to grow because successful firms are penalized by the withdrawal of support.

This policy has surely contributed to the presently unbalanced state of the Indian economic structure; the economy is dominated by a few enormous private sector conglomerates, such as the Tata and Birla groups, and nationalized firms, while there is a vast collection of 'shopkeepers and local industrial firms' (Dossani and Kenney, 2002: p.233). Firms that fall into the latter categories are clearly not attractive to the VC industry yet their activities do demonstrate a culture of enterprise and suggest the potential for much greater economic growth within both the SSI and the wider SME population.

6.5 Venture capital in India

6.5.1 History

The literature on VC in India was formerly sparse and somewhat descriptive in nature. Mishra (1996) presented a general overview of the institutional framework, but this was overtaken by a recent review of the industry (Dossani and Kenney, 2002) and an expert assessment of VC support for the IT sector (Dossani, 2003). Likewise, earlier studies (Verma, 1997; Mitra, 2000) shed some light on the practices and procedures adopted by venture capitalists, whereas Wright et al. (2002) offer a much more authoritative review of the risk assessment procedures adopted by fund managers.

The VC sector in each country reflects the characteristics of the nation's unique structures, institutions and policies (Manigart et al., 1997). India presents a fascinating opportunity for the study of VC. A number of factors suggested that VC would find it difficult to take root, notably the nation's record of state-directed institutional development, along with its antagonism to capitalism and its stifling bureaucracy. Other aspects of society and the economy offered great encouragement for VC, including the huge numbers of smaller enterprises, the widespread equity markets, the educated workforce with technological expertise, the indigenous software industry and close links to Silicon Valley (Dossani and Kenney, 2002).

The catalyst for the emergence of VC in India was the Bhatt Committee of 1972 (Nasscom, 2000). In recognition of the problems being encountered by entrepreneurs in setting up ventures, the Bhatt Committee was charged with the task of finding ways and means to develop SMEs and it recommended that an Rs1bn VC fund be established (Mishra, 1996). The Industrial Finance Corporation of India (IFCI) answered this call in 1975 by sponsoring the Risk Capital Foundation. Its objective was to supplement founders' equity and encourage talented professionals and technocrats to set up new ventures. In 1976, the Industrial Development Bank of India (IDBI) followed suit and established a division to provide seed capital for innovative projects.

Financial institutions and banks across the globe rarely have the capacity to evaluate technical developments and to nurture promising companies. India was no exception. It should be apparent from the analysis earlier in this chapter that its conservative banking community could not meet the growing demand for risk capital to support the technological revolution that swept across India in the early 1980s. In addition, enterprises with a capital base of below Rs30m could not access equity through the primary capital markets. The National Technology Policy of 1983 therefore envisaged a much greater role for VC, a stance that was confirmed in the Seventh Five-year Plan for 1985–90.

In 1984, the Industrial Credit and Investment Corporation of India (ICICI), at that time a DFI, set up a separate VC division. This division made equity investments, and conditional loans where repayment was linked to a royalty on sales; it backed companies involved in waste disposal, food products (a bubble gum manufacturer) and software services (Dossani and Kenney, 2002). One year later, the Government established an Rs100m venture fund in 1985 to support pilot projects attempting to commercialize indigenous technology (Verma, 1997).

The first stage of genuine VC activity in India spanned the period 1986–1995 (Dossani and Kenney, 2002). In the mid-1980s, only Government-owned institutions were engaged in VC operations and there were no formal guidelines to govern such activity. A 1987 evaluation of the prospects for private sector VC in India by the United Nations Development Program and the Technology Policy Implementation Committee (TPIC) was the signal for change. In 1988, the Government implemented a set of guidelines to govern the establishment and functioning of VC companies. The value of risk capital for smaller enterprises was recognized, and preferential treatment was granted for the taxation of capital gains on the divestment of shares in such companies (Mishra, 1996). These moves to liberalize the market paved the way for the entry of private sector players and, with hindsight, proved to be a watershed for the industry.

However, there was no immediate surge in the number of private venture sector funds. Dossani and Kenney (2002, p.240) explain the reasons for this reluctance: 'The funds were restricted to investing in small amounts per firm (less than Rs100m); the recipient firms had to be involved in technology that was "new, relatively untried, very closely held or being taken from pilot to commercial stage or which incorporated some significant improvement over the existing [technologies] in India".' The Government also specified that the entrepreneurs should be relatively inexperienced. In addition, investments were restricted to a mere six sectors, henceforth referred to as the 'six list': software; IT; pharmaceuticals; biotechnology; agriculture; and other items, such as patented inventions, notified by the Government.

The regulatory system introduced further bureaucracy as fund managers were permitted only to make equity investments in unlisted companies, and a ceiling was placed on individual investments (minimum five per cent and maximum 24 per cent of the value of the investment fund). The formation of every fund was subject to official approval; a Ministry of Finance Committee then had to ensure that each potential investee company operated within the somewhat ambiguous 'six list' specified above.

As a consequence of these restrictions, private sector institutions were slow to enter the VC arena, even though economic developments had made India an increasingly attractive location for VC investment. Most of the activity remained in Government-linked funds, especially after a supportive World Bank report in 1989. This Report (World Bank, 1989) pointed to a shortage of capital for young technology-oriented firms with high-growth potential and the Bank therefore committed funds that enabled four state-owned financial institutions to establish VC subsidiaries. The most prominent was the Technology Development and Information Company of India (TDICI), a joint venture between ICICI and the state-run mutual fund, Unit Trust of India (UTI). The ICICI venture division described above was merged into TDICI. For complex tax reasons, the funds were registered as UTI's VC unit schemes (Vecaus I and II); they backed a number of technology-oriented firms and made some impressive gains from IPO exits.

In 1993, the industry grouped together under the banner of the Indian Venture Capital Association (IVCA), essentially to lobby the government for concessions and also to disseminate information on its activities. The membership of the IVCA has increased in fits and starts from 11 in 1995 to 44 in 2004.

Overall, the period from 1986–1995 was: 'plagued by inexperienced management, mandates to invest in certain states and sectors, and general regulatory problems' (Dossani and Kenney, 2002, p.243). Apart from the Vecaus Funds described above, most venture funds struggled, held back by well-intentioned, but misguided intervention from Government officials. However, there was evidence of profitable investment opportunities and local venture capitalists secured valuable experience (albeit at a cost to the public purse).

The second phase of VC operations (from 1995–date) has seen foreign institutional investors become the dominant suppliers of capital, along with private sector domestic funds; non-resident Indians (NRIs) have been prepared to provide investment funds to venture funds. Government agencies or subsidiaries of domestic banks have been relegated to a much less prominent role (Wright et al., 2002). The arrival of such well-known investors as Draper International and the Walden International Investment Group (WIIG) heralded a sharp increase in investment – see Table 6.3 in the following sub-section. Other active global names are Warburg Pincus, Intel, Softbank, Carlyle, Capital International, Citibank and ING. ICICI Ventures, now operating in the private sector, has emerged as the most active local fund.

This growth in investment would not have been as rapid, had legal and regulatory changes not been introduced in 2000. Previously, three different authorities regulated the affairs of the VC sector: the Reserve Bank of India (RBI); the Securities and Exchange Board of India (SEBI); and the Central Board of Direct Taxes (CBDT). Industry practitioners had to adhere to different sets of guidelines, and there were a number of anomalies in the guidance received. Sarika (1999) pointed out, for example, that SEBI regulations provided for investments in equity shares and equity-based products, allowing fund managers to put together flexible financial packages, whereas CBDT guidelines insisted that fund managers invest only in 'pure' equity to qualify for the tax concessions.

Those responsible for the regulation of VC in India recognized the futility of operating under such a framework, and both the RBI and SEBI set up committees to review this issue. The more influential SEBI Committee completed its deliberations by December 1999, and SEBI's board adopted the Committee's recommendations in January 2000. Dossani (2003) summarized the key proposals as follows:

1. SEBI should be designated as the sole regulator of VC funds operating in or from India.
2. Once registered with SEBI, VC firms should automatically obtain the advantages of tax pass-through and repatriation of overseas capital, provided they invest at least 70 per cent of their investment pool in unlisted equity or equity-related securities, hold no more than 40 per cent of the share capital of any investee company and invest no more than 25 per cent of the fund in a single firm.
3. Domestic venture funds should be allowed to invest offshore.
4. All institutional investors (insurance companies, provident funds and so on) should be allowed to invest in VC funds, with the maximum investment level being defined by a 'prudent expert'.
5. Investee companies should be able to issue preferred stock with differential voting and dividend rights.
6. The minimum individual investment in a VC fund should be raised from Rs100,000 to Rs500,000.

In May 2000, the Ministry of Finance approved the first two proposals and the last, but took no action on the rest. The benefits of these proposals and the consequences of the Government's rejection of the integrated package of reforms put forward by SEBI are considered below.

The choice of SEBI as the sole regulator is logical (Dossani, 2003, p.160) because: 'it is the only regulator that can make decisions that integrate the interests of the capital markets with that of the regulators ... SEBI's mandate is to protect investors while overseeing the development of an equity culture.'

In relation to Proposal 2 above, most venture funds in the developed world adopt the limited partnership (LP) model described in Chapter 4. The general partners (the fund managers) are responsible for managing the investment process; in return, they are paid a management fee plus a share of any profits. The limited partners provide the investment funds but play no part in managing the investments. In the LP model, no taxes are paid at the fund level; the tax obligation 'passes through' to the individual general and limited partners. Tax-exempt investors can therefore avoid almost all liability to tax (Lerner and Pacanins, 1997).

India does not have a limited partnership law. However, it does allow trusts with the feature of tax pass-through, provided that they conduct business in a form specified by the government (Dossani, 2003). The trust structure has been utilized by venture funds,[2] although overseas VC firms still have to be registered in a tax haven such as Mauritius to qualify for tax relief. Tax advantages have accrued, provided that investments were restricted to the 'six list' outlined above. This led to confusion, disputes and unacceptable delays. The solution proposed, and accepted, was to set out more general investment guidelines (although finance and real estate investments are prohibited).

The authorities have not allowed domestic funds to invest overseas (Proposal 3), even though the rules have been relaxed on offshore funds conducting business in India. This seems illogical, especially as domestic funds are permitted to invest outside India provided that they set up separate overseas funds to do so.

Insurance companies and provident funds (who provide the bulk of funds for VC firms in the US and Europe) are still not allowed to commit funds to VC in India (Proposal 4). This restricts the amount of funds available for investment. The rejection of this proposal probably stems from a desire to avoid any repeat of previous scandals involving the heavy losses in intermediaries' investments. It is ironic that the banks, the primary home for savings in India, can invest five per cent of their new funds in VC yet they have very rarely chosen to do so.

The value of preferred stock for venture capitalists (Proposal 5) is considered in more depth in Chapter 7. In selecting the financial instruments to put together a deal, fund managers seek to protect themselves against downside risk yet maximize the incentives to the entrepreneur. This balancing act is made much easier if there is the flexibility to convert preferred stock into equity shares at key decision points. In India, this option is limited at present and the rejection of Proposal 5 means the status quo is preserved.

The adoption of Proposal 6 is sensible; the provision of VC funds should be confined to informed investors with substantial capital resources.

The introduction of some of the SEBI proposals has streamlined the bureaucracy associated with the regulation of the VC sector, but it is regrettable that the Government did not take the opportunity to adopt a more radical approach and implement all the recommendations. Venture capitalists across the globe have demonstrated the ability to select and nurture SMEs, and to increase national wealth, yet they require the freedom to operate flexibly within a supportive tax and regulatory environment.

6.5.2 Current position

There is no single authoritative source of information on aggregate VC investment in India. The Indian Venture Capital Association (IVCA) has maintained a database of its members' activity, but many deals are done by venture funds that do not subscribe to the IVCA. The figures below therefore give the reader an indication of investment trends in India, but they should be treated with caution.

Compared to established VC markets, the industry in India remains small. Table 6.3 shows a surge of investment prior to global economic uncertainty and stock market volatility in 2001, then a slump followed by a recent recovery. Apart from the fall in the amount invested, the focus switched from smaller, early stage deals to larger investments in more established companies.

The vast majority of entrepreneurs in India have little or no experience of starting and developing an enterprise (Srivastava, 2002). They have still to get to grips with the issues identified in Chapters 2 and 3, whether strategic or functional, or simply putting together a business plan. The founders often have a good idea, backed up by passion and commitment, and a readiness to take risks, but they rarely require substantial capital at the outset. In the early years of VC in India, many smaller deals were conducted and many of these were in the techno-

Table 6.3 Aggregate Venture Capital Investment in India

	Investment (US$m)	Number of ventures
1996/7	20	N/a
1997/8	80	N/a
1998/9	250	N/a
1999/2000	500	N/a
2000/1	1,200	N/a
2001/2	1,100	N/a
2002 calendar year	510	91
2003	507	56
2004	1,100	66

Source: Nasscom, IVCA, TSJ Media.

logy field. This stemmed from the VC guidelines in force from 1988. Inexperienced entrepreneurs were backed by inexperienced (mainly domestic) venture capitalists, and a high attrition rate was inevitable.

The upshot was that 2001 proved to be a watershed in VC activity. There is a more detailed analysis of pre-2001 investment trends in Chapter 8. Some key features of activity since the VC industry changed direction are presented below.

By 2002, venture funds started to favour large size deals in later stage transactions, even buy-outs. Start-ups were seen as almost a 'no go area'. The President of the IVCA and Chairman of Infinity Ventures (Srivastava, 2002) confirmed that many investment opportunities were linked to India's acknowledged expertise in the technology and knowledge-based sectors. He also pointed to significant innovation in electronics manufacturing, continuing growth in the media/entertainment sector and growing expertise in 'classic' high-technology activities, including biotechnology and pharmaceuticals. The largest deal was when Patni computer Systems, a consultancy and software company, received US$107.5m from a syndicate of US venture funds.

In 2003, the highest number of deals in any sector was computer software. This was no surprise yet there was also a broadening of investment activity. Major deals were completed for export manufacturing companies (Radhakrishna Foods), and in the media/entertainment sector (New Delhi Tele Vision; Hindustan Times). The majority of deals were for US$10–25m; it was significant that such deals were often linked to future IPOs in New York or London, rather than India.

In 2004, there was some investment in early stage ventures and start-ups, for example in firms engaged in chip design (especially where there was Indo-US collaboration). Nonetheless, the focus remained on later stage investments, including the purchase of publicly quoted securities. Many of the larger investments were in mature sectors, for example: CDC Capital Partners a UK VC fund paid the state government of the northern province, Punjab, Rs2.2bn (US$57m) for a 23.5 per cent stake and management control of Punjab Tractors. There was also support for innovation; Warburg Pincus' US$149m investment in optical storage media maker Moser Baer was the largest single investment during the year.

The links between the VC/private equity and the investment banking communities were strengthened as 30 'exits' were secured. Six venture-backed companies pulled off successful IPOs, while IBM's US$160m purchase of Daksh eServices was the largest trade sale. Private equity groups were sometimes prepared to invest in strong prospects and then take control of the management team, a sign of maturity in the market. There was also a growth in corporate VC through the activity of acquisitive companies such as Flextronics.

Some of the high profile 'mega deals' above would obviously be classed as private equity rather than VC transactions. Even if such deals are set aside as outside the main thrust of this book, the majority of the funds committed by the VC community since 2001 have been in later stage investments.

6.5.3 Prospects

In the early stages of a firm's existence, the majority of firms in India will continue to be funded by the 3Fs (founder, friends and family) or sometimes by 'angel' financiers. In the pre-2001 period, such firms might have been backed by venture capitalists. This would now be a rare event. Venture capitalists are renowned for funding high-risk, high-growth opportunities, but venture funds across the globe (including India) prefer to invest later in a firm's life. The level of risk declines, the amount of funding sought increases and the time before exit is reduced.

However, some of these small companies will be the large companies of the future and thus present opportunities for VC funding. Srivastava (2002) points to the rise in entrepreneurship in India; over 2,500 new entities were formed in the IT sector alone in 2001. He urges domestic entrepreneurs to draw inspiration from the achievements of NRIs. Silicon Valley Indians have created wealth in excess of US$250bn (at peak share values) and 25 per cent of small IT companies in the US have Indian founders. These NRIs are returning to their homeland with funds, ideas and entrepreneurial skills, but VC backing will also be required.

Investment patterns have not been uniform across either the regions or industrial sectors of India (refer to Chapter 8 for a detailed breakdown of activity).

For example, New Delhi is renowned for software services, IT and telecommunications, whereas Mumbai focuses on software services, IT, media, computer graphics and animation. However, this specialization is most apparent in the South of India. Texas Instruments, the prominent US IT firm, established a base in Bangalore in 1984, and the area has become home to global software and technology companies, including Microsoft, Motorola, SAP and General Electric. Bangalore and surrounding areas have become an important part of the global computing industry, and other high-technology activities such as wireless and telecommunications are also prominent. There has also been substantial investment by SMEs and phenomenal growth in start-ups.

About an hour by plane from Bangalore is Hyderabad, the capital of the eastern state of Andra Pradesh. This area produces a third of India's generic drugs and local officials are determined to develop its nascent biotechnology cluster. There are some 40 laboratories, research centres and universities covering disciplines such as cellular and molecular biology, and DNA fingerprinting (Merchant, K., FT, 14 August 2003).

Venture capitalists have marshalled resources and established specialist investment networks in these centres of expertise. If the nation can fulfil its aim of moving up the value chain, VC will be at the heart of such clusters. It might not be a realistic aim to create the environment of Silicon Valley (or Israel in the Yozma era) at each centre of excellence, but it should be possible to put together an interlinked network of innovators, academics, financiers, Government support and so on.

Venture funds in India have invested (and will continue to invest) across a range of industries, but a number of sectors appear to offer excellent prospects for profitable investment.

The Indian IT industry is unbalanced and based largely on contract servicing or offshore outsourcing. Writing code is relatively easy, but turning the code into a product is the challenge. Foreign giants like Texas Instruments dominate technology development at present. Domestic product development for the export market has been negligible, although the situation is changing slowly, for example Moschip designs and produces microchips for mobile phones (Merchant, K., FT, 8 June 2004). However, designing and making new technology is costly and time-consuming, with no guarantee of success in the global market. VC investors can offer both financial resources and expertise to support growth in this field.

On a similar theme, the pharmaceutical industry has been driven by cost factors. It costs around US$1.5bn to develop each new drug in the developed world yet Ranbaxy launched 20 new products in the US and another 32 in India over 2003. Its entire R&D budget amounted to just US$55m, because it was able to 'reverse-engineer' proprietary drugs. Intellectual property rights are now being acknowledged in India, and Ranbaxy (and many other firms) now have the capacity to develop new drugs. In addition, more than 100 global companies have set up R&D centres in India within the past five years, and this investment is starting to bear fruit; a breakthrough in the treatment of TB has been developed by a research institution and a Mumbai drugs company (Merchant, K., FT, 7 September 2004). Experience elsewhere suggests that this sort of activity will spill over from large firms to SMEs, and the latter will require VC funding.

India is the world's largest producer of tea and milk, and the second largest producer of fruit, vegetables, rice and sugar. However, the country is not a dominant force in these markets, because only around one per cent of these products are processed. The global processed food industry must surely offer huge scope for Indian firms to invest in technologies, skills and equipment, and VC could be the route to spearhead growth in these 'sunshine' industries.

Apart from specific sectors, there is also potential for increased activity in the buy-out market. The incumbent management might seek to purchase their company, with VC assistance, through a management buy-out; alternatively, outside expertise might be brought in via a management buy-in or some form of leveraged buy-out. There is currently a very low level of such activity in India. Even though this type of transaction is more likely to be seen in mature VC markets (Wright et al., 1992), there are a number of factors that could trigger such deals.

Four areas seem ripe for growth: listed companies that perform well but fail to catch the attention of the investors could be suitable for 'public-to-private' transactions with management at the helm; many companies are registered with the authorities as 'sick' (equivalent to Chapter 11 in US), but could be revived by VC firms that install stronger management teams; the Government's privatization policy offers opportunities for existing (or new) management teams to restructure former state-owned bodies to enhance efficiency; and, the search for core competences among diversified groups allows companies to dispose of non-core subsidiaries via buy-outs.

Finally, it is worth noting that many Indian companies have prospered without resorting to VC, for example: none of the three largest software firms (Wipro, Infosys and Tata Consultancy Services) have utilized this form of finance (Dossani, 2003). A major challenge for the VC community is to change the culture by encouraging entrepreneurs to give up some control in return for a larger 'pie' for everyone to share.

6.6 Summary

This chapter has covered a lot of ground. It started with an introduction to one of the most complex nations on earth. India is a country of contrasts. The trappings of a modern economy are enjoyed by relatively few, while most of the rural population exists on the poverty line. Nonetheless, the country has come a long way in a short period of time, it has many world-class companies and it is seen as a future economic powerhouse. The financial system has seen patchy development; the banks still lag behind their counterparts in the developed world, but the stock markets have modernized rapidly. The role of SMEs in India was examined, and the role of Government support was questioned.

Finally, the chapter covered the past, present and future of the VC sector. Venture capital has emerged as a flexible form of financing for young companies with growth potential. The formal VC sector was built on the efforts of state-sponsored financial institutions. Foreign VC institutions entered the field as the Government implemented a more relaxed regulatory framework. Venture capital can play a significant role in India's industrial progress but venture capitalists cannot exert much influence if they act alone. For the nation to move up the value chain, we suggest that it is vital to create an interlinked framework of innovators, academics, financiers, Government support and so on.

These themes are taken up in following chapters. The research programme conducted for this book adds greatly to our knowledge of the VC sector. The analysis in Chapter 7, taking account of developments in the Indian economy and society, identifies critical elements for further investigation and develops a series of propositions that were tested in the empirical work.

7

Venture Capital in India: The Analytical Framework

7.1 Introduction

Having reviewed the VC literature in Chapter 5, it was evident that the valuation, structuring and monitoring of deals have not been covered as well as the pre-investment appraisal criteria. In the context of India, Chapter 6 (Section 6.5) referred to the 'sparse and somewhat descriptive nature' of previous research on the VC market, until the arrival of recent studies by Dossani and Kenney (2002), Dossani (2003) and Wright et al. (2002). The latter study considers some of the valuation procedures adopted by fund managers, but does not tackle the issues of monitoring and control. Our research programme complements and extends greatly the work of Professor Wright and his colleagues, and the findings should be valuable for students, academics, policy makers and practitioners.

Chapter 5 discussed the investment cycle employed by venture capitalists. After the deal generation, screening and due diligence stages, fund managers seek to determine the value of the investee company, provided that the project still appears financially attractive. The valuation process might involve prolonged negotiations between venture capitalists and entrepreneurs. This is understandable, as the injection of external capital is one of the most important events in the life cycle of any firm that harbours serious growth ambitions.

Agreement on the entry price is complicated by the fact that the valuation techniques available to venture capitalists are often problematic to apply. In most cases, the valuation of a deal is primarily a function of investors' perceived risk and their target rates of return (Wright and Robbie, 1995). However, the valuation question is only part of the process of structuring the VC deal. Coase (1960) sets this point in context when he states (p.15) that: 'In order to carry out a market transaction it is necessary to discover who it is that one wishes to deal with, to inform people that one wishes to deal and on what terms, to conduct negotiations leading up to a bargain, to draw up a contract, [and] to undertake the inspection needed to make sure that the terms of the contract are being observed'. This chapter examines the issues raised by Coase from the perspective of the VC transaction.

Venture capital investing takes place in an environment of uncertainty and indeterminate risks, hence investors have developed a variety of strategies to identify and to mitigate these risks (Ruhnka and Young, 1991). The design and structure of the investment contract can go a long way to limit the downside risks and optimize the chances of a successful investment, especially where an investment is backed by intangible assets, and the venture fund puts its trust in the ethics and abilities of the entrepreneurial team (Norton, 1995). It will become apparent that such risks relate mainly to the unifying theme of the principal/agent relationship discussed in Chapter 5 (Section 5.2).

The venture capitalists are not involved in the day-to-day operations of their investee companies; information having a material affect on the success of the venture is therefore available to one party and not to the other. Comprehensive contracts are formulated to influence the agent's (entrepreneur's) behaviour, even though the VC investors are often referred to as partners. The entrepreneur has probably agreed to significant changes in the firm's ownership and organizational structure in return for the venture funding. However, the entrepreneur has to be persuaded that demands for information about the status and progress of the firm are reasonable and justified.

In these circumstances, it is imperative for practitioners and academic researchers to understand the theory and process of controlling risk, and to be able to explain the implications to those involved in raising VC (Rosman and O'Neill, 1993). For example, Norton and Tenenbaum (1992) stress the need for researchers to assess the impact of the clauses incorporated into the deal term sheet, and to investigate the reasons why some venture capitalists inject cash in exchange for common equity while others reject this form of financial instrument. The research programme conducted for this book addresses some of these key concerns.

7.2 Scope of the research

As stated above, some topics in the field of VC have been extensively researched, notably the investment criteria used in appraising investments. This research programme, by contrast, explores three areas that have been relatively neglected in previous studies, namely the valuation, structuring and monitoring of VC deals. Building on the literature review conducted in Chapter 5 and incorporating some of the specific factors explored in Chapter 6, the critical elements in each of these three areas are explored then a series of research questions and propositions are formulated.

There are two crucial dimensions to valuation:

(i) Information sources on which the valuation of a business is based.
(ii) Valuation techniques used in arriving at an entry price.

Similarly, three key constituents are considered in relation to structuring the deal:

(i) The conditions or covenants in the investment contract for limiting the downside risk of investments, including rights of the VC firm to board representation.
(ii) The milestones set as a condition for further capital disbursements (assuming that the funds are advanced in stages).
(iii) The type of financial instruments used by the venture fund.

The monitoring phase offers reassurance to the investors who provide funds to the VC firms and to the fund managers themselves that any cash injections are being deployed in line with the covenants/terms contained in the contract. The research centres on three themes:

(i) The information gathered through periodic statements and board meetings and/or other discussions between fund managers and entrepreneurs.
(ii) The degree to which CEOs in investee companies are replaced, in order to preserve and enhance the value of investments, and ...
(iii) The most common reasons cited for CEO replacement.

For the purposes of this research, a broad definition of VC was adopted, ranging from classic, early stage growth opportunities to large, later stage investments (especially management buy-outs) that overlap with the activities of private equity groups. The scope of this definition reflects global developments in VC markets, as well as the range of investment opportunities now available in India.

The focus of our research programme was the formal VC sector. Individual investors (angels) are excluded, as are private equity deals at the very top of the financing spectrum, for example mergers and/or corporate reconstructions. The venture funds invited to participate in the research have all made at least three investments. Most have made considerably more hence the participants are experienced in the valuation, structuring and monitoring of deals.

7.3 Research objectives

The VC industry outside the United States has grown explosively in recent years. This emerging global market is characterized by heterogeneity; the 'Western model' has been adapted in different geographic regions to take account of the prevailing circumstances in the host country (Bygrave and Timmons, 1992). In particular, Wright et al. (2002) argue that information asymmetry may vary between countries and this has implications for the VC funds operating in that environment.

In investigating the Indian VC market, our research programme sought to ascertain:

a) the profile of venture funds and the fund management teams, along with their investment policies;
b) the sources of information and valuation methods used by funds in arriving at an entry price;
c) the most common terms and conditions included in investment contracts;
d) the most favoured financial instruments used in making investments;
e) the detailed breakdown of information required from investee companies in monitoring VC investments;
f) whether close monitoring leads to the replacement of underperforming CEOs in the investee companies, and ...;
g) the most frequent factors that lead to CEO dismissals.

Within this overall framework, the research addresses how venture capitalists cover their downside risk in the: post-evaluation stage (valuation of deals); post-valuation stage (contracting or structuring of deals); and, post-investment stage (monitoring of deals).

RESEARCH OBJECTIVES

Characteristics of the Fund Managers and their Risk Management Stategies in India

Characteristics

Venture Fund: size, investment stage, etc
Fund Managers: age
Fund Managers: qualifications
Fund Managers: experience

Risk-management Strategies

Post-evaluation: valuation
Post-valuation: structuring
Post-investment: monitoring

7.3.1 The characteristics of venture capital funds

Representatives of 40 of the 42 most active VC firms in India contributed to the research programme conducted for this book. This is the largest sample size for any empirical study on the Indian VC sector. The interviews enabled the authors to build a comprehensive profile of the industry. Information was gathered in relation to: fund size, origin and age; investment stage and sector; portfolio size; and, investment size. (The results of this exercise are set out in the following Chapter.) The database created allowed the authors to explore how the whole VC 'community' tackles valuation, monitoring and control issues. In addition, by breaking down the information into segments, it was possible to isolate the influence of specific factors (for example, foreign versus domestic funds) in relation to the propositions set out below.

7.4 Risk management strategies

7.4.1 Valuation

The return on the investment is obviously the primary motivation for undertaking the investment. According to finance theory, the return required by an investor is a function of the non-diversifiable risk of the investment (Brealey and Myers, 1996). It is axiomatic that the higher the risk, the higher the required return should be. This principle is undisputed yet differences arise in the way that investment analysis is conducted in different countries (Manigart et al., 1997). For example, German investment analysts use technical analysis to a greater extent than their UK counterparts; the latter tend to rely more on techniques such as net asset per share and the dividend growth model (Pike et al., 1993). Given the heterogeneity of VC markets in different countries, differences may also be expected in the 'approaches to the valuation of VC projects as well as the information used' (Manigart et al., 2000, p.6).

The initial valuation has a critical impact on an investor's anticipated reward-to-risk ratio (Ruhnka and Young, 1991). In the light of the adverse selection and information asymmetry problems discussed at several points in this book, there is considerable scope for negotiation on how to value a company. However, the basic process normally comprises three sequential steps. First, information is gathered on the venture, its management team and its business prospects. Second, this information is used to appraise the risk of the venture and hence the required rate of return on the investment, and to estimate the future cash flow and profit potential. Finally, one or more valuation methods are used, integrating the various elements to arrive at an appropriate value for the company.

7.4.1.1 Valuation information

The problem of valuation is not confined to venture capitalists in the developing world; the element of subjectivity in valuations is an international phenomenon (Manigart et al., 2000). The problem is especially severe in the seed/early stages of a company's life, where information is imperfect and the true worth of a project might not be revealed for some considerable time (O'Shea, 1996; Cooper and Carleton, 1979; Bergemann and Hege, 1998).

For listed companies with a high public profile, the most influential sources of information are the company's annual audited figures (profit and loss account, and balance sheet) and its interim results, as well as public statements by the senior management of the company. By contrast, unlisted companies have far fewer statutory disclosure requirements hence potential investors find it much more difficult to gather information on such companies.

The business plan should contain significant sources of information, including historic accounting data (if available) and budget forecasts (Boocock and Woods, 1997). The managerial track record of the entrepreneur, and his familiarity with the project and the industry, may give some indication about the accuracy of the projections in the business plan (Amit et al., 1993). However, projections may be crude estimates at best, especially where innovation is involved. In addition, entrepreneurs may not disclose (deliberately or inadvertently) crucial information, or they might give a biased view of important facts that could lead to an unrealistic valuation of the business (Sahlman, 1990). The outcome is that venture capitalists rely heavily on independent reports to confirm the information put together by the management team.

Wright and Robbie (1994) established the critical value placed on the venture funds' own due diligence reports in the UK, followed by information supplied by entrepreneurs and accountants respectively. In a study covering the UK, the Netherlands, Belgium and France, Manigart et al. (1997) confirmed the prime role of due diligence reports prepared by the venture fund, followed by the overall coherence of the business plan. The financial information (whether audited, interim and/or projected), product characteristics and marketing information were judged to be of lesser importance. When the 1997 study was broadened to include the US, Manigart et al. (2000) concluded that, for valuation, the most important source of information in each country (except France) was again information gathered during the venture capitalists' due diligence process.

In a 'transition' nation, moving from a planned to a market economy, Karsai et al. (1996) found that Hungarian venture capitalists also placed most emphasis on their own due diligence reports for valuation purposes, ahead of sales and marketing information provided by the management. The business plan was ranked third in importance, followed by reports from external accountants and/or consultants. In an extension to the 1996 study, taking in the transition economies of Poland and Slovakia, Karsai et al. (1998) reinforced the importance attached to the funds' own due diligence process.

At the time of our survey, venture funds were being encouraged to back inexperienced entrepreneurs, often involved with relatively young, technology-oriented companies. The information provided by such firms in support of their funding applications would normally have been viewed as very suspect. A systematic approach to business planning is not yet part of the business culture. In the light of this, and the literature cited above, it is no surprise that our first proposition places most importance on the production of due diligence reports designed to minimize the problems associated with information asymmetry and adverse selection. It would also be interesting to ascertain whether foreign and domestic venture capital funds adopt different approaches to gathering information (Wright et al., 2002).

Proposition (1): In order to arrive at a valuation, venture capitalists in India rely more on their 'Own Due Diligence Reports' than other sources of information.

7.4.1.2 Valuation techniques

Given the critical importance of establishing an accurate valuation of potential investee companies, it is not unexpected that venture capitalists use a wide range of information and techniques for this task (Wright and Robbie, 1995). The valuation is used as a basis for determining the most appropriate financing structure, and for calculating the projected internal rate of return (IRR) on the deal – the standard performance benchmark.

There are several valuation methods advocated by practitioners and academics; sometimes these methods conflict and sometimes they complement each other. The principal approaches rely upon: discounting expected cash flows; using financial information; and finding comparable companies that display similar 'value characteristics' as the company in question (Lerner, 2000). Valuation methods have also been based on discounted dividend yield and, more recently, options theory. Finally, the VC industry has developed its own valuation tool.

Techniques based on financial information view a firm's assets from the accountants' perspective, using historic cost figures (book value) or replacement cost for valuation purposes. The use of audited information is not applicable to early stage companies that have 'short or no histories', notably companies based on intangible assets (Gompers, 1995, p.1473); historic financial information is more useful in valuing later stage investments (Wright and Robbie, 1995).

In methods using comparable companies, analysts have first to identify key characteristics that underpin profit-generating potential. This might involve 'rules of thumb' for specific sectors. For example, US venture capitalists value cable and internet businesses by a multiple of the number of subscribers at the time of the deal; biotechnology companies might be valued in relation to the number of patents awarded. Other comparisons value projects on the basis of the price-earnings ratio (p/e: share price divided by earnings per share), multiples of earnings before interest and taxes (EBIT) and/or before depreciation and amortization (EBITDA), or recent transaction prices for comparable companies (Lerner, 2000). The dangers of financial information of this nature include the difficulty of identifying suitable 'matches' for comparative purposes and the reality that a new or young company might never achieve the status of companies on the market at present.

The finance/accounting and 'comparable' methods can yield approximate values and they might be relatively straightforward to use, but valuations based on discounted cash flows offer a greater degree of theoretical validity (Manigart et al., 1997). The latter approach does not rely on historic information hence it is useful for valuing new ventures. However, it is not easy to forecast future cash flows and there are a host of assumptions involved in these calculations. For example, many analysts argue that cash flows should be discounted at a rate derived from the Capital Asset Pricing Model but the project's beta can only be estimated from 'comparable' public companies (Lerner, 2000).

Arnold and Moizer (1984, p.201) conclude that: 'although mathematically very appealing [DCF] is far too precise an estimate of a company's worth'. The prediction of future cash flows is hazardous, even though errors in forecasting may be overcome, to a certain extent, by sensitivity analysis (Wright and Robbie, 1998). Further complications are introduced when the time horizon is short. A significant part of the value of the company is captured by its residual value, and this figure is quite sensitive to the expected growth rate beyond the projected time horizon.

Manigart et al. (1997) concede that valuations based on discounted dividend yield also have theoretical merit. However, in the majority of VC deals, investee companies are cash-starved initially and the possibility of paying dividends is rare. Business value cannot be reflected in a dividend stream in the short-term; fund managers hope to make significant capital gains on exit. The dividend yield method is therefore ruled out in most cases. Dixit and Pindyck (1995) argue that real options could be used to value start-up companies in highly uncertain environments, but Manigart et al. (1997) point to problems in defining the parameters of option models and thus setting the correct valuation.

The 'venture capital method' of valuation addresses the problems associated with projects characterized by: 'negative cash flows and earnings and highly uncertain but potentially substantial future rewards' (Lerner, 2000, p.187). Venture capitalists in developed markets typically apply a p/e multiple to the earnings forecasted at some point in the future; by this time, profits will be positive and the venture fund will be looking to exit the deal, usually by way of flotation or trade sale. The p/e multiple applied to the forecast earnings is usually adjusted downwards by about a third compared to those achieved by comparable listed companies. Finally, the resulting (future) valuation is discounted at a very high rate, usually between 30–60 per cent. This figure represents the venture capitalists' target rate of return or IRR (Lerner, 2000).

Valuation problems are reduced as a firm becomes more established. Based on a sample of 371 large firms across 27 developed economies, La Porta et al. (1999) confirmed that better shareholder protection is associated with higher valuation of corporate assets. On the same theme, the stage of financing is significantly more important in determining project risk (and hence the targeted IRR) than the state of technology involved (Murray and Lott, 1995).

In the developed world, Manigart et al. (2000) found that UK venture capitalists favour the use of prospective or historic p/e multiples, whereas fund managers in the US utilize EBIT/EBITDA multiples or recent transaction prices in comparable sectors. The use of DCF techniques is most popular in Belgium and the Netherlands, while recent transaction prices are the top ranked valuation tool in France. There have been very few comparative studies on the valuation of VC investments in markets at differing stages of development (Wright and Robbie, 1998), and Wright et al. (2002) did not investigate valuation techniques in their study of VC in India.

Given the type of deals conducted (often early stage and/or technology-oriented) and the difficulty of finding comparable companies with similar value characteristics, we propose that DCF techniques will be most favoured by venture capitalists in India.

Proposition (2): Venture capitalists in India use DCF-based valuation techniques more than any other methods of valuation.

7.4.2 Structuring

This section focuses on three broad activities undertaken by venture capitalists: the contractual features (covenants) incorporated in shareholders' agreements; the extent to which the staging of investments is used as a control mechanism and the 'milestones' used to trigger subsequent disbursements; and, the financial instruments used in putting together financial packages. The 'staging' and the 'financial instruments' sub-sections overlap to a large extent.

In the finance literature, the framing of the optimal contract under conditions of uncertainty has received considerable attention. In a seminal article, Jensen and Meckling (1978, p.357) argue that: 'millions of individuals voluntarily entrust billions of dollars, francs, pesos ... of personal wealth to the care of managers on the basis of a complex set of contracting relationships which delineate the rights of the parties involved'. The asymmetry of information between investor and investee, and their different attitudes to risk, provide the basis for mutually beneficial contracting (Terry and Smith, 1998).

In the context of VC, it is worth restating the fundamental issue at stake here. Investments are high-risk, high-return projects that create: 'the opportunity and the necessity to learn more about risk, uncertainty and contracting technology' (Barry, 1994, p.3). In the light of differing objectives, management styles and risk preferences, the entrepreneur is inclined to choose actions that are consistent with his own best interests rather than those of the investor (Amit et al., 1990). In addition, the entrepreneur's capabilities are unknown at the time of contract negotiation and investment (Chan et al., 1990).

The structuring of financial contracts is therefore designed to counter the risks associated with information asymmetry and moral hazard (Gompers, 1995). Fund managers utilize a variety of strategies to safeguard themselves against the risks perceived as most threatening (Fiet and Hellriegel, 1995). The terms of a contract might specify, for example, control rights, the division of any returns and the circumstances in which debt can be converted into equity (Berglof, 1994). Nonetheless, the deal needs to be structured so that all parties (fund providers, investors and investee companies) are comfortable with their positions.

Amit et al. (1990) identified five distinguishing characteristics of VC contracts (often known as stock purchase agreements): sharing arrangements; earn out agreements; buy-out options; performance requirements; and future financing arrangements. A degree of complexity is required because the information flow from small businesses is often 'acutely opaque' (Berger and Udell, 1998, p.614). Venture capitalists want the right to intervene in the company's operations when necessary. Simple contracts are appropriate where an agent behaves in an honest manner; if the principal believes that the agent will act recklessly or dishonestly, more safeguards are put in place.

7.4.2.1 Contractual covenants

As stated above, the number and 'tightness' of covenants depends on the extent of potential agency problems. Covenants are costly to negotiate and monitor, and they should be employed only when the consequences of inaction are likely to be severe (Gompers and Lerner, 1996). They serve as: 'tripwires that enhance the flexibility and efficiency of financial contracting' (Rajan and Winton, 1995, p.1113). The secret of negotiating is to strike the right balance; covenants should not be too harsh (resulting in the premature demise of good projects) or too lenient (allowing bad projects to mature).

Many studies have examined the covenants incorporated in debt transactions, especially bank/borrower contracts. Bank loan term sheets, for example, typically specify minimum or maximum levels for certain financial ratios, place restrictions on managerial actions involving significant acquisition and/or investment expenditure, and limit a firm's action in relation to dividend payments, additional borrowing and the sale of assets. By contrast, VC investment contracts or stock purchase agreements are shrouded in secrecy, and many academic studies have made only passing reference to the negotiations on covenants. In essence, however, the contracting process focuses on a few simple questions (Sahlman, 1988, p.27): 'how is cash allocated?; how is risk allocated?; and what are the incentives for both parties in the deal?'

The distinction between 'complete' and 'incomplete' contracts was discussed in Chapter 5 (Spier, 1992). Venture capitalists prefer to work with complete contracts and they will typically specify clauses that relate to either behaviour or outcomes (Sappington, 1991; Jensen and Meckling, 1978). Examples of covenants identified in previous studies reveal the type of behaviour or outcomes that venture capitalists insist upon:

- the appointment of reputable auditors and limitations on managers' decision-making powers (Jensen and Meckling, 1978);
- the staging of the investment to ensure the optimal exercise of production capacity and/or withdrawal from operations (Sahlman, 1988 and 1990; Chan et al., 1990);
- the choice of financial instrument (Cornelli and Yosha, 1997; Trester, 1998);
- requirements to maintain minimum working capital levels, and restrictions on the disposition of assets, and merger activity (Zender, 1991);
- limits on entrepreneur compensation (Sahlman, 1990);
- co-sale clauses[1]: 'tag along' and 'drag along' rights (Berglof, 1994);
- the right to board representation (Lerner, 1995);
- the allocation of voting rights (Fenn et al., 1997);
- the ability to access directly the investee company's accounting system (Mitchell and Terry, 1998);
- the right to remove incumbent management (Ruhnka and Young, 1991).

The above list is not exhaustive. For example, venture capitalists often insist on the right to block key decisions, including the sale of the company and the timing of an IPO. The contract is also likely to contain protection in the form of anti-dilution clauses. Venture capitalists are offered enough shares to maintain the original percentage of their equity stake, even if a subsequent round of financing takes place at a lower valuation (Zider, 1998). Another key area is an insistence upon the regular submission of financial information; small firms often do not have audited financial statements, making it extremely difficult to impose ratio-related financial covenants (Berger and Udell, 1998).

The covenants above are concerned with limiting potential losses for the investors, but the contract also has to provide incentives for effort on the part of the entrepreneur(s). Performance criteria (ratchets) enable the fund managers to adjust the initial ownership of the investee company in line with, for example, achieving profit targets, filing patents or winning major contracts. The better the management performs, the more of the firm's equity they retain. On the other hand, such ratchets can penalize the entrepreneurs for poor performance!

The number of restrictions imposed depends on the scope for opportunistic behaviour, thereby increasing the potential for moral hazard (Gompers and Lerner, 1996). However, covenants are not always written in fine detail. Many are standard 'boiler-plate' clauses prepared by lawyers rather than investment managers; contracts prepared on that basis may not cover all contingencies (Sahlman, 1990; Aghion and Bolton, 1992). As a consequence, the management may be required to give general warranties to indemnify venture capitalists against (say) any outstanding litigation (Adamati and Pfleiderer, 1994).

Investors are keen to protect their key concerns with tight conditions in the contract, yet trust is crucial. Contracting parties have to balance the benefits of restricting activities against the cost of negotiating the provisions, writing the contractual clauses and monitoring compliance. The contract terms must allow the company to obtain the capital necessary for survival in (hopefully temporary) downturns while providing for the exploitation of promising opportunities. If a deal is structured in such a way that makes it almost impossible to raise additional capital, the contract will cause difficulties rather than add value to the project.

Venture funds in India were subject to tight regulation; investments were largely restricted to certain sectors and early stage deals. The vast majority of recipients would not have had any experience of dealing with venture capitalists or be aware of what was expected of them. The exit route for the venture fund would not be assured, given the uncertain climate for IPOs and the problems experienced at the OCTEI. (These comments are equally applicable to Propositions 3–5 below.) In these circumstances, it is anticipated that venture capitalists would keep their investee companies under relatively tight control to alleviate agency problems, especially moral hazard. There might, however, be important differences in the approaches of foreign and domestic venture funds.

Proposition (3): Venture capitalists in India employ a variety of covenants in shareholder agreements to combat principal/agent problems, including the right to board representation.

7.4.2.2 Staging of investments

For start-up projects characterized by great uncertainty and a high-risk of failure, investment funds are advanced in stages, provided the venture capitalists are satisfied that milestones have been achieved. Discretion over the timing and terms of future funding offers a powerful means of control. Indeed, some researchers have argued that flexibility in future pricing can make the difference between a venture succeeding and failing (Sahlman, 1988).

Gorman and Sahlman (1989, p.238) stress the desire of venture capitalists: 'to limit damage by refusing additional financing if the company is unsuccessful in the early stages'. One of the most challenging problems is to determine when to release funds for continued development and when to abandon a project. The solution is to release funds at key points in the development process, such as filing a new patent, the completion of a new product or a clearer view of the marketability of a product (Neher, 1999). For example, Lerner (1992) analyzed VC financing in two industries (biotechnology, and Winchester hard drives); he found that the likelihood of later round funding increased with technological progress (especially the award of patents) and when rising liquidity in the IPO market offered investors the encouragement of a future exit route.

The existence of these targets enables both entrepreneur and investor to take stock of progress at regular intervals. Moreover, Mukherji and Nagarajan (1995) argue that intermediate signals can be incorporated into VC contracts. Such signals can be based on 'hard' or 'soft' measures; the former are verifiable and quantifiable such as cost or profit, while the latter include more nebulous concepts like the quality of service provided and customer satisfaction.

It will be appreciated that setting milestones allows both venture fund and entrepreneur to benefit, compared to the alternative situation in which future financing terms are set irrevocably at the start of the project (Sahlman, 1988). The entrepreneur is very keen to accomplish his/her ambitions for the business; he/she may not be fraudulent in misapplying funding but might over invest in the early stages of a project then find that progress takes longer than anticipated. If capital is rationed, any tendency to over-optimism can be countered; further funding is conditional on the successful completion of earlier stages (Bergemann and Hege, 1998). The entrepreneur will usually face equity dilution at the next financing round if the project takes too much time. On the other hand, the majority of entrepreneurs have great confidence in their own abilities to meet targets and if progress is in line with, or exceeds projections, they capture a larger share of the company.

A complementary perspective is to view stage payments as the creation of strategic options (Gompers, 1992). Building such options into VC contracts helps to overcome initial differences of opinion between investor and entrepreneur about the probability of different outcomes. Sahlman (1988) argues that investors can infer information about the abilities and convictions of entrepreneurs by offering different deal terms and then gauging their response. The ability to signal intentions credibly may enable some entrepreneurs to obtain funding that would not have been available in the absence of a mechanism for communicating true abilities or convictions.

Staging should keep the entrepreneur focussed on the task at hand and may motivate a more rapid pace of activity. However, it might induce the entrepreneur to aim for short-term success rather than long-term value creation (Gompers, 1995); the entrepreneur loses sight of the larger picture by focussing too narrowly on short-term goals (Hellman, 1998). This problem can be addressed by designing short-term performance benchmarks that represent intermediate steps towards longer-term objectives. This raises the question of: 'how and when the funds should be released so as to maximize the value of the venture' (Bergemann and Hege, 1998, p.716).

Proposition (4): Venture capitalists in India use the staging of capital payments as a mechanism to control agency costs, and a variety of conditions are attached to further disbursements.

7.4.2.3 Choice of financial instruments

There has been surprisingly little research on deal structuring in VC contracts, especially in relation to how and why the various types of financial instruments are combined (Wright and Robbie, 1998). The choice between different financing alternatives and/or financial packages is motivated by a whole series of considerations, including corporate and personal tax laws (Ravid and Spiegel, 1997), and signalling expectations and control (Cooper and Carleton, 1979). Recent developments in the financial markets have greatly expanded the range of financing choices available to both investors and firms seeking funds.

Fruhan (1979) argues that all financial transactions can be classified into three categories: those that create value; those that destroy value; and those that transfer value between two or more parties. The interaction of entrepreneurs and venture capitalists has resulted in the evolution of a unique set of financial contracts where the link between value and financial structure appears strong and direct. Indeed, an effective financing structure might prove to be the difference between a flourishing and a failed enterprise (Sahlman, 1990).

The link between financial structure and control is more debatable. Some researchers argue that a firm's behaviour can be best controlled through the financial structure of the deal (Ravid and Spiegel, 1997) while others (including Hellmann, 1998) believe that control rights are independent of financial structure. Proponents of the latter school of thought argue that control is better exercised through the terms of the contract; such terms might specify the board structure from the outset or vary the voting powers attached to the venture capitalists' shareholdings to give the investors control of the board if required.

The principal choice in structuring deals is between debt and equity, although there are many variations on these basic concepts, as well as hybrid products that have characteristics of both debt and equity. Myers (1984) argues that a firm will prefer to issue fixed claim securities (debt) rather than fractional claims (equity) because of its ability to benefit from the interest tax shield. However, one of the key features of VC investment is the preference for equity. Deals are not financed purely by debt for a number of reasons.

Investors and entrepreneurs require the flexibility to deal with intermittent (or non-existent) cash flows as a project is developing. The tax shield on interest payments is of little or no benefit for firms without sufficient operating profit. The use of debt may also limit the firm's capacity to make future equity issues: 'as debt holders will have a senior claim on firm cash flow and assets' (Norton and Tenenbaum, 1993, p.34). Moreover, a project financed by debt may convey too much of the liquidation value to the venture capitalist and encourage both venture fund and entrepreneur to seek premature liquidation. Trester (1998, p.677) argues that: 'the foreclosure option embedded in a debt contract may actually create an incentive for the entrepreneur to behave opportunistically, taking whatever project payoffs are available and defaulting on the debt.'

Venture fund managers will therefore turn to equity, but investment through ordinary shares (common equity) can create problems where the venture capitalist's financial contribution far outweighs that of the entrepreneur(s). Stathopoulos (2002) illustrates the problems involved.

A start-up venture requires a total investment of £5.5m, and the founders can contribute £500,000. However, the founders insist on having 25 per cent of the company after the deal is struck. If the venture fund invests via ordinary shares, the venture capitalists would have to pay a higher price for their shares than the management team (more than three times as much per share). In the event of failure, and subsequent liquidation, the holders of the ordinary shares are entitled to receive 100 per cent of the excess of assets over liabilities but they are the last to be paid. It is therefore possible for management to make money if the project fails but for the venture fund to lose.[2]

The solution adopted by venture capitalists is 'flat pricing'. The founders and the venture fund therefore pay the same price for their ordinary shares. The balance of funds contributed by the venture capitalists is invested in 'preferred equity' or convertible debt. (The former refers to various forms of preferred ordinary shares[3] as well as, more commonly, convertible redeemable preference shares.) In the case above, Stathopoulos (2002) explains that:

- the founders subscribe £500,000 for 25 per cent of the ordinary shares (this values the total number of ordinary shares at £2m)
- the venture fund subscribes £1.5m for the remaining 75 per cent of the ordinary shares
- the balance of the venture fund's £5m investment (£3.5m) is invested in preferred equity or convertible debt.

The use of flat pricing allows for a fair distribution of gains and losses, as the venture capitalists' preferred equity ranks ahead of the ordinary shares. Flat pricing combines incentives for the entrepreneur(s) and downside protection for the venture fund (Gompers, 1995), without the loss of financial flexibility or the cash flow pressures caused by debt (Norton and Tenenbaum, 1993).

Finance theory explains the use of convertible securities by reference to information asymmetries (Harris and Raviv, 1985; Stein, 1992; and Nyborg, 1995). Such instruments fit perfectly within the culture of VC investment. Information regarding the quality of the project is revealed gradually to both venture fund and entrepreneur. Preferred stock allows investors to stage investments, allocate risk, control management, provide incentives to executives and demarcate ownership.

A number of studies have confirmed that preferred equity is by far the most common financial instrument used in VC deals, especially for early stage financing (Norton and Tenenbaum, 1992; Berglof, 1994). Debt and common equity tend to be used in later stage financing and/or in industries where monitoring is less difficult. Trester (1998, p.688) concludes that: 'It is the likelihood of asymmetric information in the projects venture capitalists finance which causes them to use preferred equity. Banks and other institutions contracting with debt are financing projects where monitoring is easier and the probability of asymmetric information is smaller'.

There are other reasons for the use of convertible instruments. Some firms would face a sharp increase in funding costs if they added additional 'pure' debt to their capital structure. On a different tack, investors might judge that the incumbent management would not be capable of managing a large organization; conversion options enable the investors to take control when the firm reaches a certain size. Venture funds can also profit where progress is satisfactory but a firm's size does not permit a public offering; capital can be recouped through the redemption of preferred stock and/or the payment of accumulated dividends (Sahlman, 1988).

The choice of investment instrument differs between developed and developing markets. Venture capitalists in developed nations have a greater range of instruments at their disposal including several varieties of preferred equity. This enables investors to use flat pricing or similar mechanisms to maximize incentives for the entrepreneur(s) and downside protection for the venture fund. Many developing countries restrict VC investors to common equity. This is not the case in India, but there is only limited flexibility in the use of preferred equity and earlier studies suggest that its use has been modest (Sarika, 1999; Wright et al., 2002). As many deals (actual and potential) are ideally suited to this form of finance, our study investigates the extent to which preferred equity has become established in the VC market in India.

Proposition (5): Preferred stock is the most frequently used financial product in India.

7.4.3 Monitoring

It is essential for the investors to monitor progress on a regular basis (Fiet, 1996). Venture capital investments are characterized by significant information asymmetries (Fama, 1991; Wright and Robbie, 1998). Projects typically involve relatively novel products and services hence risk levels and information needs are high. Robbie et al. (1997) found that the venture capitalists' reporting requirements were multi-layered, and that there was growing emphasis on a proactive approach to provide early warning signals about impending problems.

In spite of these safeguards, it is acknowledged that more than one-third of investments made by venture funds in the developed world result in losses, even though extensive monitoring has (supposedly) taken place. The pre-contractual assessment of agency risk is not sufficient; interpersonal and competitive circumstances change and are impossible to anticipate fully (Fiet and Hellriegel, 1995). A recurring theme of this chapter is that investment decisions depend upon the integrity and abilities of the entrepreneurial team. The potential for moral hazard has been stressed, especially the diversion of profits to the entrepreneur in preference to outside shareholders, by way of: '...[excessive] salary, transfer pricing, subsidised loans, non-arm length asset transactions and, in some cases, outright theft' (La Porta et al., 1999, p.6).

There is an added incentive for venture capitalists to monitor the performance of their investments (Gompers, 1995); fund managers are rewarded through 'carried interest', and bonuses are closely linked to the performance of an individual's own portfolio of investments. Indeed, many venture funds insist that investment managers invest their own money alongside that of the fund.

7.4.3.1 Monitoring mechanisms

An investee firm cannot claim to have strong prospects for growth, without supplying the data to support such claims. It is then incumbent on the investee firm to supply sufficient information to indicate the true state of its progress compared to the pre-investment forecasts (Myers and Majluf, 1984). There may be situations where, for example, entrepreneurs continue to invest even after a project ceases to be viable (Jensen and Meckling, 1978; Barry, 1994). The essence of monitoring is to anticipate problems and to respond promptly when performance falls short (Sahlman, 1990).

It is impossible for the investor to identify and counter every possible risk at the outset, but effective corporate governance systems can achieve enhanced efficiency (Wright et al., 1998). Even for quoted companies, public signals are less informative than the knowledge gained by dedicated monitoring systems (Rajan and Winton, 1995). The degree of post-investment activities ranges from '*laissez-faire*' to 'close tracker' depending on the degree of risk perceived to be associated with the venture (Steier and Greenwood, 1995). Sophisticated monitoring systems are typically required for a high-technology venture, whereas information asymmetry would not be as prominent in (say) a retailing project.

Venture funds take an active monitoring role compared to relatively passive financiers like the banks. The fund will have the right (frequently exercised) to take a seat on the board of directors, make frequent informal visits to the company, meet regularly with customers and suppliers, and participate in key personnel and strategic decisions (Lerner, 1995). Fund managers will also insist on the provision of regular financial and other reports, typically on a monthly and/or quarterly basis. The control mechanisms available include formal audit systems, budget restrictions and, as already noted: 'the establishment of incentive compensation systems which serve to more closely identify the manager's interests with those of the outside equity holders' (Jensen and Meckling, 1978, p.323).

The three core financial statements (balance sheet, profit and loss account, and cash flow statement) are usually compulsory. Annual submissions would be a minimum, although a venture fund will usually insist that these documents are provided more frequently and/or in much greater depth. Profitability might have to be segmented according to product line, with data supplied on capacity utilization, order book position and so on (Mitchell and Terry, 1998). This level of financial detail might not be appropriate in the early stages of a project, although early stage investors will insist upon the submission of non-financial indicators of performance (Wright and Robbie, 1998).

The degree of monitoring required is, once again, a question of balance. Venture funds seek to monitor their investments, yet the entrepreneur has to be given the time and freedom to run the company effectively. Experienced managers may feel that the effort expended in generating frequent reports takes valuable time that could be dedicated to other activities (Ehrlich et al., 1994). However, an inability to produce information is often associated with business failure in SMEs (Storey et al., 1987), whereas better quality information has been associated with success and survival (Hutchison and Ray, 1986).

The timely dissemination of information is crucial for taking corrective action: 'the value of information today is larger than tomorrow' (Bergemann and Hege, 1998, p.718). The quality of information provided depends on the resources committed to this activity and the purchasing of appropriate technology for monitoring purposes. However, even where the most up-to-date information systems are in place, fund managers have to remain in close contact with the company if they are to monitor the risks effectively (Barney et al., 1989).

Reid (1998) found a strong link between the quantity and quality of information provided to the venture capitalist and the level of trust enjoyed; a fruitful exchange of information results in a marked reduction in risk and a more productive relationship. On the same theme, Wright and Robbie (1998) confirmed that an absence of information, or a persistent delay in its provision, tended to undermine an investor's trust in an entrepreneur. Sapienza and Korsgaard (1996) reinforced the value of regular information flows for promoting positive relations between investor and investee company. In transition markets, especially, the rapidly changing conditions place a premium on timely receipt of information, as well as effective and flexible responses (Karsai et al., 1996).

Across the globe, there is considerable variation in the way venture capitalists conduct corporate governance. The systems adopted can be formal and/or informal, and venture funds can seek to build long-term relationships or protect themselves against short-term threats (Shleifer and Vishny, 1997). The development and enforcement of effective formal monitoring may be problematic in some environments, notably where the institutional and contractual infrastructure is weak (Wright et al., 1998).

What does the analysis above imply for the monitoring systems adopted by venture capitalists in India? The dynamic economy is characterized by changing tastes, changing technologies (some brought back to India by NRIs) and a growing population of SMEs. However, the enforcement of contracts and the protection of intellectual property have been questionable, and the quality of many entrepreneurs is still to be tested. It is therefore anticipated that monitoring will be vigorous, with the focus probably on protection against short-term threats. Venture capitalists, especially those investing in early stage deals, will require the provision of regular reports on a range of issues. Within the rather general proposition below, it will be interesting to establish the relative importance of financial and non-financial data, as well as the frequency of reports and the topics most discussed at meetings to monitor progress.

Proposition (6): Venture capitalists in India use a range of mechanisms to monitor their investee companies, calling for financial reports and other information on a regular basis.

7.4.3.2 Replacement of CEOs in investee companies

The entrepreneur's capability is a key concern of investors. It is widely acknowledged that venture capitalists prefer to invest in a Grade A man with a Grade B idea, rather than a Grade B man with a Grade A idea (Bygrave and Timmons, 1992, p.104). Bruton et al. (1997) argue that the greater confidence a venture capitalist has in the capacity of the CEO to offer sound strategic direction, the less time the fund manager/s will devote to monitoring the venture.

Despite the importance placed on assessing management ability, it is difficult for venture capitalists to predict how an individual or management team might react after the funds have been injected. The right to monitor management performance is critical in tackling conflicts of interest, in other words where entrepreneurs pursue their own ideas and ambitions at the expense of the investor's best interests. The degree of control available to the venture fund is decided in the initial negotiations. In extreme cases, fund managers can discipline wayward managers by removing or demoting them, even if the founder is the source of the problem (Sahlman, 1990; Adamati and Pfleiderer, 1994).

Such action usually coincides with an organizational crisis, and it is not uncommon. Hannan et al. (1996) suggested there was a 10 per cent chance of the appointment of a non-founder CEO in the first 20 months of the life of a firm in Silicon Valley; this likelihood increased to about 40 per cent in 40 months, and over 80 per cent after 80 months. Hall (1998) found that 73 per cent of UK venture capitalists had replaced executives while Gorman and Sahlman (1989) revealed that each US fund manager had (on average) removed three CEOs or company presidents over 2.4 years of investing. It is evident that fund managers in the UK and the US will not hesitate to replace the chief executive (and/or the management team) if the investee company is under-performing.

The high profile role of the CEO means that venture capitalists focus on his/her performance (Bruton et al., 1997). Moreover, Kunze (1990) claims that the replacement of the CEO is the single most critical point in the life of a start-up company. The time spent hiring the new CEO, the shock to the organization during the changeover, the lack of direction in the interim, the quality of the new person hired, and the speed with which he or she seizes command, all impact heavily on the health and potential of the company. This upheaval means that replacing the CEO may not prevent the failure of the company (Bergemann and Hege, 1998), especially if there is a lack of high quality replacements available.

Venture capitalists across the globe have a propensity to remove CEOs, even in emerging markets like Russia (Wright and Robbie, 1998), and we envisage that this trend will be repeated in India.

Proposition (7): Venture capitalists in India replace CEOs in order to control moral hazard and improve performance in investee companies.

7.4.3.3 Reasons for replacement of CEOs

The prime reason offered for CEO dismissal is perceived inadequacies in organizational performance (James and Soref, 1981). This begs the question of how such performance is measured and whether financial indicators should be used as the sole basis for CEO removal (Finkelstein and Hambrick, 1996; Fredrickson et al., 1988).

There is some debate as to whether a firm's success stems from the operational or strategic skills of a CEO. Some researchers have argued that operational skills, for example marketing or engineering skills, are fundamental to survival (Longenecker and Moore, 1991). By contrast, Andrews (1980) contends that strategic direction is the key to success and Bruton et al. (1997) maintain that venture capitalists look for CEOs capable of offering sound strategic direction. Whatever the merits of these competing arguments, a failure in those skills most valued by the VC community will lead to CEO removal.

In the light of the rapid developments in the Indian and global economy, we suggest that venture capitalists might place a premium on strategic skills.

Proposition (8): Venture capitalists in India will tend to replace CEOs because of perceived failures in strategic skills.

7.5 Summary

The VC industry outside the United States has grown exponentially over recent times, and this emerging global market is characterized by heterogeneity (Bygrave and Timmons, 1992; Wright et al., 2002). Our research programme focuses on the development and operations of the VC industry in India. The scope of this comprehensive study was set out in Section 7.2, and a number of research objectives were presented in Section 7.3.

The first objective is to establish a profile of venture funds in India, along with their investment policies. The chapter then drew upon the literature review in Chapter 5, as well as the economic, financial and social factors explored in Chapter 6, to formulate a series of propositions in relation to the valuation, structuring and monitoring of VC deals. In essence, the study explores how venture capitalists cover their downside risk in the: post-evaluation stage (valuation of deals); post-valuation stage (contracting or structuring of deals); and, post-investment stage (monitoring of deals).

Chapter 8 will outline the research methodology adopted for developing an appropriate survey instrument, conducting the empirical survey and analyzing the data. The authors then work through the evidence gathered and discuss whether the Propositions have been accepted or rejected.

8
Venture Capital in India: Research Methodology and Findings

8.1 Introduction

Having set out the analytical framework in Chapter 7, this chapter opens with a brief discussion of the methodology adopted for the research programme. This is followed by a summary of the data gathered from the sample as a whole. The sample is then segregated on the basis of certain factors identified in the VC literature, and the data are used to investigate the validity or otherwise of the series of propositions set out in Chapter 7. The chapter concludes with a synopsis of our research findings under the three broad headings of valuation, structuring and monitoring of VC deals, and a brief summary.

Fried and Hisrich (1994, p.29) argue that: 'traditional financial research methodologies are not well suited to an examination of the VC examination process. The transactions involved are private; what little information is available comes from secondary sources'. Over the past decade, researchers in this field have increasingly gained access to primary data, both quantitative and qualitative. To draw any meaningful conclusions on the development and operation of the VC industry in India, we believed strongly that it was essential to follow this approach.

Our findings are based on a comprehensive interview programme that benefited from unprecedented cooperation from the VC community in India. The principal source of primary data was a questionnaire, distributed before and then discussed during the interviews. There was also ample opportunity to explore related topics during the course of the discussions with the venture capitalists.

Our questionnaire drew upon survey instruments used in prior studies in the developed world, including: Tyebjee and Vickery (1988);

Sapienza (1989); Gompers (1998); Wright and Robbie (1996); and Reid (1998). The initial drafts of the questionnaire were then pre-tested with a number of practitioners in India and a selection of UK academics. The aim was to identify and eliminate potential problems of interpretation (Hunt et al., 1982; Zelnio and Gagnon, 1981); this process led to a significant strengthening in the structure, content and language of the document.

The final format comprised a general introduction, eliciting information about the fund's origin, size, management team, investment portfolio and so on. This was followed by sections covering the three key themes under investigation, namely the valuation, structuring and monitoring of VC deals. The questions called for a variety of responses, from closed questions inviting participants to use nominal, ordinal or ratio scales to more open-ended questions. The Statistical Package for Social Sciences (SPSS) was used for processing and analyzing the data.

Wright and Robbie (1998) caution against relying upon 'evidence' gained from small and potentially biased sample sizes. The Chairman of the IVCA was therefore enlisted to gain the cooperation of IVCA members (30 firms as at 2000). However, one of the authors had been involved with the VC industry for several years; he spent considerable time in India, assessing market trends and consulting with practitioners to identify active VC firms among non-IVCA members.

A provisional list of 47 VC firms was drawn up before it was discovered that five of this number had closed their operations or merged with other VC firms. The questionnaire was thus mailed to all active VC firms in India (42 in total). Forty fund managers agreed to take part in the study; this extremely high degree of participation reflected the value placed on the project by practitioners. The country was divided into four regions, and interviews took place in eight cities over 2000/2001 (Ahmedabad, Bangalore, Bombay, Kolkata [formerly Calcutta], Chennai, Hyderabad, New Delhi and Pune). The minimum duration for a meeting was 35 minutes, the maximum well over two hours, and the average (an hour and three-quarters) was much closer to the latter than the former. Although this methodology was expensive and time consuming, it proved to be time well spent in building a complete picture of the industry.

The response rate of 95 per cent (40 fund managers from 42 contacted) is exceptionally high for the VC sector. In the developed world, the maximum response rates have been around 60 per cent, for example: Fiet (1995); Wright and Robbie (1996). In their studies of European VC markets, Manigart et al. (1997) received lower response rates in the emerging markets of France (24 per cent), the Netherlands (41 per cent) and Belgium (50 per cent). Some studies of VC in the emerging markets have attracted greater interest, for example: Karsai et al. (1998) achieved an overall response rate of 62 per cent across Central and Eastern European countries. In India, Mitra (2000) surveyed 16 VC firms (around 40 per cent of active investors), while Wright et al. (2002) based their findings on a sample of 31 firms (84 per cent of active VC firms in 1999, the time of the survey). A number of the 'Wright' interviews were conducted by telephone, rather than face-to-face.

Our study is therefore based on a more complete set of responses than any previous study of VC in India. The primary data from the interviews were supplemented by further discussions of our findings with participants, as well as secondary data from a variety of sources.

8.2 Descriptive profile of survey participants

Out of the 40 participants, 16 were foreign (40 per cent), while 24 of them (60 per cent) were Indian – refer to Table 8.1 for the summary data covering this Section. The 'origin' is based on the classification by used the SEBI. VC firms that are subsidiaries of foreign banks, foreign financial institutions or multilateral financial agencies are classified as 'foreign'. All funds sponsored by Indian financial institutions, banks, high net-worth individuals or corporations (provided that all or the majority contribution came from one or more of these sources) are classed as 'domestic' investors.

The combined investment pool of these 40 firms was US$2.95bn; as at February 2001, US$2.17bn had been invested (73.4 per cent of the available funds) in 1,020 deals (some investee companies had received more than one round of funding). The average amount per investment

Table 8.1 Survey Participants

24 Domestic Funds (60%), 16 Foreign Funds (40%)	
Investment pool	US$2.95bn
Investments made	US$2.17bn
Average amount invested per VC firm	US$54.4m
Total number of investments	1,020
Average investments per firm	25.5
Average amount invested per fund manager	US$7.8m
Average time of operations in India	5.5 years

was therefore US$2.12m. The largest fund was US$400m while the two smallest each had US$3.3m to invest. The former was foreign while both the latter were Indian. Of the 40 participants, only three VC firms operated more than one fund.

A closer examination (not shown in Table 8.1) reveals that four (10 per cent) of the 40 firms were responsible for US$1.4bn of the investment pool (47 per cent of the total); likewise, this small cohort had invested about US$1.2bn (56 per cent of total investment). This degree of concentration is not unusual, for example 13.5 per cent of VC firms in the US controlled approximately 58 per cent of the total capital for investment (Sahlman, 1990). The average amount invested per VC firm was US$54.4 million in our survey. The average number of investments per firm was 25.5. [This figure was in line with the 27 found by Terry and Smith (1998), but considerably lower than the 88 reported by Lockett and Wright (1999), both UK studies.] At the extremes, two VC firms had made just three investments each, while a single firm (operating more than one fund) had completed 310 investments. All these three firms were Indian.

The oldest fund had been operating in India for over 20 years, though the average length of time was 5.5 years. Lockett and Wright (1999) reported that the comparable figure in the UK was over 15 years. The relative youth of the industry in India is confirmed by the fact that 29 of the 40 firms (72.5 per cent) had started operations within the last five years, five (12.5 per cent) between five to ten years ago, and the remaining six (15 per cent) over ten years ago.

The highest proportion of the amount invested (US$766m, 35 per cent of US$2.17bn) has been allocated at the expansion stage – refer to Table 8.2. This is followed closely by early stage investment, US$694.6m (32 per cent). Seed capital also garnered substantial funding, US$341.2m, accounting for over 15 per cent of the funds invested. The average size of deals in the 'seed' and 'early' stages was US$1.6m and US$1.2m respectively.

The investment distribution in East European countries is weighted towards start-up and turnaround finance, while expansion and mezzanine financing dominate in the developing countries in Asia (Aylward, 1998). The more mature VC markets are characterized by greater competition for deals, reduced rates of return and a dominance of later stage investments such as buy-outs (Murray, 1994; Wright et al., 1992). The investment profile in India at that time was clearly much closer to the investment profile found in transition economies. This is not surprising because the Indian regulatory bodies directed venture capitalists to

Table 8.2 Stage of Investments

	Seed	Early Stage	Expansion	MBO	Pre-IPO	Securities Purchased
Amount (US$m)	341.2	694.5	776.1	81.6	126.0	156.2
% of total	15.6	31.9	35.7	3.8	5.8	7.2
Number of investments	214	571	191	7	30	7
% of total	21.0	56.0	18.7	0.7	2.9	0.7
Average investment (US$m)	1.6	1.2	4.1	11.7	4.2	22.3

invest substantial amounts in relatively new companies, and the VC sector in transition economies also tends to be Government-dominated.

In relation to the *number* of deals, the early stage topped the list with 571 transactions, representing more than half (56 per cent) of all the deals executed. The seed stage with 214 investments comprised about a fifth (21 per cent) of the total number, followed by the expansion stage with 191 deals (19 per cent). There were a total of 44 deals in later stage, 'post-expansion' deals (4.3 per cent), including seven management buy-outs – the future for buy-outs in India was considered in Chapter 6 (Section 6.5).

It is interesting to note (not shown in Table 8.2) that three of the four largest VC firms in India were foreign. However, the three foreign firms invested in only 39 deals between them, a mere four per cent of the deals in our study, whereas the only Indian player in the top four invested in 310 deals, over 30 per cent of the total. The authors appreciate that this is a selective use of the data, but there is a stark contrast between the investment preferences of foreign and domestic investors.

Turning now to consideration of investment sectors, nearly half of the funds invested (US$1.06bn, 48.7 per cent) were directed towards the IT, media and telecommunications sectors ('ITMT') – refer to Table 8.3. This outcome was predicted in our analysis of the Indian economy, SMEs and VC in Chapter 6, and it confirms earlier studies of the VC sector in India (Verma, 1997; Mitra, 2000; Wright et al., 2002). Pandey and Jang (1996) found a similar investment pattern in Taiwan; the authorities also encourage investment in ITMT activities.

Infrastructure was the second largest recipient at US$461.5m (21.3 per cent), mainly in projects connected with energy and transportation; foreign investors dominated this activity. The 'manufacturing' sector accounted for aggregate investment of US$368.3m (17 per cent); this covers a number of activities, including the clothing and food/beverages industries. The final prominent category was a somewhat eclectic grouping of the healthcare, life sciences and pharmaceutical sectors, together with retail/other services. This category attracted US$223.2m, just over ten per cent of funds invested. The contrast between the affluence associated with certain sectors of economy (notably ITMT) and the rural poor is highlighted by the fact that VC activity has barely touched the agricultural sector, despite this activity contributing more than 25 per cent of the nation's GDP.

With regard to the *number* of investments made in each of the above categories, Table 8.3 shows that ITMT attracted the most (480 deals, 47.1 per cent of 1,020 transactions). The infrastructure sector, though

Table 8.3 Sector of Investments

	ITMT	Infrastructure	Manufacturing	'Healthcare'	Other
Amount (US$m)	1058.8	461.5	368.3	223.2	61.5
% of total	48.7	21.3	17.0	10.2	2.8
Number of investments	480	22	340	97	81
% of total	47.1	2.2	33.3	9.5	7.9
Average investment (US$m)	2.2	21.0	1.1	2.3	0.8

it was ranked second in terms of the amount invested, accounted for only 22 deals (2.2 per cent of transactions). This is plausible as infrastructure projects have massive capital requirements.

Apart from the number and size of deals, country of origin and so on, we also gathered information on the expertise within fund management teams: 'The most important element ... is the quality of the team, the people who run the fund' (Fassin, 1998, p.133). We ascertained the number of fund managers in each VC firm, as well as their educational qualifications, age and previous work experience. This information is presented below, in summary form only.

The 40 participants in the research programme employed a total of 279 investment executives; the average amount invested per fund manager was US$7.8m. The participating firms employed on average almost seven fund managers, ranging from a single individual to a maximum of 20. Over 60 per cent of the managers had an MBA, frequently combined with an engineering degree or diploma. Over half of the sample (148 out of 279) was aged 26–35 years (53 per cent) and 79 executives fell within the 36–45 age range (28 per cent). These results confirm that relatively young professionals manage VC funds (Hoffman, 1972). The vast majority of the sample had previous experience in industry, merchant banking or management consultancy. Very few had worked in commercial banking. This is no surprise as a very different skill set is required to assess business potential and/or the capabilities of the management to meet projected targets, rather than simply relying upon collateral.

Venture capital firms have different objectives, strategies, resources and so on. 'This diversity needs to be understood and incorporated into well-focussed research design if studies of the VC industry are to be most productive' (Timmons and Bygrave, 1986, p.163). The authors therefore considered it essential to categorize the sample in relation to certain critical factors identified in the literature. These factors are set out below:

- Fund Origin (Indian/Foreign) – to take account of any cultural differences (Karsai et al., 1996; Wright et al., 2002);
- Investment stage preference (Early/Late) – to allow for possible behavioural differences among investors at different stages (Wright and Robbie, 1995, 1998; Karsai et al., 1998);
- Sector preference (Technology/Non-technology orientation) – the global VC industry has backed many successful technology companies (Tyebjee and Vickery, 1988; Pandey and Jang, 1996; Gompers,

1998), but there has been less focus on how venture capitalists assess technology-oriented proposals (Lockett et al., 2002);
- US$m invested per fund manager (Higher/Lower) – to explore whether the size of portfolio influences fund managers' behaviour (Gompers, 1996);
- Size of investment pool (Smaller/Larger) – to examine whether the funds at the disposal of the fund managers have any impact on prevalent practices (Timmons and Bygrave, 1986; Scheela, 1994; and, Elango et al., 1995);
- Length of time in India (Older/Younger) – to investigate whether the time of operations in India affects behaviour (Chiampou and Kallett, 1989);
- Number of investments made (Greater/Fewer) – to analyze if the firms pursuing an aggressive investment policy and making a large number of investments behave differently from the more selective investors.

Table 8.4 shows the division of the sample based on the categories above.[1]

The method of dividing the sample was relatively crude; the data were divided on the basis of above/below 'average', except for the categories covering origin, and investment sector and stage preferences.[2]

In investigating the series of propositions set out in Chapter 7, the responses from the sample as a whole are considered first. Basic statistical tools (frequency analysis, mean and standard deviation) are used to present an aggregate picture. The authors then utilized the categories described above (foreign/domestic and so on) to explore how VC firms form clusters that adopt different approaches to their valuation, structuring and monitoring practices.[3] The ability to identify common characteristics of VC firms within clusters gave the authors deeper insights into the responses to the various propositions. It will become apparent

Table 8.4 Key Characteristics of VC firms

Fund origin	Indian, 24	Foreign, 16
Investment stage preference	Early, 20	Late, 20
Technology/non-technology orientation	T, 25	N/T, 15
US$m invested per fund manager	Higher, 12	Lower, 28
Size of investment pool	Smaller, 30	Larger, 10
Length of time in India	Older, 17	Younger, 23
Number of investments made	Greater, 8	Fewer, 32

that different clusters were isolated for different propositions, although certain factors (notably investment stage and technology-orientation) appear to exert a major influence on how the clusters are formed.

The Chi Square test and logistic regression techniques have also been widely used in VC research. The authors used the former to identify significant differences between groups and the latter to explore the collective effect of independent variables on valuation, structuring, and monitoring practices in India. The statistical data derived from these two techniques are used selectively below. In most cases, the authors rely upon the basic statistical tools (especially the means of the Likert scale responses).

8.3 Investigating the propositions

The questionnaire data are now combined with key elements from the sample profile in Section 8.2 to investigate whether the research propositions set out in Chapter 7 hold true.

Proposition (1): In order to arrive at a valuation, venture capitalists in India rely more on their 'Own Due Diligence Reports' than other sources of information.

The Likert scale scores for each potential source of information were averaged – see Table 8.5. The factor perceived to be the most valuable and hence with the lowest average was 'Own Due Diligence'; in this case, 85 per cent of participants viewed it as 'essential', ten per cent 'important' and five per cent 'desirable'. (The averages only are presented from now on.) The full sample (40) responded to every question except where indicated otherwise.

The results in Table 8.5 seem logical. Venture capitalists place maximum emphasis on their own due diligence, and this process could encompass a variety of activities, including interviewing key employees, checking out the CV of the management, investigating technical information and so forth. The average score for 'due diligence by financial advisers' is relatively low but its standard deviation is relatively high; some respondents obviously attach much greater significance to this issue than others.

The importance placed on 'own due diligence' accords with previous studies – Karsai et al. (1996, 1998) in Hungary and Central Europe, and Manigart et al. (1997, 2000) in Europe and the US. Two other points are worth highlighting. First, 'other venture capitalists'

Table 8.5 Sources of Information for Valuation Purposes

	Mean	Standard Deviation
1. Own due diligence	1.20	0.52
2. Interviews with key employees	1.23	0.48
3. CV of the management	1.30	0.56
4. Product, technical and marketing information	1.38	0.54
5. Cohesive business plan	1.45	0.55
6. Audited balance sheet and P&L accounts	1.67	0.89
7. Un-audited management projections	1.85	0.80
8. Exit timing and mechanism	1.93	0.83
9. Due diligence by external financial advisers	2.15	1.00
10. Information from other venture capitalists	2.53	0.96

Note: 1 = Essential; 2 = Important, 3 = Desirable; 4 = Irrelevant

as an information source was the lowest ranked in both Hungary and India; the VC community was emerging in both countries hence the sharing of information and syndication of deals would be relatively rare in both countries. Second, product and marketing-related information was ranked in ninth place in Europe yet fourth in India – explored further below.

It is clear that many sources of information are perceived to be of importance to venture capitalists in India (Table 8.5). However, the fact that 'own due diligence' attains the lowest overall mean score is evidence that this information source is the most favoured. It is therefore reasonable to accept Proposition (1) for the sample as a whole but with the caveat that 'own due diligence' should be viewed as the first among equals rather than a clear 'winner'. Cluster analysis reveals some distinct patterns amongst the respondents' preferred information sources. Three clusters emerged, with 26, eight and six members respectively.

Cluster One (the largest) is selective in choosing its information sources. These firms rely almost exclusively on 'own due diligence' and generally reject advice from 'external advisers' or 'other venture capitalists'. When describing this cluster in terms of key characteristics (Table 8.4), it should be noted that this group contains more foreign VC firms than the sample as a whole; the members are also larger, more established and have made a greater number of investments. In addition, the fund managers tend to favour later stage, technology-oriented investments, and they are also responsible for higher value investment portfolios. Fund managers in this cluster place less trust in information from other sources. The implication is that foreign investors use their own research to check out market potential (within India and globally) and the technological feasibility of the project (confirming Wright et al., 2002); these firms work on the principle that committing resources to research at the outset will lower the likelihood of problems in future.

Cluster Two firms (eight in number) consider fewer sources of information as 'essential' and seem prepared to value projects on the basis of more limited data. Three quarters of the cluster comprise older, Government-sponsored funds (the Government launched the earliest venture funds). Such firms employ more fund managers than private sector VC firms. It is ironic that the funds with more staff place more reliance upon, for example, the applicant's business plan as opposed to their own research. Such firms might utilize other sources of information (such as personal references) that were not included in the questionnaire, or they might simply take a more 'relaxed' approach to appraisal, aiming to meet social rather than commercial objectives.

At the other extreme, the six firms in Cluster Three make fewer investments than the norm yet view almost all information sources as 'essential'. They are hungry for information. Government-backed funds again form the majority in this cluster. Their caution in seeking information and making fewer investments probably reflects a desire to be seen as 'professional' in their approach to investing.

The reader will appreciate that the cluster analysis has offered deeper insights into the ways in which VC firms use the various information sources; it should be emphasized again at this point that different clusters of respondents will be identified in relation to the propositions below.

Proposition (2): Venture capitalists in India use DCF-based valuation techniques more than any other methods of valuation.

In selecting quantitative techniques for valuation purposes, the IRR and net present value (NPV) methods were marked as 'essential' by 29 and 16 respondents respectively. This resulted in the lowest average Likert scores for these two factors – refer to Table 8.6.

The reader will appreciate that the top two items are closely interlinked – the IRR is the rate of discount that makes the NPV equal to zero. It is evident that the majority of venture capitalists in India utilize discounted cash flow forecast (DCF) based valuation techniques. The next most popular is the multiple of earnings before interest, tax, depreciation and amortization (EBITDA) approach. The EBITDA method is an important component in the 'venture capital method' of

Table 8.6 Valuation Techniques used by Venture Capitalists

	Mean	Standard Deviation
1. Internal rate of return	1.48	0.91
2. Net present value	1.98	1.03
3. EBITDA multiple	2.35	1.05
4. Payback period	2.93	1.02
5. Book value	3.13	1.11
6. Accounting rate of return	3.30	0.85
7. Dividend yield	3.40	0.87

Note: 1 = Essential; 2 = Important; 3 = Desirable; 4 = Irrelevant

valuation described in Section 7.4.1. The very basic payback technique also scores higher than accounting-based techniques. The dividend yield method is rarely used. This ranking is broadly in line with the findings of previous studies (Karsai et al., 1998; Lockett and Wright, 1999; Manigart et al., 1997, 2000), and Proposition (2) is accepted.

Cluster analysis in this case identified three groups of firms with 7, 22 and 11 members respectively. Cluster One (7 members) comprises smaller funds that favour early stage investments; the VC firms apply a variety of techniques before deciding on the valuation and hence are termed 'cautious investors'. Cluster Two firms (22 in number) are larger, focus on later stage investments and rely upon fewer techniques compared to Cluster One. Finally, the 11 firms in Cluster Three preferred investments in the technology sector albeit at a later stage and did not consider any of the techniques as essential.

Some differences in using DCF valuation techniques emerged when the sample was split according to the origin of the fund and the length of time that it had been operating in India. Based on our sample, Indian funds have generally adopted DCF techniques, although some of the long established domestic VC firms appeared reluctant to forego their traditional methods of valuation. One possible explanation for this behaviour is that Indian venture capitalists tended to rely upon earnings multiples to value their investee companies, until the arrival of the foreign funds that favoured DCF-based techniques.

The questionnaire also covered the qualitative techniques used by fund managers. These techniques are sometimes rather esoteric, allowing the personal whims or preferences of the venture capitalist to take precedence. However, the standard methods are shown in Table 8.7.

Venture capitalists typically seek to multiply their initial investment by a factor of 5–10 times on exit, as MacMillan et al. (1985) proposed some 20 years ago. This test is still widely applied and venture capital-

Table 8.7 Qualitative Valuation Methods used by Venture Capitalists

	Mean	Standard Deviation
1. Multiple of initial investment on exit	1.85	1.05
2. Industry benchmarks	1.88	0.82
3. Turnover (or subscriber) multiple	2.40	1.01
4. Brand equity	2.43	1.01
5. Rules of thumb	2.58	0.98

Note: 1 = Essential; 2 = Important; 3 = Desirable; 4 = Irrelevant

ists in India are no exception to the general rule! Industry benchmarks, including comparable transaction prices, are also preferred options. The remaining qualitative methods were not favoured, probably because (say) rules of thumb tend to develop by custom and practice in more mature markets (Manigart et al., 1997).

Our data also revealed that venture capitalists in India, as elsewhere, use more than one valuation technique for determining the entry price of investments (Wright and Robbie, 1998; Manigart et al., 1997). This process provides a range of values that can serve as the basis for negotiations. Venture capitalists also adjust the DCF techniques according to the stage or sector of investment (Lam, 1991). Fund managers in our study applied varying discount rates at different stages of investment, ranging from 50–70 per cent for seed capital to 25–35 per cent for pre-IPO deals. Likewise, investors in the ITMT sectors applied higher discount rates, ranging from 36–65 per cent, compared to infrastructure deals that were usually discounted at 10–35 per cent.

Early stage and technology-oriented investors apply higher discount rates than their counterparts investing in later stage, more stable and/or asset-based sectors. Lockett et al. (2002) revealed that venture capitalists moving into the field of technology sought very high rates of return to compensate for the perceived high level of risk, irrespective of the stage of investment. This trend is evident in India.

Proposition (3): Venture capitalists in India employ a variety of covenants in shareholder agreements to combat principal/agent problems, including the right to board representation.

Based on an extensive literature review (summarized in Section 7.4.2.1) and specimen share subscription agreements gathered during the pre-testing phase of our research programme, a list of 25 covenants was included in the final questionnaire. This list might be thought to be excessive, but it does reflect current practice; previous studies may have been incomplete because venture capitalists have been reluctant to give researchers sight of confidential documentation (Norton and Tenenbaum, 1992).

It was suggested in Chapter 7 that VC fund managers in India would keep their investee companies under relatively tight control. This claim appears to be justified, as the average scores for each factor (refer to Table 8.8 below) indicate that many of the 25 covenants are considered to be essential or important. Venture capitalists insist upon including a variety of covenants in their shareholders' agreements hence Proposition (3) is accepted.

Table 8.8 List of Structuring Covenants used in India

	Mean	Std Deviation
1. Approval for additional borrowing and/or equity dilution (*)	1.23	0.42
2. Approval for restructuring and consolidation	1.25	0.54
3. Approval for changing M and As of association (*)	1.33	0.57
4. Right to inspect books and visit facilities (*)	1.43	0.68
5. Exit timing and mechanism (*)	1.43	0.75
6. Drag-along & tag-along rights (*)	1.45	0.71
7. Right of first refusal in future fund raising	1.50	0.72
8. Proportional board representation (*)	1.55	0.81
9. Approval for capital expenditure (*)	1.55	0.71
10. Intellectual property rights to be owned by investee company	1.55	0.88
11. Approval for appointing auditors	1.60	0.78
12. Employee stock ownership plan	1.60	0.67
13. Approval before selling major assets (*)	1.68	0.89
14. Equity ratchets for entrepreneurs (*)	1.88	0.79
15. Right to appoint key functionaries (*)	1.88	0.88
16. Right to send observers in important meetings	1.90	0.93
17. Monthly financial reporting (*)	1.93	0.94
18. Staging of disbursements/drawdown (*)	2.08	0.97
19. Approval for all major contracts (*)	2.13	0.88
20. Right to set executive remuneration (*)	2.15	0.86
21. Post completion audit	2.18	1.01
22. Approval for treasury operations (*)	2.75	0.90
23. Maintenance of escrow account	2.75	0.87
24. Nominating the chairman	2.80	0.99
25. Installing specific accounting package	3.20	0.88

Note: 1 = Essential; 2 = Important; 3 = Desirable; 4 = Irrelevant

* Statistically significant differences between technology and non-technology investors.

The most important factor was the right to prior approval of any attempts to raise further finance or to alter the financial structure of the company. The desire to review any changes in the Memorandum and Articles of Association is placed high on the list, but would probably not affect many investee companies. The need to secure an exit route is vital (factors 5 and 6) and applies to every deal.

Cluster analysis showed few differences in response patterns. There were two 'outliers' that responded very differently, but they are not critical in considering the overall picture. The vast majority of the sample views most of the covenants as either essential or important. However, there were significant differences of approach when the sample was split according to the VC firms' preferences for investment stage and sector.

Investors focussing on early stage deals use a more comprehensive menu of covenants than their late stage counterparts. Likewise, the 'technology' group has statistically significant differences for 15 of the 25 covenants (marked with asterisks in Table 8.8), compared to their 'non-technology' counterparts. Specialists in technology place greater importance on certain covenants, based on their experience in addressing the risks involved in high-technology projects. For example, technology investors were especially concerned with the appointment/removal of key personnel and the formulation of performance-linked ratchets in the contract.

Before we move on from Table 8.8, two further points are worthy of note. First, the rights to board representation and to nominate the chairman were placed only at Numbers 8 and 24 (contrary to previous findings: Gompers et al., 1998). This could be taken to imply that a physical presence on the board is not the principal concern of investors, and that other covenants can offer sufficient protection against moral hazard (Gompers and Lerner, 1996; Mitchell and Reid, 1998). This is not the case in India. Fund managers marked the right to visit the firm (Number 4 on the list) marginally higher than formal board representation (Number 8), yet both factors are seen as essential in most cases. The topics discussed at meetings (board or informal) are considered below in relation to Proposition (6).

The second point of interest from Table 8.8 is that the staging of investments features only at Number 18 on the list. A more detailed exploration of this factor forms the subject of Proposition (4).

Proposition (4): Venture capitalists in India use the staging of capital payments as a mechanism to control agency costs, and a variety of conditions are attached to further disbursements.

Table 8.9 shows that 70 per cent of respondents considered the staging of investments as either essential or important. Proposition (4) is therefore broadly accepted.

We then asked about specific milestones that investee companies have to achieve before further funds are released. (The full list of factors is not shown here.) The venture capitalists viewed the 'achievement of budgets' and 'recruitment of key employees' as the most important staging points, in line with earlier studies (including: Sahlman, 1988; Bergemann and Hege, 1998; and Neher, 1999). The achievement of budgets is the acid test that funds have not been diverted to the entrepreneur (moral hazard) and that the firm is on course for success. The founder(s) often came from a technical background hence the recruitment of key employees was vital to build a balanced management team. Chi Square tests on the data revealed that technology-oriented funds saw the 'appointment of key functionaries' as a critical milestone compared to their non-technology counterparts; this demonstrates clearly the significance of human capital in knowledge-based sectors.

The value of the cluster analysis was again confirmed for this proposition. Cluster analysis produced two clusters of VC firms responding very differently to the 'milestones' variables. The larger cluster (27 members) comprises smaller funds that tend to favour early stage deals; this cluster generally viewed the achievement of milestones as essential/important before releasing further funds. Members of the smaller cluster (13 in number) are generally larger funds that prefer to invest in later stage deals. This cluster 'rarely' tied the release of funds to milestones. The stage of the deal is clearly a significant factor here; the value of

Table 8.9 Venture Capitalists' Preferences for the Staging of Investments

	Responses	Per cent	Cumulative per cent
Essential	13	32.5	32.5
Important	15	37.5	70.0
Desirable	8	20.0	90.0
Irrelevant	4	10.0	100.0
Total	40	100.0	

the investee company is more established in later stage deals and the venture capitalists are more confident in advancing the funds immediately to finance (say) a major contract or the purchase of an expensive fixed asset.

Proposition (5): Preferred stock is the most frequently used financial product in India.

Preferred stock is by far the most common financial instrument used in VC deals across the globe; it allows investors to stage investments, allocate risk/return equitably, provide incentives to executives and so on (Trester, 1998; Berglof, 1994). Preferred stock can also counter asymmetric information, a particular problem for early stage financing. Debt and common equity are used more frequently in later stage financing and/or in industries where monitoring is comparatively easy. There is limited flexibility in the use of preferred stock in India, and it will be recalled from Chapter 6 that the authorities rejected SEBI's proposal for more freedom in this respect.

Participants in our survey expressed a preference for 'plain' equity across all stages and sectors. Despite this preference, further probing revealed that the vast majority of fund managers had made investments that combined financial products – the preferred combinations are shown in Table 8.10.

Table 8.10 reveals that preferred stock was used by over half of the respondents. The authors were not able to establish with any certainty the split between pure equity and combination deals, but the indications are that Proposition (5) should be rejected. The difficulty of drawing a definite conclusion on this issue is reinforced by our

Table 8.10 Use of a Combination of Financial Products (37 respondents only)

Combination of Financial Products	Responses	Per cent	Cumulative per cent
Equity + preferred stock + convertible debt	12	32.5	32.5
Equity + convertible debt	9	24.3	47.8
Equity + preferred stock	9	24.3	72.1
Equity only	7	18.9	100.0

earlier analysis of structuring covenants (Table 8.8). Equity ratchets are closely associated with preferred stock; conversion rights depend upon performance. While this factor was ranked only 14 in a list of 25 structuring covenants used in India, its Likert scale average of 1.88 implies that most respondents viewed ratchets as essential or important.

Cluster analysis identified the characteristics of VC firms that favoured: equity (ten VC firms); equity and convertible debt (nine); equity and preferred stock (nine); and a combination of equity, convertible debt and preferred stock (12). Those firms that utilized the latter combination had portfolios comprising mainly early stage investments; the combination of three financial instruments gives maximum flexibility to manage risk. At the other extreme lie the ten VC firms that preferred equity only. These firms are mainly of Indian origin and they have a strong technology bias, even though most of the investments are in later stage deals where the risk-return profile is more stable. The authors suggest that this cluster probably consists of less sophisticated investors.

The cluster opting for the combination of equity and convertible debt (nine VC firms) contained mainly foreign investors relatively new to India that had made few investments; the investments were mainly of the 'non-technology' nature and could service debt commitments from cash flow. The final cluster (also nine in number) favoured equity and preferred stock; the group had marginally more foreign investors, and comprised mainly large funds that had made relatively few investments. The key factor behind the use of preferred stock rather than convertible debt was their preference for technology-based investments.

Logistic regression analysis highlighted the fact that technology-oriented investors utilized preferred stock at the seed and early stages.

Proposition (6): Venture capitalists in India use a range of mechanisms to monitor their investee companies, calling for financial reports and other information on a regular basis.

Any monitoring system is designed to reduce the problems of information asymmetry and moral hazard. In the fast changing Indian economy, we suggested that monitoring would be vigorous, with the focus on protection against short-term threats rather than long-term relationship building. The specific reports requested are set out in Table 8.11; lower averages for the Likert scores reflect a desire for more frequent information.

Table 8.11 Monitoring Reports used by Venture Capitalists in India

	Mean	Standard Deviation
1. Profit and loss accounts	1.43	0.50
2. Sales reports	1.53	0.72
3. Cash flow statements	1.63	0.63
4. Balance sheets	1.68	0.66
5. Project implementation report	1.75	0.74
6. Budgets versus actual	1.75	0.81
7. Default reports	2.05	0.81
8. Sales budgets	2.05	0.93
9. Working capital reports	2.08	0.89
10. Recruitment/loss of key personnel	2.13	1.18
11. Capacity utilization reports	2.13	0.97
12. Creditors and debtors reports	2.20	0.82
13. Inventory reports	2.38	0.95
14. Market share analysis	2.40	0.81
15. Payroll sheets	3.10	1.08

Note: 1 = Monthly; 2 = Quarterly; 3 = Yearly; 4 = Never

Over half of respondents monitor the performance of their investee companies through a monthly profit and loss statement, and the remainder receive these statements on a quarterly basis. This mirrors the practice of VC firms in the developed world (Reid, 1998). The emphasis on accounting reports is reinforced by the requirements for budget variance analysis, as well as cash flow, working capital and balance sheet information. Capital expenditure is also tightly monitored; cost overruns in the early stages of a company's life can often lead to ultimate failure. Sales and marketing is another key concern, along with the recruitment and retention of key personnel. The broad thrust of Proposition (6) is therefore accepted.

Cluster analysis revealed three groups that differed in their attitudes to monitoring reports. The groups comprised 17, 16 and 7 members respectively. The largest cluster favours later stage deals. These VC firms monitor extensively, but less frequently than those in the second largest cluster where early stage investors dominate. The cluster with seven VC firms comprises mainly smaller funds, relatively new to India, that invest in technology-based projects. This group monitors most frequently, suggesting once again that the risk involved in funding high-technology proposals is perceived to outweigh that of early stage deals.

The venture capitalists not only receive reports, but also visit their investee companies for board meetings or informal discussions. The vast majority of respondents exercised the right to formal board representation, and they were keen to engage in ongoing dialogue; one participant stated that: 'I invariably send five questions to the Chief Financial Officer, after examining the periodic statements'. There is ample evidence of 'multi-layered monitoring' (Robbie et al., 1997). The main purpose of the meetings include: reviewing progress, especially the generation of sales revenue; considering strategic issues, rather than operational matters; acting as a sounding board; and monitoring product development, particularly for technology-oriented companies. The investors are also prepared to engage in troubleshooting, to counter the teething problems encountered by many start-up businesses (Terry and Smith, 1998).

Additional statistical tests revealed that early stage VC firms favouring technology investments focussed on longer-term, strategic issues rather than short-term financial matters.

Proposition (7): Venture capitalists in India replace CEOs in order to control moral hazard and improve performance in investee companies.

The replacement of CEOs in investee companies is accepted as a feature of mature venture capital markets (Gorman and Sahlman, 1989; Fiet and Hellriegel, 1995; Kanellos, 1996) and it is also prevalent in emerging markets (Wright et al., 1998). In our survey, 16 respondents (40 per cent of our sample) had not taken this action yet – see Table 8.12.

As 40 per cent of respondents had never replaced the CEO in an investee company, these results provide only partial support for Proposition (7).

Of the 20 respondents who had replaced a few CEOs in their investee companies (Row 2 in Table 8.12), three quarters of the group are

Table 8.12 Percentage of CEOs Replaced by the Venture Capitalists

% of CEOs Replaced	Frequency	Per cent	Cumulative per cent
None	16	40.0	40.0
1–5 %	20	50.0	90.0
6–10 %	1	2.5	92.5
> 10 %	3	7.5	100.0
Total	40	100.0	

Indian; most of these funds have been in existence for some time and they are primarily early stage investors. These firms have also made fewer investments than our full sample and the fund managers therefore concentrate on monitoring a smaller portfolio. One participant commented that: 'We would like to replace more CEOs, but finding a suitable replacement is difficult!'

Of the four VC firms that have displayed a greater propensity to replace CEOs, all are foreign. Any conclusions have to be tempered with caution, owing to the small number of VC firms involved, but this study provides some evidence that foreign funds are more aggressive in dealing with perceived management failings. This impression is strengthened because these firms have typically not been operating for long in India. They have thus taken decisive action early in their relationship with the investee company. It is also significant that they have invested more in the technology sector. VC firms in the developed world do not hesitate to replace a technology-oriented founder by a CEO with commercial experience; this practice appears to have been imported into India.

Proposition (8): Venture capitalists in India will tend to replace CEOs because of perceived failures in strategic skills.

There is a debate in the literature on whether a firm's success stems from the operational or strategic skills of a CEO. In the light of the rapid developments in the Indian and global economy, we proposed that venture capitalists might place a premium on strategic skills. Nevertheless, the data in Table 8.13 suggest that venture capitalists in India hold operational and strategic skills in almost equal regard.

Table 8.13 Lack of Skills Responsible for the Dismissal of Investee CEOs

	N	Mean	Standard Deviation
Operational skills	24	1.88	0.90
Strategic skills	24	2.04	1.04
Financial skills	24	2.21	1.02
Drive and vision	24	2.25	1.11
Integrity	24	2.54	1.38
Interpersonal skills	24	2.58	1.18
Communication skills	24	2.88	0.95

Note: 1 = Always; 2 = Mostly; 3 = Rarely; 4 = Never

The reasons for the replacement of CEOs vary, and the standard deviations for some factors are quite high, for example: the importance of strategic skills. (Logistic regression analysis revealed that investors in technology-based projects valued such skills very highly.) A lack of interpersonal or communication skills are clearly less likely to lead to the removal of a CEO; the participants' relative indifference to these factors is somewhat puzzling because one of the most challenging tasks facing CEOs is team building, a task that requires strong interpersonal skills.

Cluster analysis revealed two groups, with 14 and 10 members respectively. The larger cluster considered 'financial skills' as more important whereas the smaller cluster rated 'integrity' as the critical factor. The two clusters were remarkably similar in many characteristics, except that the smaller group contained a much higher proportion of Indian investors. This concern for integrity over financial skills might reflect the traditional concept of *baniya* (Hindi for trader) where trust precedes everything else and transactions worth millions of dollars are executed in cash, purely on the basis of trust. Integrity has thus long been the hallmark of Indian business culture. India is not alone in this respect; business in a large part of the Arab world is also conducted in this fashion.

Proposition (8) is therefore rejected, but only marginally. Moreover, strategic skills are very highly valued for investments in certain sectors, especially those associated with technology.

8.4 Conclusions

The database constructed for this research programme enabled the authors to build a comprehensive picture of VC activity in India. In investigating the propositions set out in Chapter 7, the high response rate can give the reader confidence in the findings. Moreover, the ability to describe the sample in relation to categories was very useful in identifying common characteristics of VC firms within clusters. The Chi Square test and logistic regression were used sparingly to reinforce key findings.

8.4.1 Valuation

The importance placed on 'own due diligence' as a source of information for valuation purposes was evident. The foreign VC firms led the way in using their own research to check out the market potential and technological feasibility of their projects; the Indian (mainly

Government-sponsored) VC firms were either 'information hungry' or prepared to invest more intuitively.

The prime importance of DCF techniques for valuation purposes was confirmed for the sample as a whole, and there was some evidence that Indian venture capitalists are adopting the quantitative valuation methods used by their foreign counterparts. The quantitative techniques will increasingly be used in tandem with qualitative methods as the VC market in India matures. It was interesting to note that both early stage and technology-oriented investors apply higher discount rates to compensate for the risks involved, with the technology element perhaps exerting more influence on the choice of discount rate.

8.4.2 Structuring

A striking feature was that many of the covenants in common use (25 in all) were considered to be essential or important. The top-rated covenants included those aimed at preventing investee companies from raising other sources of funding or restructuring, those giving the VC firm the right to discuss progress informally or through board representation, and those concerned with the venture capitalists' exit route. In themes that are already starting to emerge, early stage investors insist upon more covenants than those favouring later stage deals, and technology-oriented VC firms focus on a different set of covenants compared to their 'non-technology' equivalents.

The majority of investors also consider the staging of investments as either essential or important. The release of further funds was most often linked to the achievement of budgets and, perhaps more surprisingly, to the recruitment of key employees. (The latter was especially important to technology-oriented VC firms.) Cluster analysis revealed that smaller, early stage investors place much greater emphasis on the achievement of milestones than larger firms with a preference for later stage deals.

In relation to the financial instruments used in structuring deals, the participants claimed to favour 'plain' equity across all stages and sectors. This bucks the global trend for using preferred stock. However, the majority of fund managers in India had made investments that combined financial products, and the use of equity ratchets (often linked to preferred stock) was commonplace. Preferred stock featured mainly in financial packages for seed and early stage deals, especially technology-based investments.

8.4.3 Monitoring

Respondents monitor the performance of their investee companies by calling for regular financial reports, and by keeping a close eye on capital expenditure and the recruitment and retention of key personnel. The degree and frequency of monitoring was higher in early stage and technology-linked deals; the risk associated with technology investments again appeared to weigh heavily on the minds of venture capitalists in India. In meeting the investee companies through board representation or informal discussions, the venture capitalists' main concerns were to review progress, especially where product development is involved, and to offer strategic input. There is obviously less need to review operations in early stage companies.

The replacement of the CEO in an investee company can have severe repercussions for all parties and 16 respondents (40 per cent of our sample) had not pursued this course of action. This might be explained by the difficulty of finding suitable replacements in India. It is not easy to decide the point at which a CEO should be replaced; the CEO would normally be given time to prove his/her worth. Of the 60 per cent of respondents that had replaced CEOs, a small group of foreign VC firms revealed a willingness to take decisive action early in their relationship with the investee company. Non-Indian firms seemed to be prepared to bring in a CEO with commercial experience, as a condition of investing in a technology-based firm.

In replacing a CEO, venture capitalists in India hold operational and strategic skills in almost equal regard. Strategic skills are very highly valued for investments in certain sectors, especially those associated with technology. Indian VC firms proved to be more concerned with integrity than financial skills, whereas foreign VC firms took the opposite view.

8.5 Summary

This chapter described the research methodology adopted for our study of the VC industry in India. The data were gathered in a resource-intensive programme of interviews that enabled the authors not only to build a picture of VC activity as a whole, but also to investigate the influence of how (say) clusters of VC firms with certain characteristics adopted different practices to manage risk. Further statistical analysis confirmed how, for example, fund origin affects the attitudes and actions of venture capitalists. The propositions set out in Chapter 7 were accepted in most cases and rejected in others (refer to Table 10.1 in the concluding chapter). A number of themes emerged in the synopsis of our research findings presented in Section 8.4 above, notably the impact of early stage and/or technology deals on the behaviour of venture capitalists in India. The implications of our findings for policy makers, entrepreneurs and VC practitioners are explored in Chapter 10.

Before then, Chapter 9 examines the emerging market for Islamic finance in India and describes the affinities between VC and Islamic finance. The ethical principles of Islam offer one way to address the principal/agent problems that have been a recurring theme of this book.

9
Business Ethics and Venture Capital in Islam

Mansoor Durrani

9.1 Introduction

The main theoretical themes running through this book have been agency theory and the associated problems of adverse selection, information asymmetry and moral hazard. In an effort to control the behaviour of managers (agents) and the workforce, the focus of attention for academics and practitioners has been on techniques to improve corporate governance. Others have put forward more imaginative solutions to address potential conflicts of interest. For instance, tapping into the employees' Emotional Quotient (Goleman, 1998) or allowing them to find expression through art (www.artquotient.com) may improve productivity and thus enhance shareholder value. This chapter develops this theme by focussing on the 'Spiritual Quotient' (SQ), a dimension that is usually neglected but one that may have a crucial role to play in addressing the problems associated with agency theory.

The first part of this chapter (up to and including Section 9.6) describes some of the consequences of growth when it is not tempered by moral concerns and then guides the reader through the Islamic injunctions (collectively called SQ) that offer an alternative approach to business; the second part (Section 9.7 onwards) examines venture capital as an emerging asset class within the Islamic financial architecture. The latter includes an evaluation of our three key themes – valuation, structuring and monitoring – from an Islamic perspective. Author's intention is neither to present a detailed exposition of the Islamic faith, nor to offer a full review of the concepts of Islamic banking and finance (for the latter, the reader is referred to Iqbal and Molyneux, 2005).

9.2 The adverse consequences of growth

The industrial and technological revolutions have brought mixed results. Economic development has registered impressive gains, including: 'unprecedented prosperity in certain regions of the world, technological progress, improvements in productivity and efficiency, (and) thousands of new products' (Ahmad, A. 2000, p.86). Yet, Ahmad argues that such development has led to increased pollution, environmental damage and moral degeneration.

At the organizational level, other stakeholders (especially investors and employees) suffer when its owners and/or senior managers pursue selfish interests or engage in dubious business practices to achieve growth. A number of high profile corporate court cases have recently featured in the global media, for example Hollinger International, Enron and WorldCom. At best, a firm's share price has fallen sharply after such 'show trials'; at worst, companies have disappeared altogether. Other organizations (such as Nike) have changed their employment practices in the face of allegations about the payment of low wages in the developing world. The ethical and social responsibilities of the business community have thus become a matter of serious public concern.

Moral values have existed in all religions and societies throughout human history. Koontz (1990) argues that a state religion can constitute a central source of authority to influence ethical practices; in the US, however, there are so many cultures and religions that it is impossible to identify a church, Government, educational institution or other private association as the source and centre of ethical tradition. Prince Charles expressed similar sentiments about a lack of values in the developed world (Dunning, 2003, p.viii): 'Apart from anything else, it had become clear to me that, while producing a generation of excellent corporate managers, business schools were failing to inculcate in their students a value-based system ... After all, values and a moral compass are surely essential.'

In the absence of absolute moral values, ethical standards tend to evolve by experience and/or a 'feeling' for what is acceptable at any given time. Indeed, Webster's Business Dictionary (2001, p.95) defines ethics as: 'conduct one may expect from a reasonable person under normal circumstances'. What is 'reasonable' and 'normal' may vary from person to person, group to group, city to city and country to country. If money and profit become the dominant if not the sole criterion of success in life and business, societies disintegrate and corruption flourishes (Chapra, 1992). In the wake of allegations of financial impropriety at Enron and elsewhere, the regulatory bodies in the industrialized nations have had to react swiftly to ensure that this situation is averted.

Notwithstanding such action, it is legitimate in the current climate to consider three questions posed by Dunning (2003, p.1):

1. 'What must be done to upgrade moral standards?
2. What role should incentive structures, formal and informal rules, and enforcement instruments play? And ...
3. What is the influence of religious thought and practice?'

9.3 An alternative view

'The Islamic model [of corporate governance] ... transcends national barriers, but the common bond comes from religious precepts which lay down how trade and commerce should be conducted by an adherent to the faith' (Lewis, 1999). Islam places the highest emphasis on ethical values in human life; these ethical principles are eternal and absolute.

Prophet Muhammad (peace be upon Him – PBUH), regarded by Muslims as the last Messenger of Allah, said (*Bukhari*): 'I have been sent for the purpose of perfecting good morals'.[1] The Holy Book of Islam, source of guidance containing the message of Allah to mankind, states: 'O believers! Do not consume each other's wealth unjustly, but only [in lawful] business by mutual consent' (*Qur'an*, 4: 29). Islam thus recognizes the desirability of engagement in business activity, and it also encourages fair trade, commerce and an entrepreneurial culture.

This ideology implies that an entrepreneur who performs his business operations in accordance with the commands of Allah will also reap handsome reward in the Life After, an article of faith for Muslims. Business activities can become a part of *Ibadah* (worship and obedience of Allah) if they are performed in accordance with the Islamic code of conduct. Pilgrims are allowed to undertake business transactions even during Hajj, the annual pilgrimage to *Makkah*, the highest form of worship in Islam (*Qur'an*, 2: 198). Islam declares that the search for one's livelihood through fair business is like seeking the blessing of Allah (*Qur'an*, 62: 10).

9.4 Ethical principles in Islam

It is believed that Islam is based on Divine commands and guidelines available in the *Qur'an* and the sayings of Muhammad (PBUH). This section summarizes some fundamental moral values in Islam; these principles have practical implications across all spheres of life, including business. This will become evident as we explore a selection of Islamic principles relating to business ethics in Section 9.5 below.

Truthfulness: is a basic ethical value in Islam. 'O believers! Fear Allah and speak [always] the truth' (*Qur'an*, 33: 70). This instruction has profound implications for establishing a flourishing business environment. All business dealings must be managed in an honest, truthful and straightforward manner.

There is no scope for cheating, misrepresenting and misleading in the Islamic framework. The principles of truthfulness and honesty are not followed merely as a matter of business strategy rather they are the obligation of a true Muslim in all his dealings, including politics, diplomacy, judiciary, governance, administration and economic activities. *Qur'an* describes Prophet Joseph as 'man of truth' (12: 46). Another unique feature of the Islamic economic system is that its moral values are fortified through institutional arrangements in the form of an *hisbah* (ombudsman) for fair business.

Trust: A business enterprise is viewed as a trust from Allah between the society and entrepreneurs or sponsors. A businessperson is required to treat all business resources as a Divine trust. Hence, s/he is expected to make the most efficient and socially desirable use of business resources. Prophet Moses is described as 'trustworthy', one of the traits critical for his future role (*Qur'an*, 28: 26). This concept of trust highlights the sense of responsibility towards all stakeholders, and holds true even where those entrusting something to Muslims are non-Muslims.

Justice: The whole universe is based on the concept of justice and balance. Justice means every one should be treated, as s/he duly deserves without discrimination. It includes fair treatment, equality and a sense of proportion and balance. Justice is a dynamic characteristic that each Muslim is required to develop. *Qur'an* states: 'O Believers! Stand out firmly for Allah as witness to fair dealing and let not the hatred of others [non-Muslims] prevent you from justice. Be just; that is next to piety; and fear Allah for Allah is well-acquainted with all that you do' (5: 8). Justice is a prerequisite for successful business and trade as it encompasses the entire gamut of corporate life (Ahmad, M., 1999). It permeates almost every business decision – pricing, product quality, human resource policy, corporate governance, financial disclosures, environmental protection and so on.

Competence: Competence is highly valued in Islam, even to the extent that a competent but 'Islamically weak leader may be preferred to an incompetent leader who is Islamically more knowledgeable' (Beekun and Badawi, 2000; p.39). Notwithstanding this assertion, the most preferred set of qualifications is surely a combination of competence and knowledge. *Qur'an* (28: 26) describes Prophet Moses as *al-qawi* (the most competent or qualified) and declares that Allah granted him 'wisdom and knowledge' (28: 14). In striving for excellence, *Qur'an* assures: 'whoever pledges his life to Allah and his deeds are excellent, his reward is with his Creator' (2: 112), and Prophet Muhammad (PBUH) states: 'You should not be extremist, but try to be near to perfection' (*Bukhari*). A distinction is also drawn between knowledge (*ilm*) and one's ability (competence) to put this knowledge into practice (*hikmah*). The combination of these two concepts encourages entrepreneurial initiatives among the followers of Islam (Ahmad, M., 1999).

Sincerity and humility: Islam attaches enormous importance to humility and sincerity in every department of life. The performance of duties to perfection requires individuals to work with sincerity and devotion, and discourages manipulation or exploitation for personal gains (Ahmad, M., 1999). Accordingly, a sincere businessperson refrains from cheating or harming his/her business associates deliberately. *Qur'an* describes Muslims in general as 'those who walk on the earth with humility' (25: 63). Even affluent Muslims are not permitted to spend their wealth extravagantly; they are urged to spend cautiously so that economic resources are allocated only to productive assets (*Qur'an*, 17: 26–29).

Brotherhood: Islam declares all human beings as one single community (*Qur'an*, 10: 19). This has profound implications for the way in which (say) entrepreneurs treat employees, customers, suppliers, shareholders and other stakeholders. Business dealings should not be conducted with the aim of personal gain, or the defeat and humiliation of business adversaries; rather, they should be driven by the desire to add value to the general welfare of the society. Competition is then replaced with cooperation, but not at the expense of the efficient allocation of society's resources.

Zakah: forms one of the five fundamental pillars of Islam. This is a mandatory charity that, beyond a threshold of one year's accumulated wealth, every Muslim has to pay to the poor and needy. If implemented sincerely, this is a social self-help system that embeds welfare at the heart of society and results in complete eradication of poverty. The optimum use of *zakah* increases purchasing power in society and plays a vital role in maintaining sustained levels of demand and supply in the economy. However, this unique instrument for establishing economic justice based on Islamic values is being ignored, even in Muslim societies (Chapra, 1992; Qardawi, 2003).

Knowledge and science: Islam makes it obligatory for Muslims to seek knowledge and obtain excellence in performance. Islam encourages dynamism, fosters initiative and enjoins Muslims to work persistently for progress and advancement, both materially and spiritually. Research and development is highly valued in Islam. The Prophet (PBUH) urged Muslims to travel as far as China (the most distant country known to the Arab world in the 6th Century) in search of knowledge. This passionate quest for knowledge and science brought unprecedented glory and success to Islamic civilization between the 6th and the 14th Centuries. Indeed, it is believed in some quarters that the decline of Islamic civilization was set in train by a progressive reduction in resources allocated to education and human capital development after the 14th Century.

9.5 Business ethics in Islam

The generic Islamic principles above lay the foundation for the Islamic moral system. The injunctions give rise to specific ethical guidelines for business; many of these have practical relevance in addressing agency problems including information asymmetry, adverse selection, moral hazard and corporate governance.

9.5.1 Ethical investments

A number of business sectors (including alcoholic drinks, gambling, pornography, tobacco and the arms industry) are perceived as socially harmful and hence are not permitted as Islamic investments. The *Qur'an* warns: 'O believers! Intoxicants and gambling, and *Al-Ansab* [animals that are sacrificed in the name of idols] and *Al-Azlam* [arrows thrown in a search for luck or as an aid to decision-making] are an abomination of Satan's handiwork. So avoid that [abomination] in order that you may be successful' (5: 90).

9.5.2 Compliance with contracts

The fulfilment of contracts and promises forms the core of Islamic ethical system, reflecting the basic principles of truth, honesty and trust. *Qur'an* declares successful Muslims to be: 'those who faithfully adhere to their *Amanah* [honesty, moral responsibility and trusts] and to their covenants' (23: 8).

Business growth is impossible without mutual trust and confidence. There is no scope for opportunism and the unilateral violation of contracts and promises in Islam. (There is no doctrine of *caveat emptor* in

Islamic Law: Lewis, 1999.) A Muslim entrepreneur is expected to honour his/her trusts, promises and contracts. Indeed, Prophet Muhammad (PBUH) called the violator of a covenant a 'hypocrite', one of the most repugnant titles in Islam. It is therefore desirable to use unequivocal language in all business contracts and dealings. Prophet Muhammad (PBUH) stated: 'Whoever is making such contracts, let it be in a well defined measure and well defined price and well defined time frame' (*Muslim*[2]*: Chapter al-Baya*).

While *Qur'an* urges Muslims to 'fulfil all obligations' (5: 1), Prophet Muhammad (PBUH) states that this injunction does not apply where the fulfilment of a contract would not be acceptable (Iqbal and Llewellyn, 2001), for example: if an entrepreneur discovers a contract is associated with the supply of intoxicants.

9.5.3 Deceptive advertising and misrepresentation

Customers should be treated fairly and not be subject to misleading advertisements and publicity campaigns. Islam strongly condemns such practices: 'Give full measure and weigh justly and do not deprive people of their due, and do not abuse on the earth, spreading corruption' (*Qur'an*, 11: 85). On a similar note, Islam prescribes a strong dress code for its followers, and the sale proceeds of products that are perfectly permissible in Islam (such as chocolates or perfume) become tainted when promoted by indecently dressed female or male models.

9.5.4 Accurate measurement and weights

Qur'anic instruction is explicit on this issue: 'Give full measure when you measure, and weigh with a balance that is straight. That is good [advantageous] and better in the end' (17: 35). This command is frequently disregarded, especially where consumer rights are not protected adequately by the legal system. Those who undertake such practices increase their rights at the expense of others, but they have to face the consequences. Elsewhere in the *Qur'an,* it is warned: 'Woe to *Al-Mutaffifin* [those who give less in measure and weight], those who, when they have to receive by measure from people, demand full measure, and when they have to give by measure or weight to people, give less than due. Do they not think that they will be resurrected [for reckoning], on a Great Day, the Day when [all] mankind will stand before the Lord?' (83: 1–6).

9.5.5 Hoarding and destruction of surplus produce

Prophet Muhammad (PBUH) declared: 'One who hoards things for increasing their prices for Muslims is a wrong doer' (*Mustadrik Hakim,*[3]

Volume 2). On the same theme, many producers are accused of destroying surplus produce, with a view to restricting supply and hence maintaining high prices. Islam attributes the ownership of goods and resources to Allah and views man as merely a trustee; the destruction of surplus produce is regarded as a form of *fasad* (atrocity), which is reprehensible in the eyes of Allah. Producers, whether individual organizations or national/international bodies, are therefore encouraged by Islam to explore ways and means to utilize their surplus produce for the betterment of mankind.

9.5.6 Fair recruitment practices

Islam views a public office or a corporate position as a Divine trust that should be offered to the most deserving person. Responsibility must be given only to those who have the capability to justify their position on the basis of merit. *Qur'an* demands: 'O believers! Betray not Allah and His Messenger, nor betray knowingly your *Amanah* [things entrusted to you and all the duties Allah has ordained for you] (8: 27). Prophet Muhammad (PBUH) warned: 'Whoever employs a person out of favouritism, when there is a more competent candidate, has committed a breach of trust with God, His Prophet and all Muslims' (*Mundhari*,[4] 1986: Vol. 3, p.175). The offering of employment opportunities on the basis of nationality, favouritism, cronyism or even gender is forbidden; recruitment should focus on competence and trustworthiness alone.

9.5.7 Human resource practices

It is the obligation of business organizations to take care of the overall welfare of their employees and to provide opportunities for their advancement. Business organizations are therefore obliged to provide fair remuneration, a decent working environment, reasonable working hours and so on. Muhammad (PBUH) counselled as follows: 'Allah says that I will act as plaintiff, on the Day of Judgement, against the person who engages someone on work and takes full work from him but does not give him [full] wages' (*Bukhari*); and, 'It is essential to feed the slave [worker], clothe him [properly] and not burden him with a task beyond his power' (Khan, 1989).

9.5.8 Corporate governance

The essence of corporate governance is accountability. This concept accords with the fundamental Islamic premise that all deeds of mankind will be accounted for on the Day of Judgement. Indeed, Muhammad (PBUH) declared: 'Every one of you is a guardian and is accountable for his charge and his subjects' (Khan, 1989). This principle demands that those holding powerful positions should not show favouritism towards a particular group or community. More generally, Islam expressly forbids the accumulation of wealth by illegal means. Funds should not be misappropriated for personal gain; individuals must not accept public office solely for financial reward.

Qur'an emphasizes the standards expected in these words: 'O believers, eat not up your property among yourselves unjustly except it be a trade among you by mutual consent' (4: 29). The following passage confirms the importance of good governance. A man came to Prophet Muhammad (PBUH) and asked when the doomsday would occur. The Prophet (PBUH) replied: 'When deposits in trust would start being lost, then wait for the doomsday.' He was again asked, what is the meaning of loss of trust? The Prophet (PBUH) replied: 'When responsibilities are entrusted to unfit persons then wait for the doomsday' (*Bukhari*).

9.5.9 Environmental protection

It is a fundamental principle of Islam that no individual or organization has the right to utilize resources in a way that damages nature or causes inconvenience to the society in general (Llewellyn, 1984). Prophet Muhammad (PBUH) prohibited the cutting of any tree in the desert that provides valuable shade or sustenance to humans or animals (*Mishkat al-Masabih*, [5] Vol. 2, p.125, No. 2970). Muslim rulers enforced this instruction religiously when they barred their armies from destroying the crops, orchards and livestock of their enemies (Hamidullah, 1973).

Uncontrolled industrial development leads to environmental pollution (Ahmad, A., 2000). The destruction of nature for the sake of profit is condemned in Islam. The goals of 'profit-maximization' and 'customer-satisfaction' should thus be subordinate to societal needs and governed by environmental friendly practices. The focus must be on providing useful products and services without causing damage to nature or society. Similarly, Islam places obligations on the current generation to be sensitive about the needs of coming generations, and urges its followers neither to over-consume existing resources nor to waste them.

9.5.10 Wealth distribution

Islam warns against the concentration of wealth in fewer hands, and the creation of small islands of prosperity in an ocean of poverty (Ahmad, K., 2000). The early chapters of this book emphasized that SMEs generate employment and innovation, provide opportunities for social inclusion and produce a more equitable distribution of wealth. Efforts to promote the SME sector are therefore eminently compatible with Islamic principles (Chapra, 1992). Since most of the Islamic world is under-developed, a long-term, coherent vision of economic development, underpinned by SME growth, could bring both economic prosperity and social justice. In practical terms, this could involve (say) bringing large and small enterprises together in dedicated industrial clusters.

9.5.11 Prohibition of interest

Islam regards money as a means of exchanging value rather than a valuable commodity itself (Naqvi, 1987). In Islamic doctrine, the charging of interest is considered not only a form of *zulm* (exploitation) but also a far greater sin than even adultery and consumption of alcohol. Prophet Muhammad (PBUH) equated wilful dealing in interest with committing adultery 36 times or being guilty of incest with one's own mother (*Bayhaqi;*[6] *Shuab al-Iman*).

The *Qur'an* states that: 'Those who deal in *riba* [interest] will not stand [on the Day of Resurrection] except like the standing of a person beaten by *satan* leading him to insanity. That is because they say: "Trading is only like *riba*", whereas Allah has permitted trading and forbidden *riba*. So whosoever receives an admonition from his Lord and stops dealing in *riba* shall not be punished for the past; his case is for Allah [to judge]; but whoever returns [to *riba*], such are the dwellers of the Fire – they will abide therein' (2: 275).

Islam identifies *riba* as the root cause of a number of economic evils. However, Islam differentiates between genuine business profits and interest; the former is desirable, the latter is not. Islam requires an interest-free financial system, primarily based on the principles of *Mudarabah* and *Musharakah* (these concepts are explained below). At the most basic level, Islam stresses the need to share rather than transfer the risk. The rationale behind this approach emanates from the justice system of Islam. Justice demands that the capital provider is entitled to a return in excess of original investment only if the recipient of capital (the entrepreneur) makes profits. In the case of losses, the capital provider must share those losses. This leaves no justification for interest in Islam, whether in commercial or non-commercial transactions. Chapra (2001, p.11) states that: 'However, it is not Islam alone which has prohibited interest. Other major religions like Judaism, Christianity and Hinduism whose followers constitute two-thirds of the world population have also done the same [banned interest at some time]'.

The profit sharing approach would see the evolution of a 'real' economy based on genuine asset creation; if all business transactions were based on the underlying value of tangible goods and services, a more stable and sustainable economic outlook should ensue. The alternative is a speculative economy with a tendency to create 'fiduciary bubbles'. It is estimated that more than 96 per cent of global currency trades are speculative, and that such transactions exceed US$1.5 trillion daily (Chapra, 2001). Speculators can provide liquidity to markets and offer risk protection, but they have also been associated with the risk of over-inflated paper assets that collapse in value and bring misery to investors and other stakeholders.

9.6 The differentiator

The moral values set out above (both personal and business) reflect the values of many societies across the globe, particularly those that have been influenced by religion. However, where individuals or organizations seek to serve self-interest at the expense of all other factors, ethical values or rules of behaviour are rarely observed (Dunning, 2003).

In the Islamic view of the world, the concept of Hereafter provides the necessary motivating force to act in an ethical manner. This belief is so strongly embedded that a person will cease to be a Muslim if s/he doubts the prospect of accountability on the Day of Judgement and refuses to shape his/her lifestyle accordingly. People may be able to serve self-interest in this world by violating moral values, but they serve their self-interest in the Hereafter only by observing the moral values described above. Islamic doctrine therefore suggests that the well-being of humanity in this world and Hereafter converge because of adherence to these values.

The need to regulate human behaviour is observed in every society. Moore (1972, p.81) pointed out, correctly in author's view, that: 'no human society can afford to permit all kinds of human behaviour. If it did permit them, it would soon cease to be a society'. The significance of the Divine law in general, and the means to operationalize it in human society in particular, has been a subject of intense debate throughout history.

The rationale for the Islamic view on the need of accountability at the end of this life is outlined below:

1. The Divine sanction makes the rules of behaviour absolute and beyond dispute (Chapra, 1992). Without the Divine sanction, rules

can become the subject of personal judgement and dispute; indeed, the value of these rules 'came to be questioned all together' in secular societies (de Beus, 1985, p.71). Historians have concluded that: 'There is no significant example in history, of a society successfully maintaining moral life without the aid of religion' (Durant and Durant, 1968, p.51).

2. If humans were to try to develop these norms themselves, there would be a natural tendency on their part to frame rules that are skewed in favour of the rich and powerful. In such circumstances, even the slightest doubt about impartiality would negate the chances of a consensus.
3. Human beings have only limited capacity for assessing the harmful effects of their own actions on others. An unbiased and knowledgeable adjudicator is needed, one who is capable of visualizing such effects and who can offer rules of conduct that prevent them occurring.
4. The Creator of human beings alone is capable of understanding their nature, their needs, their strengths and their weaknesses, and of serving as the Sole Guide and the Only Source of all values. He has not left human beings to grope in the darkness and has provided the needed Guidance, through a chain of prophets starting from Adam, that can ensure the well being of all (Chapra 1992).

These themes illustrate the importance of integrating the Spiritual Quotient (SQ) into mainstream corporate practices. The explicit recognition of the spiritual dimension might present a solution to the problems associated with information asymmetry, adverse selection, moral hazard and corporate governance, and hence offer more protection to all stakeholders.

While the author that the SQ could play a key role in reducing agency problems and enhancing corporate practices, it has to be integrated with existing financial systems and procedures. Our focus has been on VC, a concept that has many of the profit/loss sharing principles of Islamic finance (Anderson, 1994). The links between VC and Islamic finance form the subject of the next section.

9.7 Venture capital and Islamic finance

VC is risk capital, and risk-taking involves a willingness to commit to a course of action that leads to rewards or penalties associated with success or failure (Welsch and Young, 1982). Equity investments in permissible sectors are allowed in Islam (Siddiqi, 1985; Chapra, 1992), as are investments in companies having a zero conventional debt capital structure (Khan, 1989; Khan, 1995). The provision of equity-based capital for SMEs also accords with the Islamic desire for wider economic development and a more equal distribution of wealth.

The global Islamic finance industry (almost exclusively Islamic banking) is almost three decades old, and it is valued at over US$150bn (Iqbal and Molyneux, 2005). However, Islamic finance has not been linked to economic development to the same extent as VC, and there have been very few innovations in Islamic financial instruments. Over 65 per cent of Islamic funds are currently invested through *murabaha,* an Islamic debt instrument that is used to purchase real assets for onward sale at a fixed mark-up rate.

In setting out a framework for Islamic VC, there are primarily two reasons to justify this form of finance. First, the state of economic development in the Muslim world has remained at the lower end of the scale for more than a century (Ahmed, 2004). As this book highlights, the benefits associated with equity finance, technological innovation and entrepreneurial assistance point to VC as a vital contributor to a long-term strategy of economic growth. Second, it is believed by Islamic economists that VC finance has its original roots in the Islamic world, especially in the concept of *mudarabah.* This funding mechanism provides support to those with entrepreneurial skills but lacking financial resources. The entrepreneur or the recipient of capital is termed the *Mudarib* while the provider of capital, the venture fund, is known as *Rabb al-mal.*

The basic theoretical model of an Islamic bank, according to Iqbal and Molyneux (2005), has been developed along the lines of the Two-Tier *Mudarabah* Model (TTMM). The rate of interest brings the asset and liability sides of conventional banking into equilibrium, whereas *mudarabah* is the primary profit and loss sharing (PLS) vehicle of asset and liability creation in Islamic banking. The bank is positioned between surplus groups (investors/depositors) and deficit groups (borrowers/beneficiaries). The TTMM is an equity-based structure. On the liability side, the Islamic bank is assumed to play the role of *Mudarib* for the suppliers of capital (*Rabb al-mals*), while on the asset side it acts as the equity financier (*Rabb al-mal*) for entrepreneurs (*Mudaribs*). The bank's return is therefore determined by a share of the profits on both sides of the TTMM; banks share profits with their depositors and also with their beneficiaries. If a business venture fails, the capital provider (bank) loses its capital and labour provider (entrepreneur) loses his/her time and efforts.

Another prominent form of Islamic finance is *musharakah;* in this equity-based structure, two or more partners with a given amount of capital come together in a business venture. They share profit in a pre-determined ratio (Siddiqi, 1985). Entrepreneurs are permitted to contribute to the total funds requirement, but it is only in *musharakah* that the partners may incur a financial loss, strictly in proportion to their capital contribution.

Both *mudarabah* and *musharakah*[7] are equity-based, profit sharing structures, although there are some key differences between the two forms of funding. The main difference is that the entrepreneur offers no capital contribution in *mudarabah,* and therefore s/he is not liable to incur any financial loss apart from losing his/her effort (cost of labour) if the venture fails. Moreover, the bank is not authorized to participate in the management of a *mudarabah* project hence this form of financing carries a greater degree of risk. In a project financed by *musharakah,* the bank has right to participate in management unless it deliberately waives the right to do so.

The key question is where the contemporary practice of VC financing fits within the PLS techniques of Islamic finance. Two alternative approaches that might be used for Islamic VC are now explored in greater depth.

The first option describes how the TTMM could be used to refocus conventional methods of Islamic finance within a formal Islamic VC structure. The TTMM closely resembles what we have termed 'formal VC funds' throughout this book. However, the current operation of TTMM has been largely unable to fulfil the PLS objectives of Islamic finance. The principal/agent problem, and the associated issues of information asymmetry, moral hazard and adverse selection, has restricted the use of 'profit-sharing' finance. The current Islamic banking portfolio is therefore loaded heavily in favour of fixed return structures such as *murabaha, ijara, istisnaa* and other debt generating instruments (Iqbal and Llewellyn, 2001, detail these specialized forms of Islamic finance).

The more dominant Islamic PLS structure, *mudarabah,* is especially liable to the risks of adverse selection and information asymmetry because it relies on trust between the capital recipient and provider. By contrast, *musharakah* gives investors the option to engage (directly or indirectly) in the management of investee companies. In reality, however, the banks' right to participate in the management of firms funded by *musharakah* deals is almost invariably waived, mainly because this degree of involvement would be prohibitively costly. The somewhat ironic outcome is that SMEs (often ideal candidates for equity finance) approaching Islamic banks face very similar barriers to those erected by conventional banks (Masood, 1983).

The problems associated with the use of *mudarabah* and *musharakah* provide some justification for the current predominance of debt-based instruments within Islamic banking assets. There is also a degree of inertia, in that Islamic banking emerged in the 1970s while VC in its contemporary form has edged its way into the Islamic world over the 1990s. Bankers are resistant to change!

In an effort to overcome the problems described above, *mudarabah* has been combined with another financial structure, *wakalah*, whereby clients authorize a bank or fund manager to invest funds on their behalf, in return for a predetermined fee. This structure is widely used by Islamic mutual funds (Iqbal and Molyneux, 2005) and a combined TTMM-*Wakalah* structure could offer a suitable model for an Islamic VC initiative.

However, there is a major problem to be addressed in *mudarabah* deals. In the *mudarabah* structure, both the financial institution and the recipient can agree on any covenants at the time of the disbursement of the funds. If the project does not proceed as originally planned, then covenants cannot subsequently be changed unless both parties agree. It would be difficult for investor and entrepreneur to resolve disputes on (say) product development, replacing the CEO and so on. The Islamic resistance to changing the terms of the deal stems from the principle that the outcome of the entrepreneur's efforts should not be at the mercy of the capital provider. In *mudarabah* structures, therefore, all possible outcomes and their consequences have to be agreed upfront. This arrangement could present problems for the way in which venture capitalists structure the contracts with their investee companies.

The second option for the development of Islamic VC stems from the *shir'ka al-inan* financial structure (Siddiqi, 1985). In the Ottoman State, the manufacture and trade of fabrics, the production of pillows and shoes were funded in this way (Cizacka, 1996). In *shir'ka al-inan*, two or more members invest a certain amount of capital and share the benefits on a pre-agreed basis. This approach permits the capital provider to place any number of restrictive covenants on the functioning of fund managers and/or entrepreneurs (Fethi, 2000). In the VC context, *shir'ka al-inan* is a genuine partnership hence both parties are equally involved in any decision to change the strategy of the investee company, even after the disbursement of funds. This approach provides an acceptable risk mitigation mechanism, and a hybrid of *mudarabah* and *shir'ka al-inan* might offer a more suitable investment vehicle for the Islamic VC sector.

It is encouraging to see that Islamic economists have lately devoted considerable attention to resolving the risks of information asymmetry in the Islamic PLS architecture (Ahmed and Chapra, 2003). Islamic finance involves sharing risk; institutions must be able to assess and then manage that risk effectively. Some of the risk management techniques applied at various stages of the VC investment cycle could assist Islamic financiers to develop an equity-based approach to SME financing. The variety of techniques used by venture capitalists to reduce agency problems will now be viewed from an Islamic perspective, to assess their suitability for use in the Islamic financial sphere.

9.8 Acceptable Islamic VC procedures

The analysis above demonstrates that a hybrid of *mudarabah* and *shir'ka al-inan* would give capital providers many of the powers available to established venture capitalists; in particular, the investors can insist upon the inclusion of covenants in the contract and they can make post-investment adjustments/interventions to ensure that the investee company stays on course for success. Likewise, *mudarabah* in conjunction with *wakalah* provides another option for venture capitalists (albeit less flexible), because the *wakeel* (representative) may be allowed to carry out business activities within mutually agreed parameters.

Both of the two approaches above offer advantages compared to (say) an Islamic VC institution that were to invest solely through *mudarabah, musharakah* or a combination of the two (m&m). In the final analysis, a successful format for VC funds will evolve only when we move beyond theoretical discussions to the operation of Islamic VC in practice. Any such fund has to operate in accordance with Islamic principles and, critically, conduct its business with a view to securing the fundamental Islamic objectives of socio-economic justice and development.

Whichever fund structure is adopted, a contractual relationship is formed between the fund managers as *Mudarib* and capital contributors as *Rabb al-mals*. VC contributors (typically insurance companies and pension funds) seek long-term investments hence they target capital gains to match their future liabilities. The fund management team has to protect the investors' funds yet invest in projects with the capacity to generate the targeted rates of return. Ahmed (2004) contends that Islam allows the fund managers to have fixed and variable elements within an overall compensation package, provided these arrangements are set out in separate contracts. The well-established limited partnership form of legal structure could thus offer real benefits for the development of Islamic VC.

The fund managers will generate, screen and evaluate potential deals. Having decided to invest, cash is injected through equity-based instruments. The venture fund's status changes from an agent of the investors to a principal in relation to the entrepreneur. Depending on whether the VC fund provides all the required finance or whether the entrepreneur contributes, the fund managers will sign a *mudarabah* or *musharakah* contract (the equivalent of a shareholders' agreement) with the entrepreneurs. In neither of these cases will the fund managers be involved in the routine operational management of the business; their involvement centres on the supervisory and monitoring roles that reduce the risks of information asymmetry and thus generate the desired rate of return.

In principle, the author can see no clear Islamic objection to any of the seven stages of the VC investment cycle (fund raising, deal generation, initial screening, due diligence and valuation, structuring, post-investment monitoring and exit). However, possible concerns over the 'valuation' and 'structuring' stages are addressed below, and the author presents solutions that, in his view, accord with Islamic philosophy and principles.

9.8.1 Valuation

Viewed from the Islamic perspective, the need for a valuation conducted with due diligence and rigour cannot be undermined. A *musharakah* contract, for example, cannot be concluded without clearly specifying the distribution of the prospective profits between the VC fund and entrepreneur(s). Any uncertainty or ambiguity in the distribution of equity shares introduces an element of excessive uncertainty (*gharar*) into the partnership (Al-Dhareer, 1997).

It might be argued that the **valuation techniques** currently adopted by the global VC community involve the use of interest rates (*riba*) that are forbidden under Islam. Valuation practices vary across the world (refer to Section 5.3.5). Some techniques, such as the multiplication of past or future earnings by a comparable price-earnings ratio, do not involve any explicit reference to interest rates. However, Islamic objections do arise in respect of the most popular techniques used by venture capitalists, the discounting of future cash flows. The DCF approach usually discounts forecast cash flows by a 'benchmark' rate of interest, to arrive at a fair valuation or entry price of a project; the interest rate reflects the degree of risk inherent in the proposal.

The principle of discounting *per se* is not a prohibited practice. The time value of money is well recognized in Islamic jurisprudence, provided that it relates to trade rather than the lending and borrowing of money (Khan, 1995). Zarqa (1983) distinguishes clearly between using interest rates as a means of financing and using them to compare the viability of rival projects. For the latter purpose, any sensible discount rate can be adopted. In essence, the use of interest in financial transactions is prohibited, whereas it may be acceptable to use interest rates as a benchmark to gauge a project's relative value.

As stated above, the interest rate also measures the degree of risk associated with a project. The interest rates used in conventional DCF analysis are often thought to carry a premium compared to the prevailing rates on government bonds or treasury bills (the 'risk-free' rate of return). The use of interest rates for such comparative purposes remains the subject of intense debate in Islamic finance. However, academic studies of VC (and the research programme conducted for this book) demonstrate that the discount rates applied by venture capitalists reflect the target rate of return sought on specific investments, rather than any comparison with the risk-free rate of interest.

The broad spectrum of discount rates used in valuing VC investments in India starts from a higher base than prevailing interest rates and covers a much wider range. The lower end of the spectrum (20 per cent) is applied to infrastructure investments while high-technology ventures attract a discount rate of 70 per cent to indicate the perceived risk in such projects. The use of such rates does not imply that the VC firm is negotiating a fixed return with its investee companies hence this approach seems acceptable within Islamic principles.

9.8.2 Structuring

The critical question is whether Islamic profit-sharing contracts (*musharakah* or *mudarabah*) can provide the required flexibility for efficient risk management. This question can be explored in relation to two fundamental dimensions of the structuring process: contractual structuring (the covenants included in shareholders' agreements and any staging agreements); and, the selection of financial products, namely the choice between equity, debt or hybrids.

In Islamic jurisprudence, parties are free to structure a contract to achieve their mutual economic interests, provided that basic Islamic principles are not violated (Ahmed, 2004). The commonly used covenants in VC shareholders' agreements and/or the conditions for investment staging could be applied to *mudarabah* and *musharakah* structures, provided that such instruments were used in conjunction with *shir'ka al-inan* or *wakalah.*

Practices acceptable to Islam within conventional VC financing are presented in Table 9.1 below.

It is evident from Table 9.1 that widely practised risk management techniques in conventional VC very rarely contradict the Islamic principles. With minor adjustments and innovation, VC can thus be added to the list of high priority asset classes that Islamic financiers should target. However, the use of two techniques for structuring VC deals – ratchets and share options – is perhaps open to question hence they are briefly discussed below.

At the start of the project, fund managers set targets for the entrepreneurs that should be challenging but achievable, normally within specified periods of time. Equity ratchets offer incentives to exceed or at least meet the original business targets. Entrepreneurs will own more of the company if progress is sound, or suffer a dilution in their equity stake if results are disappointing. The targets and resultant rewards are laid down explicitly at the outset. Islamic investors can thus minimize their downside risk using ratchets; these

Table 9.1 ***Shari'ah*** **View of Some Key Practices in Venture Capital Financing**

Conventional Venture Capital Practice	Islamic View
Limited partnership structure	Acceptable
Long terms contracts	Acceptable
Contracts can be nullified	Acceptable
Restrictions placed on the activities of fund managers	Acceptable
Equity ratchets to entrepreneurs	Acceptable
Investments in equity, fully convertible bonds (zero coupon)	Acceptable
Preferred stocks, preference shares or convertible debt	Not Acceptable
Greater control rights through restrictive covenants	Acceptable
Board seat	Acceptable
Staged financing	Acceptable
Replacement of management (CEO)	Acceptable
Liquidation rights	Acceptable
Provision of non-financial services (strategic advice etc.)	Acceptable
Application of discount rate for valuation	Acceptable

Source: Based on Ahmed, H. (2004).

covenants offer rewards for success and, at the other extreme, they provide retribution for failure.

Fiqh Academy of the Organization of Islamic Countries has strictly prohibited the use of financial options by Islamic banks (Khan, 1999). The rationale for this view is that gains are prohibited in respect of trading in financial instruments that are not backed by assets. However, the widespread use of Employee Stock Options Programmes (ESOPs) for key employees, primarily in knowledge-based industries, as a part of compensation packages is a different form of option. In ESOPs, equity shares are offered at a discounted value to employees in order to retain their services. The employees have the right but not an obligation to purchase the shares at a predetermined price. If the share price is higher than their acquisition price, employees will exercise the option; otherwise, the option will not be exercised. This practice does not appear to conflict with Islamic rules.

Turning to the **selection of financial products**, the use of common equity in VC financing (as revealed in our study of India) is an encouraging sign from the Islamic perspective. However, venture capitalists invest for capital gains rather than dividend income. The deal structure has to provide downside protection, until a successful exit is achieved via (say) an IPO. Our study confirmed that venture capitalists do not usually commit themselves to pure equity at the initial stages of a start-up enterprise. The risks are just too high. Common equity is usually combined with preferred stock, preference shares or convertible debt. These financial instruments are not acceptable. It is vital to develop more Islamic alternatives to the conventional versions of these instruments, to give Islamic VC funds the capacity to offer flexible financial packages. A number of *shari'ah* compliant alternatives have been developed, and these are described below.

The idea of differential or disproportionate revenue sharing between two classes of 'equity' investors has already been approved in Islamic jurisprudence (Ahmed, 2004). This concession applies provided that the party offering finance also contributes to the management of the project. A modified version of preferred stock could create two classes of shares, with each being entitled to different percentages of profit beyond a defined threshold (Zarqa, 1992).

Another financial product that meets the needs of entrepreneurs while simultaneously limiting investment risk is *'diminishing musharakah'* (Bendjijali and Khan, 1985). This structure can be fully secured by using company assets as collateral, thus protecting the original capital to some extent until the project achieves profitability. From cash generated through profits, the entrepreneur can begin to repurchase the equity issued to the venture capitalists. (This arrangement resembles the option in VC deals that gives the entrepreneur the right of first refusal to 'buy-back' equity held by outside investors.) Overall, the venture capitalists' return varies according to the investee company's profitability. This gain plus a gradual redemption of part of the invested capital appears Islamically acceptable.

Turning to debt, the deployment of interest-bearing financial instruments is prohibited in Islam; loans (even if convertible to equity) and preference shares with a fixed cumulative dividend cannot be used (Ahmed, 2004). As an alternative, Islamic convertible bonds could be utilized to provide part of the initial capital for start-up enterprises (Khan, 1995). For example, *murabaha* and *ijara* bonds could be used for funding plant and machinery. If appropriate milestones are achieved, these bonds can be converted into equity on the basis of a predetermined conversion formula. Venture capitalists will not be totally exposed to equity risk before the business operations of the investee company stabilize, and the staging of investments can be practised within accepted Islamic principles. Another option would be to create a zero coupon convertible bond structure that complies with Islamic injunctions. Both of these approaches involve exchanging virtual debt in the form of *murabaha* or *ijara* for equity, provided that targets are achieved.

9.9 Summary

Islamic finance is mainly confined to the provision of banking facilities in a limited number of countries. The sector currently offers invaluable services to retail and corporate clients, and its global coverage is increasing rapidly. Nevertheless, many Islamic economists have been calling for a re-orientation of this sector towards a greater role in profit-sharing and risk capital participation (Iqbal, 2004; Chapra, 2001).

Islamic banks have been hindered in their efforts to increase PLS assets within their portfolios by the presence of information asymmetry, adverse selection and moral hazard. Financiers have traditionally used contractual obligations to counter such problems, yet solutions based on the Islamic injunctions (collectively termed the Spiritual Quotient) could serve to mitigate agency risks. It is argued that the prospect of accountability on the Day of Judgement will bring about positive behavioural changes among the recipients of capital.

At this stage, the time is ripe for institutions to offer long-term equity financing in accordance with global VC practices. This would broaden the appeal of the Islamic financial spectrum to corporate clients. An Islamic VC industry could apply almost all of the conventional valuation, structuring and monitoring techniques used for risk mitigation purposes. In setting up institutions to offer VC, the widely used LP structure can be adopted. VC as an asset class is very close to PLS-based Islamic finance structures, notably *mudarabah* and *musharakah*, although these have to be adapted to create the flexibility required by venture capitalists. Certain types of financial instruments, notably preferred stock, are forbidden yet Islamic variants can be utilized. The Islamic finance industry can therefore begin to make safe forays into VC investment and could even incorporate some of these practices into Islamic banking procedures. This change of emphasis may help to improve the risk profile of the banks' portfolio, enhance their return on investment and bring them closer to the founding objectives of PLS-based financing.

10
Conclusions

10.1 Introduction

This chapter revisits the key themes in each of the previous chapters, summarizes the key findings of the research programme in India, and draws some implications for VC practitioners, SMEs, academics and policy makers. The focus of attention is on India, but there are many lessons for other countries facing similar issues and problems.

10.2 Review of key themes

After a brief introduction, Chapters 2 and 3 deal with the role of SMEs. The SME sector provides a variety of economic and social benefits, including the creation of employment opportunities, the promotion of flexibility and innovation, and the generation of export revenues. There is also growing recognition that SMEs can play an important role in social and economic restructuring. Smaller enterprises dominate the industrial and commercial landscape of national economies, in developed as well as developing countries. The contribution of SMEs in creating jobs has been the subject of much debate; this is not surprising in a sector characterized by such diversity. It is accepted that jobs are created in the 'churn' of micro firms and that only a few high-growth firms contribute a large proportion of the employment generated by SMEs.

There is no dispute, however, that established patterns of business and trade are breaking down in the face of rapid technological change, for example: recent advances in the fields of telecommunications and data transfer techniques have opened up unprecedented commercial avenues for smaller enterprises. SMEs have also demonstrated the capacity to innovate, delivering new products and services with speed and stealth, and even the smallest and newest organizations can play prominent roles in international business activity. High-technology SMEs, in particular, have reached overseas clients through strategic alliances, technology transfer arrangements or rapid organic growth.

The definitions of micro, small, medium and large firms are generally based on employment or other quantitative measures such as shareholders' funds or turnover. India is unusual in defining small firms in relation to their asset base. Whatever definition is employed, it is accepted that SMEs operate in ways that are quantitatively and qualitatively different from those of large organizations.

The motivations of key players might conflict with the 'profit maximization' assumption of conventional wisdom, especially in family-owned firms. The highest goal to which many small firms aspire is survival and/or the generation of a basic income for the founder. Shareholding is often concentrated in a small group of individuals who also exercise executive powers, and the CEO is usually in a powerful position to dictate company strategy. SMEs face other constraints that stem from their smallness in relation to other market participants. They can overcome these constraints by, for example, building network relationships, conserving the resources at the heart of the firm's competitive advantage and investing in IT to improve their efficiency.

The failure rate of small firms is high; over 20 per cent of new ventures fail within one year while 66 per cent fail within six years (Timmons, 1994). Apart from the lack of resources cited above, the main reasons for failure are the poor quality of the original business idea and management shortcomings. The founders often find it difficult to attract human capital as the firm develops. Many firms do not fail outright, but they supply only a small segment of a local market.

The focus of attention for this book (and the VC community) is entrepreneurial firms with a desire to achieve rapid growth, a determination to innovate rather than stagnate, and so forth. These 'star performers' usually ascribe their success to a combination of factors, including: satisfying an enduring customer need; operating in high-growth industries facing substantial technological or regulatory changes; differentiating products or services in ways that are meaningful to customers; and dominating the market segments in which they compete. There is no single route to growth, and the combinations for success might change as the business develops and market circumstances alter.

Some firms have the potential to achieve success yet they encounter barriers to growth. Our main concern is the inability of SMEs to access credit, a global constraint on the growth and development of smaller enterprises.

Assuming that internal funds are not available (or are insufficient for their needs), SMEs look first to raise bank finance. High transaction costs are a reality in this market, while information asymmetries create imperfections. The upshot is that banks raise interest rates for SMEs to a point where excess demand still exists or they insist upon collateral. Both of these actions lead to adverse selection, leaving the lenders with a higher risk portfolio. The failure by banks to monitor borrowers adequately results in moral hazard.

Chapter 3 also explored the extent of any 'equity gaps' affecting SMEs. The consensus of opinion in the UK is that funding gaps are reducing in importance, but the provision of relatively small amounts of equity capital for growth-oriented, innovative firms is a continuing problem. This does not appear to be an issue in the US, where smaller enterprises take advantage of the massive depth and breadth in financial markets. (US firms also benefit from a much larger domestic market and a vibrant source of technological ideas from the major universities.) However, funding problems still constitute a major impediment to the growth of SMEs in many countries, even in those countries that have taken steps to liberalize their financial markets.

In these circumstances, it is no surprise that governments assist SMEs. It is not possible (or desirable) to offer help to every new start-up firm; many are not worthy of support. At the other extreme, it is not easy to target firms with the capacity for sustained growth. Governments usually offer assistance to firms across the SME spectrum, from potential start-ups to well-established, medium-sized companies. Government schemes will typically include, for example: finance for R&D; and, help with business planning. However, the diversity of growth patterns for SMEs, and the variety of barriers faced by such firms, makes it difficult to provide customized assistance for smaller enterprises within an integrated framework of support.

Chapter 4 introduces the concept of VC, a form of finance that had its roots in the 15th Century activities of the merchant venturers in the Far and Middle East. In its post-World War II modern reincarnation, VC was associated first with patient investments in small enterprises operating in the high-technology sphere. Such companies are characterized by uncertain cash flows and a lack of collateral; they face problems in raising bank finance yet they are too small for public equity markets. VC investors sought to exploit this niche created by the structure and rules of capital markets and thus generate long-term capital gains.

The VC industry today covers a host of institutions; every VC firm makes equity-based investments, usually in unlisted companies, yet venture capitalists differ in their approach to (say) deal size and sector focus. The two main categories of VC funds are independent and captive, and there are four broad categories of investor: formal VC; corporate VC; social VC; and business angels. There are no fixed barriers between these categories; syndicated deals between different types of VC fund are common. The focus of investments for formal VC has switched from early stage deals to relatively late stage investments, notably buy-out funding. At the top end of the financing spectrum, 'private equity' providers compete with VC firms to conduct transactions outside normal public markets.

It is widely believed that a flourishing VC industry underpins a vibrant, entrepreneurial economy. VC-backed firms contribute to wealth creation; they achieve higher revenues and generate more employment. The failure rate of investee companies is substantially lower than 'conventional' SMEs, and shares in such companies also perform better than average after flotation, even though VC firms rely upon one 'home run' in every ten investments to deliver the desired returns (Zacharakis and Meyer, 2000).

The VC industry is not an instrument for general SME support. However, it can play a critical role in supplementing official support for smaller enterprises. Venture capitalists provide 'smart money' that supplements cash with advice on issues such as strategic planning, product development, networking, recruitment and marketing; this might involve (say) identifying an overseas partner for a firm seeking to exploit international markets. The VC and private equity sectors have also assisted governments with the privatization of state-owned enterprises.

There has been a massive expansion of VC activity from the US into Europe, Asia and Australia. The VC sector returned the highest yield to US investors over the period 1945–1997 (although the dot.com and technology stock reverses brought sharp losses soon after). As Western economies have slowed and VC investment opportunities have shown signs of saturation, venture capitalists have turned to other markets.

This process has been hastened by the desire of many governments across Eastern Europe and Asia to encourage the growth of VC by laying the groundwork for this sector and removing major hurdles in its development. Official assistance for VC can take many forms; the most successful support programmes for VC have been those funded by governments but managed by private sector professionals. In the Yozma initiative in Israel, a key factor was that a healthy level of VC investment was maintained after direct Government support ended.

Chapter 5 explores the stages in the VC investment process, from raising the investment pool through to the final exit from the deal. An improvement in the quality of propositions will reduce the time venture capitalists spend in rejecting unwanted proposals during preliminary screening. A mere ten per cent of proposals reach the due diligence stage and merit thorough investigation. The time and resources required for due diligence helps to explain why venture funds specialize in certain sectors and/or financing stages. If all parties can agree on a valuation for the project, the venture capitalists are in a position to approve and then structure the deal. Covenants and milestones align the interests of venture fund and entrepreneur(s), and ensure the regular provision of information. The existence of a range of exit mechanisms is crucial.

Attention then turns to the theoretical foundations of VC financing, and the unifying theme of research in this field is agency theory. Most VC models view the relationship between VC firm and entrepreneur(s) from the principal-agent perspective. Many studies have been concerned with the appraisal criteria adopted by venture capitalists. However, these criteria form only part of the package of measures by which venture capitalists counter potential agency problems over the VC cycle. There have been far fewer studies on the valuation, structuring and monitoring of VC deals. These three areas allow venture capitalists to mitigate risk yet create value for all parties to the deal.

The correct valuation of a business is essential in determining the entry price for any deal. As a rule, entrepreneurs tend to overstate the value of their ideas, technologies and projects. If the valuation process is inefficient, adverse selection will mean that good quality projects are driven away. Once the investment has been approved and the valuation accepted, the VC contract has to be structured with great care and attention. The interests of investors and entrepreneurs tend to diverge after the funds have been disbursed. VC firms utilize staged financing, and funds are released against measurable performance outcomes. On the same theme, the entrepreneurs are responsible for day-to-day operational decisions hence effective governance mechanisms are required.

Chapter 6 presents an overview of Indian economy then discusses the financial system, and the status and contribution of SMEs. This sets the context for an analysis of the evolution and prospects for the VC industry. Since independence in 1947, the Indian economy has developed to a remarkable extent – from dependence on food aid in the 1960s to its present status as one of the 'BRIC Four' economic powerhouses.

The architects of India's independence movement had socialist leanings, an attitude that put a large number of companies and sectors under direct state control. The private sector operated, for the most part, under tight state supervision and this held back progress in key areas. The collapse of Soviet Union (an important Cold War ally of India), the unprecedented success of its South East Asian neighbours, and a number of domestic economic crises forced the Indian Government to embrace the market economy.

This policy shift started in the 1980s and gathered pace in the early 1990s. The main driver was large-scale capital market reforms to attract much needed foreign capital. Some FDI constraints were also relaxed. A privatization programme was instigated then put on hold until its recent revival (now termed 'disinvestment'). The value of relaxing Government controls is illustrated by the fact that the services sector, the least regulated in the economy, continues to be the strongest performer, while manufacturing, the most regulated, is the weakest.

The banking system in India was characterized by many of the imperfections described earlier, especially adverse selection and moral hazard, although the situation has improved since the system was opened up to private sector participation. A modest programme of reform has led to efficiency improvements, for example: the banks have penetrated rural areas of India and taken their services to small firms. Nevertheless, bureaucratic hurdles stemming from Government ownership and control of the largest banking organizations still distort this market. There is no incentive to develop credit appraisal skills in the presence of targeted lending programmes that fulfil political ends, and there is a high incidence of non-performing loans (NPLs).

In relation to equity finance, Indian capital markets have achieved global standards, for example: on-line securities trading has improved transparency and boosted the confidence of foreign investors. However, the top tier stock markets offer only limited opportunities for firms to raise long-term capital and follow-on funding. The second tier exchange, OTCEI, designed to give SMEs access to a public market and to provide exit opportunities for VCs, has largely failed to achieve its objectives.

Since independence, the Indian Government has expressed special interest in the growth and success of SMEs; this sector has generated jobs, earned foreign exchange and contributed to India's manufacturing base. Preferential financing has been available through the banks and dedicated financial institutions. Even so, SMEs still complain of a lack of appropriately priced funds. The Government has established a large network of business support agencies, at both central and state government levels. Unfortunately, this support system is piecemeal in nature and bureaucratic in its operation. Registering a new business in India can take months! There is also a fallacy at the heart of the Government's strategy. It protects SMEs from domestic competition by reserving a number of sectors exclusively for them, a policy that is unsustainable in an era of globalization.

The VC industry has provided much needed capital to entrepreneurs with attractive business propositions. After an uncertain period from 1986–1995, plagued by regulatory hurdles, VC investment has surged ahead in the more liberalized economy. The VC sector depended initially upon substantial Government support, but investment is now dominated by foreign venture funds. (ICICI is the only significant domestic player). VC firms were investing over US$1bn annually by 2001, helped by the introduction of legal and regulatory changes in 2000. After a retrenchment in the face of global economic problems, investment recovered over 2004.

Over recent years, venture funds have favoured large size deals in later stage transactions; start-ups are comparatively rare in the venture capitalists' portfolio. Many investments have been in sectors where India has acknowledged expertise, namely the technology and knowledge-based sectors. VC firms also invest in the fields of electronics manufacturing, the media/entertainment sector and 'classic' high-technology activities, such as biotechnology and pharmaceuticals. Venture capitalists have also demonstrated a willingness to invest in mature manufacturing sectors such as tractors; some of the larger deals have seen private equity groups strengthen the existing management team as a condition of investment.

Our contention is that the VC sector in India can play an increasingly crucial role in bridging the gaps between bank finance and government assistance on one extreme, and the existing equity markets on the other. Experienced fund managers with global exposure are positioned to capture significant gains from this enormous upside potential.

The reasons for this assertion are, *inter alia*, that India has: the largest pool of English speakers in the world outside those countries where English is the sole language; world-class technology and medical research institutions that generate high quality intellectual capital; and, a burgeoning middle class population that provides a captive market for many products. However, there are a number of areas for the authorities and practitioners to tackle before the VC market can fulfil its maximum potential; the authors put forward recommendations to address these issues later.

Having described key features of the Indian economy, Chapter 7 returns to the consideration of how venture capitalists cover their downside risk at the:

- Post-evaluation stage – valuation;
- Post-valuation stage – contracting or structuring;
- And, post-investment stage – monitoring.

At the time of our survey, venture funds in India (mainly Government-backed) had been encouraged to support inexperienced entrepreneurs, often involved with relatively young, technology-oriented companies. In such circumstances, information asymmetry is endemic and adverse selection is the almost inevitable outcome; good projects fail to receive funding and/or weak proposals are overvalued and hence accepted. We anticipated that venture capitalists would produce their own due diligence reports to counter this problem. Given the type of deals available to VC investors, typically early stage and/or technology-oriented, and the difficulty of finding comparable companies with similar characteristics, we proposed that DCF techniques would be most favoured for valuation purposes.

In the post-valuation phase, covenants are formulated to give special rights to the VC firm, while restricting actions by the entrepreneurs that could destroy or diminish the value of the investment. Our research explored the type and frequency of covenants utilized in India. All parties agree upon short-term performance benchmarks that represent intermediate steps towards longer-term objectives (hence 'staging'). In the event of cost and/or time overruns, entrepreneurs see their share of equity diluted in favour of external investors. In extreme cases, the venture fund has the option to discontinue funding and to cut its losses. On the other hand, should entrepreneurs exceed targets, performance ratchets work to their advantage. We investigated the extent of staged financing and examined the milestones set for investee companies.

This structuring process is eased greatly by the range of instruments at the disposal of the venture capitalists. VC-funded projects usually experience negative cash flow at the outset hence it is virtually impossible to service debt. The tax shield from debt is also worthless. Equity is more appropriate. While common equity gives more control to the venture fund, the most suitable financial structure is a hybrid instrument that combines the features of both equity and debt. Preferred equity enables investors to use flat pricing or similar mechanisms, offering incentives for the entrepreneur(s) and downside protection for the venture fund. We examined the use of preferred stock in India.

The vast majority of VC deals involve unlisted companies; such companies have little or no statutory obligation to disclose financial information and/or other information of interest to outside investors. Apart from the three traditional financial statements (P&L account, balance sheet and cash flow statements), venture capitalists gather information on employee turnover, market share, product prices and costs, and so forth. Fund managers also meet regularly with entrepreneurs, key employees, suppliers and customers, to gain first hand information on (say) R&D progress or levels of customer satisfaction.

The supply of accurate and timely information reduces information asymmetry and strengthens the venture capitalist-entrepreneur relationship. (There are also advantages for investee companies; for instance, firms with transparent operating procedures, and sound management and/or financial information systems are valued at a premium by capital market investors.) In the context of India, venture capitalists operate in a dynamic economy characterized by changing tastes, changing technologies and an evolving population of SMEs, while the enforcement of contracts and the protection of intellectual property have been questionable. In such a climate, we anticipated that monitoring would be vigorous, seeking early warning signals about impending problems.

It is accepted that the success of an investee company depends largely on the quality of entrepreneurial team and, especially, the CEO. Progress towards milestones is monitored through regular meetings (both informal and board representation), supported by powers to remedy perceived failings in management. In the event of consistent underperformance, CEOs come under threat. The vast majority of investments in India were less than three years old at the time of our survey. Nonetheless, we sought to ascertain the degree to which venture capitalists had used the ultimate sanction of replacing a CEO.

Our final research question related to the reasons for CEO dismissal. Some researchers argue that operational skills are essential in CEOs, while others place a premium on strategic skills. In the light of the rapid developments in the Indian and global economy, we proposed that a lack of strategic skills would be the prime reason for dismissal.

10.3 Key findings of the research programme

In Chapter 8, the research findings were presented. The conclusions were based on evidence gathered from representatives of 40 of the 42 active VC firms in India. These firms managed an investment pool of US$2.95bn funds, and had invested US$2.16bn in a total of 1,020 transactions. The high response rate allowed the authors to explore how the whole VC 'community' tackles valuation, monitoring and control issues. It was also possible to isolate the influence of specific factors (for example, foreign versus domestic funds) in relation to the eight research propositions. Summary findings are set out in Table 10.1.

The importance placed on 'own due diligence' as a valuation source (P1) as was especially strong among foreign VC firms; these investors almost invariably insisted upon using their own research to check out the market potential and technological feasibility of projects. The Indian (mainly Government-sponsored) VC firms used either many information sources or invested on the basis of a more general impression of a project's merits.

Table 10.1 Summary of Key Findings[1]

(P1)	Preference for own due diligence report	Accepted
(P2)	Use of DCF-based valuation techniques	Accepted
(P3)	Widespread use of covenants	Accepted
(P4)	Staging of investments	Accepted
(P5)	Preferred stock favoured[2]	Rejected
(P6)	Extensive monitoring	Accepted
(P7)	Replacement of CEOs[3]	Weakly accepted
(P8)	Lack of strategic skills in CEOs[4]	Marginally rejected

Notes:

(1) The acceptance/rejection of the propositions is usually based on a broad assessment of the data rather than stringent statistical tests.

(2) The majority of participants claimed to favour 'plain equity', although preferred stock *was* widely used.

(3) On the basis that 40 per cent of sample had *not* replaced CEOs.

(4) Marginal preference for lack of operational skills as the reason for the replacement of CEOs.

The use of DCF techniques for valuation purposes (P2) was evident across the sample as a whole. Indian venture capitalists had started to adopt the quantitative valuation methods used by their foreign counterparts. However, the most striking feature was the extent to which early stage and technology-oriented investors applied higher discount rates to compensate for the risks involved in such projects; the technology element appeared to exert more influence on the choice of discount rate. Over time, we suggest that quantitative techniques will increasingly be combined with qualitative methods as the VC market matures. Practitioners will establish rules of thumb for valuing certain types of projects and use these benchmarks to supplement quantitative methods.

The three structuring propositions (P3–P5) are now considered. Many of the 25 covenants in common use are considered to be essential or important; likewise the majority of investors view 'staging' as essential or important. The top rated covenants were concerned with preventing investee companies from raising other sources of funding or restructuring, allowing fund managers to discuss progress informally or through board representation, and clarifying the venture capitalists' exit route. Staging was most frequently linked to the achievement of financial targets. In selecting investment instruments, the participants claimed to favour 'plain' equity across all stages and sectors. Nevertheless, many respondents had made investments that combined financial products, and the use of equity ratchets was commonplace.

Early stage investors insist upon more covenants, and they place much greater emphasis on the achievement of milestones. Technology-oriented investors rely upon a different set of covenants to their 'non-technology' counterparts; for example, the recruitment of key employees was of special concern to technology investors. Preferred stock featured mainly in financial packages for early stage, technology-based deals, where it is critical to balance incentives for the entrepreneur with protection of the interests of the VC firm.

Respondents monitor the performance of their investee companies (P6) on a regular basis, paying most attention to financial reports and capital expenditure budgets. The recruitment and retention of key personnel was another key factor. It is not unexpected that early stage and technology-linked deals (especially the latter) were associated with higher levels of monitoring. When meeting investee companies, the key areas were to review product development and/or offer strategic input. The need for operational advice on (say) improving production and delivery systems was more relevant for later stage deals.

The replacement of the CEO (P7) is a radical move that can have severe consequences; 60 per cent of respondents had pursued this course of action. Some of the others might have done so except for a dearth of suitable replacements! Foreign VC firms had taken decisive action early in their relationship with the investee company; they seek to install a CEO with commercial experience, before investing in a technology-based firm. Venture capitalists held operational and strategic skills in almost equal regard (P8). It was interesting that strategic skills are highly prized for technology-based projects, and that Indian venture capitalists value integrity very highly – this is a fundamental part of the Hindu psyche.

10.4 Islamic finance

In Chapter 9, the focus of attention switched to a more general consideration of finance and business ethics, with specific reference to Islamic principles. Islamic banking is the fastest growing sub-sector in the global banking industry, and there is growing recognition that clients seek financial alternatives that are acceptable to Islam, for example: some UK banks now offer Islamic mortgages. However, the range of Islamic financial instruments has been relatively static, with *murabaha* accounting for over half of the assets in the global banking system. The *musharakah* and *mudarabah* (m&m) financing structures are technically very close to VC, and the balance of opinion is that it should be possible to introduce VC as an asset class, provided that m&m are combined with other Islamic alternatives. Islamic VC could also fuel the growth of the SME sector and lead to a more equitable distribution of wealth.

10.5 Implications for policy makers, SMEs/entrepreneurs, finance practitioners and academics

Taken as a whole, the findings of our research programme, our analysis of the literature and the experience of other countries have a number of implications for policy makers, SMEs/entrepreneurs, VC practitioners, those involved with Islamic finance, and academics. The recommendations below are mainly aimed at the authorities in India yet they should have relevance for other developing countries.

10.5.1 Policy makers

For the *economy as a whole*, it is important to build on existing strengths. If the performance of the economy could improve still further, this would benefit the whole population – from large organizations and SMEs through to individuals in cities and rural communities. There has been a big improvement in economic fundamentals and a broad consensus on the way forward. The Indian economy is too complex to be reformed at a stroke, but some or all of the following issues could be addressed over time:

- Government machinery at local and national level is still inefficient – much needs to be done to curb official 'meddling', corruption and obstructionism; the thriving IT sector shows what can be done when the Government takes a different approach – in Technology Parks, for example, bureaucratic hurdles have been reduced, the infrastructure has been improved and official licences are swiftly made available. It was argued earlier that entrepreneurial talent within India will be released only when there is less Government rather than more (Towe, 2001).
- Sustained growth will require an ongoing commitment to fiscal deficit reduction and wide ranging structural reforms. This will also attract a greater level of foreign direct investment (FDI).
- Bank reform should continue; at present foreign banks can only take a five per cent stake in 'healthy' local banks and a 74 per cent stake in banks in need of restructuring. There will not be a level playing field between foreign and domestic banks until 2009, and this process should not be delayed.
- Official attempts to preserve employment have been counter-productive because restrictions on removing employees have discouraged private sector employers from taking on new staff. The Government recently proposed the establishment of special economic zones that would bypass strict labour laws; this imaginative proposal was subsequently withdrawn.
- A reduction in import barriers would enhance the rate of technology transfer and force domestic producers to restructure their operations and improve efficiency.
- Continued investment in education will be a key factor in improving the quality of human capital.
- Likewise, investment in the infrastructure should be stepped up, for example: to increase the capacity of the ports, to improve the reliability of energy supplies and to enhance the quality of roads and highways. Investment on the scale required will call for the mobilization of private savings and (possibly) the creation of public/private sector partnerships.

Turning to the *SME sector*, there are a host of small firms at one extreme and many large organizations (both public and private) at the other, but the 'middle-ground' of medium-sized firms is under-represented. The present imbalance has to be addressed if the SME sector is to achieve its full potential for social and economic restructuring. The recommendations below constitute an integrated package of measures, rather than the somewhat piecemeal approach offered by the Government at present. The SME support network should address current 'bottlenecks' in the development of entrepreneurship within India. There are also specific proposals relating to the banks, centres of excellence and so on.

- Indians have never lacked the spirit of entrepreneurship (Sinha, 2003) yet salaried employment in large domestic companies or multinationals is still the prime goal of students (and their parents). In addition, many Indians are fatalistic and the creation of wealth is not given a high priority. It is impossible to change a nation's psyche overnight yet it should be possible to publicize the achievements of Indian entrepreneurs, to inspire those with the potential to follow in their footsteps.
- It is legitimate to offer official assistance to start-ups in the vulnerable early stages of their existence. A positive first step in India would be to ease the bureaucratic constraints in registering a firm for official assistance (registration takes 70 days on average across the 29 States at present). The Government could also offer 'soft' help with (say) business planning; this would allow small firms to approach the banks for funding on a commercial basis rather than operating an inefficient system of targeted lending (this point is developed below). Some countries set aside a certain proportion of Government contracts for SMEs or encourage multinationals to outsource their local requirements to this sector; this is generally accepted as a reasonable degree of protection ...
- However, there is a fine line between allowing small firms to gain a foothold in the market and offering unwarranted assistance. The wholesale preservation of certain categories of product and/or service for small firms has led to market distortions and, once again, Government policy has proved counter productive. At present, a growth-oriented firm is penalized because it does not qualify for help when it outgrows the small firm classification hence many firms fail to grasp opportunities to increase in size. The Government has recognized this paradox at the heart of its SME policy and the restricted categories are being phased out, albeit slowly.

- Very few firms in India are engaged in manufacturing. The IT industry currently employs around one million of the 'educated elite' in the population, and there are some signs that this industry is moving up the value chain by developing 'hard' products for the global market. However, these efforts pale in comparison to the 100 million plus semi-skilled or skilled blue colour workers employed in China's manufacturing sector. If job opportunities are to be captured (in the IT and other industries) for the large section of the Indian population currently faced with social exclusion, the official support network must assist SMEs as they increase in size and complexity. Such assistance could include grants or fiscal incentives for: R&D; the development of human capital; marketing activity; and so on.
- The Government has had some success (as noted above) in promoting technology and/or science parks, but these centres of excellence could be extended to (say) pharmaceuticals, biotechnology, machine tools, and business process outsourcing; such centres would enhance networking among SMEs specializing in that activity and promote good practice.[1] The benefits of such activity will spill over from firm to firm, industry to industry, and then to the wider society.
- In developing centres of excellence, whatever the activity in question, it is important for the Government to know when to step aside. Public/private sector partnerships are essential, especially in a developing nation like India. The Government can provide the basic infrastructure in the form of land and/or purpose-built units, uninterrupted power and water supplies, and broadband communication networks, as well as academic support from government-owned educational institutions. Private sector companies would occupy these centres but there would be no restrictions on their ability to, for example, set strategic direction, invest in equipment, screen and select manpower, evaluate technology at each stage of development and (eventually) commercialize viable technologies.
- Bank reform was mentioned earlier. In a regime of targeted bank lending programmes that fulfil political ends, there is no incentive for banks to develop skills in appraising proposals from SMEs. All parties know that the Government will offer 'comfort' in the event of losses; there is thus no incentive to improve credit appraisal skills or undertake due diligence, and it is no surprise that there is a high incidence of non-performing loans (NPLs) in targeted advances. This system has to be phased out. Domestic banks have

to be convinced that it is possible to make satisfactory returns on a portfolio of SME lending; again, this could be achieved by opening up the market to foreign competition and bringing in expertise from abroad.
- Many traditional businesses in India are run by the extended family, and they tend to be very conservative in outlook (Sinha, 2003). While such firms fulfil a valuable role, the management of 'knowledge assets' and innovation is the key to success in the new world order. The industrial profile is changing across the globe. Most academic courses in India (from MBAs to school qualifications) have long been aimed at enhancing the performance of employees in large companies. A paradigm shift is now required to introduce enterprise and entrepreneurship into the curriculum across the educational spectrum. Over time, this should enhance the performance of family-run firms and large organizations, as well as encouraging individuals to set up their own business.

In relation to *venture capital*, there is a clear need in India for risk finance that can leverage innovation, promote technology and harness knowledge-based ideas. A vibrant VC community enables SMEs to unlock new sources of finance to support worthwhile projects.

In the early years of VC in India, the regulatory authorities imposed very restrictive investment guidelines and the tax regime favoured domestic VC firms. Even with a level playing field between foreign and domestic players, venture capitalists based abroad would have been reluctant to invest in early stage, technology-intensive proposals without some form of risk mitigation offered by the Indian Government. In the absence of interest from foreign VC firms, the Government committed large sums to VC. However, government-sponsored bodies could not offer the same range of skills as experienced venture capitalists. There was also a culture of state support, where losses were condoned (reflecting the experience of the public banking sector). Many VC investments failed to prosper and the market did not develop as hoped.

The Government deserves credit for recognizing the shortcomings of the domestic VC sector and implementing legal and regulatory changes in 2000. The market has grown rapidly as the Government has become progressively less visible and foreign investors have become the dominant force. The market is more sophisticated, foreign investors are well-established and domestic venture capitalists have grown in experience. However, the authorities have proved reluctant to devolve all responsibility for VC investment to the private sector, and the package of proposals put forward by SEBI in 2000 was not adopted in full.

The recommendations below set out some general principles for the VC sector, and they also build on those in the SEBI Report (2000). Our proposals are designed to give venture capitalists the freedom to operate more flexibly within a supportive economic, taxation and regulatory environment.

- Venture capitalists have already established specialist investment networks in areas where there is a concentration of investment opportunities – Bangalore, Mumbai and so on. VC firms have been an important part of the network of support (although perhaps not to the same extent as, for example, Israel in the Yozma era). As stated earlier in this section, it is hoped that centres of excellence will be extended to more sectors and more parts of the country. Venture capitalists should thus be able to exploit economies of scale as they develop expertise in the appraisal of similar projects.
- In emerging clusters, however, many businesses will not be ready for VC; policy makers have to appreciate that venture capitalists focus on commercial imperatives rather than economic/social development. The Government might have to co-invest in venture funds with the private sector (as exemplified by the recently-launched initiative by the Regional Development Agencies in the UK); in these circumstances, it has to be recognized that seed funds will almost inevitably struggle to achieve worthwhile (if any) returns. The Government could also act in a coordinating role to direct companies seeking funds to business angel networks, appropriate grants or subsidized loans, and so on.
- Apart from contributing funds for investment, there is scope for the Government to assist in the generation of VC deals. This role addresses the demand side of the equation, and it is a function of science policy, fiscal measures, infrastructure development, and so on (Harding, 2000). An essential element of this function is the promotion of an enterprise culture; non-resident Indians, returning to their homeland with capital, ideas and entrepreneurial skills, could play a key role in this process.
- There may also be a role for Government in improving the quality of proposals put to VC firms; an improvement in the quality of

applications will assist venture capitalists to make the most efficient use of their time. If the Government could offer an independent appraisal service to assess (say) market potential or technological feasibility, this may reduce the need for the venture capitalists to devote resources to 'own due diligence'.

- Finally on the demand side, the Government has to work with the VC community to encourage entrepreneurs to give up some control in return for a larger 'pie' for everyone to share (this point is taken up in the recommendations for entrepreneurs below).
- The limited partnership (LP) structure provides operational leverage to venture capitalists as well as tax benefits. Domestic and foreign investors should be able to structure their operations in the LP format; this will bring much-needed FDI 'onshore', at no expense to the Government.
- On a similar note, VC firms should be allowed to issue preferred stock with the conversion options and/or voting rights enjoyed by the global VC community; this will give venture capitalists in India more flexibility to minimize investment risk and maximize incentives to the entrepreneur(s).
- Venture capitalists will be more inclined to invest if their investee companies operate in a fair and 'secure' trading environment. To assist in achieving this goal, special courts/tribunals could be set up to redress business disputes on a fast-track basis (it can take over a thousand days to enforce a contract in India); likewise, recent moves to protect patents and copyrights should be accelerated.
- The availability of exit routes is crucial. The National Stock Exchange (NSE) of India and other major exchanges now offer a large and efficient capital market infrastructure. Nonetheless, many recent flotations have been scheduled for New York or London. In 2004, there has been a welcome rise in IPOs in India, and this trend should continue, provided that liquidity and transparency are maintained in the exchanges. The main source of concern for venture capitalists is the second-tier market (OTCEI) that has largely failed to achieve its founding objectives. We suggest that OTCEI could be merged with NSE; the latter's sound infrastructure would then be available to companies whose turnover and/or profit record do not justify a quote on a major exchange. SMEs would be able to mobilize resources efficiently and venture capitalists could secure an exit route.

10.5.2 SMEs/entrepreneurs

There are lessons that existing and aspiring entrepreneurs can draw from the literature surveyed for this book and the research programme conducted:

- Many individuals seek to start their own companies. In addition, large organizations are tending to flatten and to evolve into a spectrum of hybrids from partnerships and subsidiaries, to joint ventures and spin-outs, hence there are many opportunities for entrepreneurial activity. We emphasize that small enterprises are not just scaled down versions of the larger counterparts and illustrate how SMEs can adopt successful strategies in relation to innovation, internationalization, networking, marketing, HR, IT, TQM and so on.
- The book also outlines the typical barriers faced by smaller enterprises, financial and non-financial, and gives guidance on how new entrepreneurs can prevent failure – summed up by Burns (2001): understand your customers and ensure that your product or service provides more benefits than those offered by competitors!
- This book has described the investment criteria of venture capitalists in selecting a project for investment, and it should therefore enable entrepreneurs to maximize their chances of securing venture funding. The development of a comprehensive business plan is usually the first step for successful fund raising; this book highlights the key areas that have to be present in such a plan. It has also spelt out the qualities that CEOs must possess to drive a project to success, for example: strategic planning skills are crucial in today's competitive environment.
- Indian entrepreneurs are reluctant to allow VC firms to supply capital that will reduce their personal ownership below 51 per cent at any stage of the financing process; this mentality has to change if the full benefit of VC is to be realized by both parties. This is all part of a wider process by which entrepreneurs align their interests with those of the investor(s). By setting out how (and why) venture capitalists value a high-technology project, for example, entrepreneurs should be able to appreciate why a valuation will be scaled down compared to their initial expectations.
- On the same theme, our research programme highlighted the importance of communication. Entrepreneurs have to accept a high degree of monitoring for innovative, early-stage investments; however, the regular contact with a VC firm should not be seen as a burden, rather as a way of increasing the firms' capacity to network,

for example, by introducing the investee company to a vital contact in overseas markets.

10.5.3 Venture capitalists

The findings of our research programme, information gathered from ongoing discussions with the VC community, and secondary data from specialist research agencies and the financial media enable venture capitalists across the world to enhance their understanding of the VC market in India. The points below cover points of interest for practitioners and highlight new investment opportunities.

- VC firms can benchmark the profile of their investment teams against the preferences for VC firms operating in India in the early part of the decade, in relation to qualifications, prior experience, age group and so on (Tables 8.1 to 8.4). Likewise, VC firms can compare their individual investment strategy with the industry's preferences for different sectors and stages.
- Each VC firm will tailor its activities according to its investment portfolio, but our research programme should enable practitioners to assess the efficiency and effectiveness of their valuation, structuring and monitoring techniques in the light of industry practice. The behaviour of different clusters should also be an area of particular interest to venture capitalists.
- Our research findings suggest that VC firms generally focus on protecting their investments. It is still relatively early in the evolution of the Indian VC market, but the venture capitalists have now invested in the most lucrative deals (often described as picking the 'low hanging fruit' in the orchard!) In established sectors (IT, BPO and so on), competition for deals is likely to intensify; the investors will be those VC firms that are seen to be building genuine partnerships and adding value without stifling the creativity and growth prospects of the entrepreneurs.
- Some opportunities for future deals have already been mentioned, for example: 'hard' IT products, and management buy-ins where managers are brought in to revive underperforming companies. Investments are likely to feature in new markets, new deal types and new industries (such as biotechnology and bioinformatics). As employment grows and average incomes increase, more will be spent within India, especially on consumer goods that have been tailored to the tastes of the home market; for example: Indian consumers value cars that last a lifetime and that have a high percentage of locally-sourced components.

10.5.4 Islamic finance

Asset allocation in Islamic banking currently favours fixed-income structures such as *murabaha* and *ijarah,* whereas the introduction of financial instruments more akin to VC could bring Islamic banks and other financial intermediaries closer to their original mission of offering a PLS based financial system. A VC regime based on Islamic principles would give Muslim entrepreneurs a flexible source of finding and allow them to benefit from the support offered by venture capitalists, thus enhancing their ability to compete both domestically and globally.

The central thrust of Durrani's argument is that the underlying spiritual quotient (SQ) in Islam will mitigate problems stemming from adverse selection, information asymmetry and moral hazard, just as much (if not more so) than the present reliance upon mathematical valuation techniques, tight shareholder agreements and extensive monitoring mechanisms. In addition, the three main themes of our research programme, the valuation, structuring and monitoring of VC deals, were considered from an Islamic perspective and found to be generally acceptable (Table 9.1).

There appears to be scope for developing Islamic VC in countries such as Bangladesh, Indonesia, Malaysia, Pakistan, Iran, Saudi Arabia, Egypt and Turkey. These countries have suitable industrial and capital market infrastructures (fully-fledged Islamic Banking systems already operate in Pakistan and Iran), although the appetite for VC investments would have to be assessed. Moreover, any new Islamic financial structures will have to be introduced incrementally to ensure that they operate in strict accordance with the spiritual dimension of the Islamic economic system.

With more than 150 million followers of Islam, the second largest Muslim population in the world, there should also be a captive market for such developments in India (even though over 80 per cent of the population follows the Hindu religion). There have been rudimentary efforts to implement Islamic financial principles, generally in the form of small-ticket *murabaha* deals. However, progress has been hindered by a number of problems.

Apart from accusations of financial irregularities, the business models adopted by emerging financial intermediaries have not been appropriate. Fund managers have raised capital from the salaried class or small shopkeepers who had 'emotional attachment' to Islamic principles but who could rarely afford to invest for the long-term. High net worth individuals or major corporate investors would have had longer staying power and the ability to evaluate the financial viability of the projects being funded. Investment was mainly in equities hence small investors were exposed to stock market volatility. To generate a sense of stability in this market, funds could have been allocated to relatively safe investments that were acceptable to Islam, such as commercial leasing and mortgage financing.

From this precarious base, it is essential to proceed with caution; the suggestions below refer to Islamic VC and also to existing forms of Islamic finance.

- Special incentives should be provided to encourage institutions such as insurance companies and pension funds to invest in Islamic VC funds.
- Islamic banks could play a part in supporting the centres of excellence described above, for example: using surplus funds to assist premier engineering bodies and technical educational institutions to develop local indigenous technology.
- Under current legislation, non-banking finance companies can offer Islamic finance. Such institutions could also offer corporate advisory services, advising Muslim-owned businesses on how to restructure their balance sheets – replacing interest-bearing debt with Islamic debt. This approach would require greater expertise in corporate finance, as well as a much larger capital base (around US$20/25m as a minimum) to weather economic volatility.
- On a different tack, Muslims in India have substantial funds for investment yet they are reluctant to invest in securities that may not be permitted under Islam. Apart from sectors like alcohol, tobacco, conventional finance, arms and ammunitions, and entertainment, investments are not allowed in companies whose interest income exceeds five per cent of their total income or whose total assets are less than 55 per cent of balance sheet size. These restrictions provide an opportunity to develop an Islamic Index on the National Stock Exchange, on the lines of those pioneered by Dow Jones in the US and the authorities in Malaysia. Such an initiative will release additional capital for productive purposes (previously retained as cash or invested in assets such as precious metals).

10.5.5 Academic researchers

The research programme conducted for this book gave a full picture of the VC industry in India the early part of the new millennium; it is now time for a follow-up study to check developments in valuation, structuring and monitoring practices.

From a policy perspective, it would be helpful to have a clearer idea of the need for small scale VC in India; it is difficult to identify high fliers that never fly because of a lack of finance yet it should be possible to assess the extent of any unsatisfied demand for VC. The performance of Government-sponsored VC funds should also be assessed. If such funds have suffered severe losses, this could indicate a lack of expertise in selecting and/or managing risky investments, or that projects should not have received funding (or some combination of these and other factors). However, some failures might have achieved social returns to offset the cost to the public purse.

Academic researchers could also evaluate a number of specific issues, including:

- The success of VC firms in supporting high-technology activity.
- The scope for reducing the discount rate applied to high-technology proposals – do current rates discourage worthwhile investments?
- Whether valuation techniques rely over excessively upon the DCF methodology rather than qualitative approaches?
- Many covenants viewed as 'essential'; does this reflect an excessive need for control by the venture capitalists?
- Whether foreign venture capitalists are too quick to replace CEOs, or should the domestic VC firms be more decisive in this respect?
- Evidence for convergence in the techniques used by foreign and domestic VC firms – is this always appropriate?

Notes

Chapter 6 An Introduction to India: The Economy, Financial System, SMEs and Venture Capital

1. A number of these markets, such as the Unlisted Securities Market (USM) in the United Kingdom and the Parallel Market in the Netherlands, launched in 1980 and 1982 respectively, have struggled to survive in volatile economic times. The USM was phased out in the mid-1990s and replaced by the Alternative Investment Market. This chequered history has been mirrored in other countries; for example the MESDAQ market in Malaysia has recently been subsumed into the main KLSE.
2. The trust structure offers taxation benefits, but it does not allow limited life funds – a key feature of the limited partnership model. If investors wish to liquidate a venture fund, the entire trust has to be closed down. This creates an unnecessary administrative burden.

Chapter 7 Venture Capital in India: The Analytical Framework

1. 'Tag along' rights allow the venture fund to sell shares on the same terms to the same purchaser; 'drag along' rights come into play when the venture capitalist sells his shareholding and requires other shareholders to sell their shares to the same purchaser.
2. Stathopoulos (2002) gives two exit scenarios for the case study – with and without flat pricing.

	Venture capitalist		Management	
	£000	£MoI	£000	£MoI
1. Newco sold for £4m				
Without flat pricing	(2,000)	0.6X	500	2.0X
With flat pricing	(1,125)	0.8X	(375)	0.25X
2. Newco sold for £20m				
Without flat pricing	10,000	3.0X	4,500	10.0X
With flat pricing	10,875	3.2X	3,625	8.25X

In case 1, without flat pricing, the venture fund owns 75 per cent of the ordinary shares hence the venture capitalists receive £3m on exit. This loss of £2m on the original investment of £5m produces a multiple of investment (MoI) of 0.6. The founders, on the other hand, have made a profit. They have realized £1m for an original investment of £500,000, a profit of £500,000 and

MoI of 2.0. With flat pricing, however, the venture fund has first call on the preferred equity investment of £3.5m then the remaining proceeds of £0.5m are distributed to the ordinary shareholders. Although both parties lose money, the loss is shared on a more equitable basis and the interests of private equity investors and management are properly aligned.

In case 2, a profitable exit, both parties achieve a satisfactory outcome. The MoI of the management falls under flat pricing (10 to 8.25); however, they are still 'better off', in that the deal might not have gone ahead without flat pricing or the management might not have been allowed to retain as much of the equity.

3. Preferred ordinary shares include cumulative convertible participating preferred ordinary shares (CCPPOs); these instruments carry a base dividend that is cumulative, conversion rights into ordinary shares, a further dividend that is paid when profits rise above a specified level, and preferential rights in liquidation.

Chapter 8 Venture Capital in India: Research Methodology and Findings

1 It is evident that the data are skewed in three sub-categories (size, number of investments and US$m invested per fund manager). This phenomenon could have been overcome by dividing the sample on the basis of median rather than mean. However, the objective of this exercise is not to make the sample statistically more efficient, but rather to examine the underlying behavioural characteristics of funds clustered according to certain factors.
2. The 'origin' category is based on actual numbers. The sector preference was determined by the amount invested in the ITMT category; all firms where investment in ITMT accounted for more than 60 per cent of their total investment were classified as 'technology-oriented'. Likewise, the stage preference was ascertained by combining the 'seed' and 'early stage' investments; where these two stages together comprised more than 60 per cent of the total amount invested, the firm was classified as an 'early stage investor'.
3. Cluster analysis encompasses a number of multivariate techniques that attempt to classify objects (VC firms in this case) according to their characteristics. The authors adopted the agglomerative, hierarchical approach and utilized Ward's method with the Euclidean measure of distance between objects in each cluster. The literature in this field generally supports this approach as the best method of finding clusters (Punj and Stewart, 1983).

Chapter 9 Business Ethics and Venture Capital in Islam

1. *Bukhari* is one of the most authentic collections of the sayings of Muhammad.
2. *Muslim* is the second most authentic collection of Prophetic sayings.
3. *Mustadrik Hakim* contains an authentic collection of Prophetic sayings.
4. *Mundhari* contains a number of authentic statements of Prophet Muhammad.
5. *Mishkat* is one of the six most authentic collections of Prophetic statements.
6. *Bayhaqi* is another authentic collection of prophetic sayings.

7. Choudhury (2001) suggests that *mudarabah* and *musharakah* have inherent problems (especially when combined in joint venture financing instruments) because they do not attain the ideal of co-operative participation. They lack precision in capitalizing the value of time or wages that workers and other participants contribute in any joint venture with the capital providers. He argues that the profit sharing ratios remain poorly determined, and sets out a more exact representation of the intent of Islamic law *(maqasid as-shari'ah)* in an Islamic joint venture enterprise.

Chapter 10 Conclusions

1 For example, the 'Six Sigma' (SS) methodology provides the techniques and tools to improve the capability and reduce the defects in any business process. Pioneered by Motorola and General Electric, SS relies heavily on statistical techniques to reduce defects and measure quality. This approach can also be applied effectively by SMEs to enhance the quality of their products and services. SS tends to be adopted as a result of pressure from customers or from recommendations from neighbouring SMEs.

References

ACOST, *The Enterprise Challenge: Overcoming Barriers to Growth in Small Firms* (London: HMSO, 1990).

Adamati, A.R. and P. Pfleiderer, 'Robust Financial Contracting and Venture Capitalists', *Journal of Finance*, 49 (1994) 371–402.

ADB, *A Study of SMES with Special Reference to Technology Development*, Staff Working Paper, April, Manila: Asian Development Bank Programmes Department, East (2000).

Aghion, P. and P. Bolton, 'An Incomplete Contracts Approach to Financial Contracting', *Review of Economic Studies*, 59 (1992) 473–494.

Ahmad M., *Business Ethics in Islam* (New Delhi, India: Kitab Bhavan, 1999).

Ahmad, A., 'Economic Development in Islamic Perspective Revisited', *Review of Islamic Economics*, 9 (2000) 83–102.

Ahmad, K., 'Key note address: 4th International Conference on Islamic Economics and Finance' (UK: Loughborough University, August, 2000).

Ahmed, H. and M.U. Chapra, *Corporate Governance in Islamic Financial Institutions* (Jeddah, Saudi Arabia: Islamic Research & Training Institute, 2003).

Ahmed, H., *'An Islamic Framework of the Venture Capital Cycle'*, Paper presented for research seminar on 'Non-bank Financial Institutions: Islamic Alternatives' (Kuala Lumpur: Malaysia, March 1–3, 2004).

Akerlof, G., 'The Market for "Lemons": Quality, Uncertainty and the Market Mechanism', *Quarterly Journal of Economics*, 84 (1970) 488–500.

Al-Dhareer, S.M., *'Al Gharar in Contracts and its effect on Contemporary Transactions'*, Eminent Scholars Lecture Series, No. 16 (Jeddah, Saudi Arabia: Islamic Research and Training Institute, 1997).

Almus, M. and E.A. Nerlinger, 'Growth of New Technology-based Firms: Which Factors Matter?', *Small Business Economics*, 13(2) (1999) 141–154.

Amihud, Y. and B. Lev, 'Risk Reduction as Managerial Motive for Conglomerate Mergers', *Bell Journal of Economics*, 12 (1981) 605–617.

Amit, R., J. Brander and C. Zott, 'Why do Venture Capital Firms Exist? Theory and Canadian Evidence', *Journal of Business Venturing*, 13 (1998) 441–446.

Amit, R., L. Glosten and E. Muller, 'Challenges to Theory Development in Entrepreneurship Research', *Journal of Management Studies*, 30(5) (1993) 815–834.

Amit, R., L. Glosten and E. Muller, 'Entrepreneurial ability, venture investments and risk sharing', *Management Science*, 36 (1990) 1232–1245.

Anderson, B.J., 'Venture Capital and Securities Market Development in Malaysia: The Search for a Functioning Exit Mechanism', *Wisconsin International Law Journal*, 12(1) (1994) 1–28.

Anderson, V.A. and J.G. Boocock, 'Learning to manage and managing to learn: the internationalisation of small organisations', *Human Resource Management Journal*, 12(3) (2002) 5–24.

Andrews, K.R., *The concept of corporate strategy* (IL, U.S.: Irwin Homewood, 1980).

Ardichvili, A., B. Harmon, R.N. Cardozo, P.D. Reynolds and M.L. Williams, 'The new venture growth: Functional differentiation and the need for human resource development interventions', *Human Resource Development*, 9(1) (Spring, 1998) 55–70.

Ariss, S.S., T.S. Raghunathan and A. Kunnathar, 'Factors affecting the adoption of advanced manufacturing technology in small firms', *S.A.M. Advanced Management Journal*, 65(2) (Spring, 2000) 14–21.

Arnold, J. and P. Moizer, 'A Survey of the Methods Used by UK Investment Analysts to Appraise Investments in Ordinary Shares', *Accounting and Business Research* (Summer, 1984) 195–207.

Arzeni, S., 'Entrepreneurship and job creation', Organisation for Economic Cooperation and Development, *The OECD Observer; Paris* (December 1997/January 1998) 18–20.

Atje, R. and B. Jovanovic, 'Stock Markets and Development', *European Economic Review*, 37 (1993) 632–640.

Autler, G., *'Global Networks in High Technology: The Silicon Valley-Israel Connection'*, Master's Thesis, Department of City and Regional Planning (Berkeley: University of California, 2000).

AVCJ, *The Guide to Venture Capital in Asia* (Hong Kong: AVCJ Holding Ltd., 1993).

Axelsson, B. and G. Easton (eds), *Industrial Networks: A New View of Reality* (London: Routledge, 1992).

Aylward, A., *'Trends in Venture Capital Financing in Developing Countries'*, Discussion Paper No. 36 (Washington, DC: IFC, 1998).

Babbie, E., *Survey Research Methods* (USA: Wadworth Publishing Company, 1973).

Balasubramanyam, V.N., *The Economy of India* (London: Weidenfeld and Nicholson, 1984), pp.1, 3, 6, 39, 41.

Banerjee, A.V., S. Cole and E. Duflo, *Bank Financing in India*, IMF Seminar, New Delhi (November 2003). (www.imf.org/external/np/apd/seminars/2003/newdelhi/banerjee.pdf).

Bank Negara Malaysia (Various), *Annual Report* (Kuala Lumpur: Bank Negara Malaysia).

Bank of England, *Finance for Small Firms* (London: Bank of England, March, 2001).

Barley, G. and B. Kleiner, 'Small business management: Ensuring your clients success', *National Public Account*, 35(2) (1990) 30–33.

Barney, J.B., L. Busenitz, J.O. Fiet and D. Moesel, *'The Structure of Venture Capital Governance: An Organisational Economic Analysis of Relations between Venture Capital Firms and New Ventures'*, Best Papers Proceedings of Academy of Management: Washington (1989), pp.64–68.

Barry, C.B., 'New Directions in Research on Venture Capital Finance', *Financial Management*, 23(3) (Autumn, 1994) 3–15.

Beamish, P.W., 'The Internationalisation Process for Smaller Ontario Firms: A Research Agenda', in Rugman, A.M. (ed.), *Research in Global Strategic Management* (Greenwich: JAI Press Inc, 1990) 77–92.

Beaver, G., *Small Business, Entrepreneurship and Enterprise Development* (Harlow, UK: FT, Prentice Hall, 2002).

Becherer, R.C. and J.G. Maurer, 'The proactive personality disposition and entrepreneurial behavior among small company presidents', *Journal of Small Business Management*, 37(1) (January, 1999) 28–36.

Beekun R. and J. Badawi, *Leadership in Islam* (US: Amanah Publication, 2000).

Bell, J. and S. Young, 'Towards an Integrative Framework of the Internationalization of the Firm' in Hooley, G., R. Loveridge and D. Wilson (eds), *Internationalization: Process, Context and Markets* (London: Macmillan, 1998) 5–28.

Bendjijali, B. and T. Khan, *Economics of Diminishing Musharakah*, Research Paper No. 31 (Jeddah, Saudi Arabia: Islamic Research and Training Institute, 1985).

Bennett, R.J., P. Wicks and A. McCoshan, *Local Empowerment and Business Services: Britain's Experiment with Training and Enterprise Councils* (London: UCL Press, 1994).

Bergemann, D. and U. Hege, 'Venture Capital Financing, Moral Hazard, and Learning', *Journal of Banking and Finance*, 22 (1998) 703–735.

Berger, A.N. and F.G. Udell, 'The Economics of Small Business Finance: The Roles of Private Equity and Debt markets in the Financial Growth Cycle', *Journal of Banking and Finance*, 22 (1998) 613–673.

Berger, A.N. and F.G. Udell, 'Collateral, Loan Quality and Bank Risk', *Journal of Political Economy*, 25, January (1990) 21–42.

Berglof, E., 'A Control Theory of Venture Capital Finance', *The Journal of Law, Economics and Organisation*, 10(2) (1994) 247–267.

Berle, A.A. and G.C. Means, '*The Modern Corporation and Private Property*' (New York: Macmillan, 1932) 6.

Besser, T.L., 'Community Involvement and the Perception of Success Among Small Business Operators in Small Towns', *Journal of Small Business Management*, 37(4) (1999) 16–29.

Bhattacharya, S. and U.R. Patel, *Reform Strategies in the Indian Financial Sector*, IMF Seminar, November, New Delhi (2003). (www.imf.org/external/np/apd/seminars/2003/newdelhi/patel.pdf).

Biekpe, N., '*Micro-finance, Venture Capital and the Unbanked: Review of Some Key Models and Way Forward in Africa*', Paper Presented at the International Conference on Development & Business Finance: Policy & Experience in Developing Countries, at Institute for Development Policy & Management, University of Manchester, April, 5–6, 2001.

Binks, M.R. and C. Ennew, 'Profiting from a closer banking link', in Birley, S. and D.F. Muzyka (eds), *Mastering Entrepreneurship* (London: Prentice Hall, 2000) 140–144.

Birch, D., 'The Job Generation Process', in *MIT Program on Neighborhood and Regional Change* (Cambridge, MA: MIT Press, 1979).

Birchall, D.W., J.J. Chanaron and K. Soderquist, 'Managing Innovations in SMEs: A Comparison of Companies in the UK, France and Portugal', *International Journal of Technology Management*, 12(3) (1996) 291–305.

Bleackley, M., M. Hay, K. Robbie and M. Wright, *Entrepreneurial Attitudes to Venture Capital Investments Realization: Evidence from the UK and France*, CMBOR, Occasional Paper No. 53 (1995) 1–27.

Bloodgood, J.M., H.J. Sapienza and J.G. Almeida, 'The internationalization of new high-potential U.S. ventures: antecedents and outcomes', *Entrepreneurship Theory and Practice*, 20(4) (1996) 61–76.

Bolton Report, *Report of the Committee on Small Firms*, Cmnd. 4811 (London: HMSO, 1971).

Bonaccorsi, A., 'On the Relationship between Firm Size and Export Intensity', *Journal of International Business Studies*, 23(4) (1992) 605–635.

Boocock, J.G., '*Venture Capital in Malaysia: The Criteria used by Fund Managers*', Research Paper No. 103 (UK: Loughborough University Banking Centre, July, 1996).

Boocock, J.G. and I.A. Wahab, 'The Financing of Small Firms: Different Continents, The Same Problems?', *New England Journal of Entrepreneurship*, 4(2) (2001) 13–31.

Boocock, J.G. and M.M. Woods, 'The Evaluation Criteria used by Venture Capitalists: Evidence from a UK Fund', *International Small Business Journal*, 16(1) (1997) 36–57.

Brealey, R. and S. Myers, *Principles of Corporate Finance*, 5th Edition (NY: McGraw-Hill, 1996).

Bridge, S., K. O'Neill and S. Cromie, *Understanding Enterprise, Entrepreneurship and Small Businesses*, 2nd Edition (Basingstoke, UK: Palgrave Macmillan, 2003).

British Venture Capital Association (various), *Reports on Investment Activity* (London: BVCA).

Bruton, G., V. Fried and R.D. Hisrich, 'Venture Capitalist and CEO Dismissal', *Entrepreneurship Theory and Practice*, 21(3) (1997) 41–54.

Bryce, M.D., *Policies and Methods for Industrial Development* (New York: McGraw-Hill, 1965).

Buckley, P.J., 'Foreign Direct Investment by Small and Medium-Sized Enterprises: The Theoretical Background', *Small Business Economics*, 1 (1989) 89–100.

Burns, P., *Entrepreneurship and Small Business* (Basingstoke, UK: Palgrave, 2001).

Burns, P., 'The Significance of Small Firms', in Burns, P. and J. Dewhurst (eds), *Small Business and Entrepreneurship* (London: Macmillan Business, 1996) 1–19.

Butchart, R.L., 'A New UK Definition of High Technology Industries', *Economic Trends*, 400 (1987) 82–88.

Bygrave, W., 'Syndicated investments by venture capital firms: a networking perspective', *Journal of Business Venturing*, 2(2) (Spring) (1987) 139–154.

Bygrave, W.D. and J.A. Timmons, *Venture Capital at the Crossroads* (Boston, Massachusetts: Harvard Business School Press, 1992).

Bygrave, W.D. and J.A. Timmons, 'Venture Capital's Role in Financing Innovation for Economic Growth', *Journal of Business Venturing*, 1 (1986) 161–176.

Calof, J.L., 'The Impact of Size on Internationalisation', *Journal of Small Business Management*, 31(4) (1993) 60–69.

Calof, J.L. and P.W. Beamish, 'The right attitude for international success', *Business Quarterly*, Autumn (1994) 105–110.

Cambridge University SBRC, *The State of British Enterprise* (Cambridge: Cambridge University Press, 1992).

Caves, R.E., *Multinational enterprise and economic analysis* (Cambridge: Cambridge University Press, 1982).

Chan, Y.S., D. Siegel and A. Thakor, 'Learning, Corporate Control and Performance Requirements in Venture Capital Contracts', *International Economic Review*, 31(2) (1990) 365–381.

Chapra, M.U., *Islam and the Economic Challenge* (Leicester, UK: The Islamic Foundation, 1992).

Chapra, M.U., '*Prohibition of Interest: Does it Make Sense?*' (Durban, South Africa: IDM Publications, 2001).

Chi, T. and D.J. McGuire, 'Collaborative ventures and the value of learning: integrating the transaction cost and strategic option perspectives on the choice of market entry', *Journal of International Business Studies*, 27(2) (1996) 285–307.

Chiampou, G.F. and J.J. Kallett, 'Risk/Return Profile of Venture Capital', *Journal of Business Venturing* (January, 1989) 1–10.

Choudhury, M.A., 'Islamic venture capital: a critical examination', *Journal of Economic Studies*, 28(1) (2001) 14–33.

Choy, C.L., 'Sources of Business Financing and Financing Practices: A Comparison among US and Asian Countries', *Journal of Business Venturing*, 5 (1990) 271–275.

Christensen, C., T. Crai and S. Hart, 'The Great Disruption', *Foreign Affairs*, 80(2) (March/April 2001) 80–95.

Churchill, N.C., 'The six key phases of company growth', in Birley, S. and D.F. Muzyka (eds), *Mastering Enterprise* (London: Prentice Hall, 1997) 213–219.

Cizacka, M., *A Comparative Business Partnership: The Islamic World and Europe, with Specific Reference to the Ottoman Archives* (Leiden: E.J. Brill, 1996).

Cizacka, M., *Encyclopaedia of Islamic Banking and Insurance* (London, UK: Institute of Islamic Banking and Insurance, 1995) 145–158.

Clark, R., *Venture Capital in Britain, America and Japan* (London: Croom Helm, 1987).

Clay, H., '*The Financing of Industrial Enterprise*' (Transactions of the Manchester Statistical Society, March 9, 1932) 205–227.

Coase, R.H., 'The Problem of Social Cost', *Journal of Law & Economics*, 15 (1960) 143–150.

Cobham, C. and R. Subramaniam, 'Corporate Finance in Developing Countries: New Evidence for India', *World Development*, 2(6) (1998) 1033–1047.

Collier, P. and C. Mayer, 'The Assessment: Financial Liberalization, Financial Systems and Economic Growth', *Oxford Review of Economic Policy*, 5(4) (1989).

Cook, P. and F. Nixon, '*Finance and Small and Medium Sized Enterprise Development*', Finance and Development Research Programme, Working Paper No. 14 (University of Manchester: Institute for Development Policy and Management, April, 2000).

Cooke, P. and D. Wills, 'Small Firms, Social Capital and the Enhancement of Business Performance Through Innovation Programmes', *Small Business Economics*, 13(3) (1999) 219–234.

Cooper, A.C., T.B. Folta and C.Y. Woo, 'Entrepreneurial information search', *Journal of Business Venturing*, 10(2) (1995) 107–120.

Cooper, I.A. and W.T. Carleton, 'Dynamics of borrower-lender interaction: partitioning final payoff in venture capital finance', *The Journal of Finance*, 34(2) (1979) 517–533.

Coopers and Lybrand, '*A Report on the Characteristics of Venture Backed Small Enterprises*' (US: Coopers and Lybrand, 1993).

Cornelli, F. and O. Yosha, '*Stage Financing and the Role of Convertible Debt*', Discussion Paper No. 1735 (London, UK: Centre for Economic Policy Research, November, 1997).

Coviello, N. and K. Martin, 'Internationalization of Service SMEs: An Integrated Perspective from the Engineering Consulting Sector', *Journal of International Marketing*, 7(4) (1999) 42–66.

Coviello, N. and A. McAuley, 'Internationalisation and the Smaller Firm: A Review of Contemporary Empirical Research', *Management International Review*, 39(3) (1999) 223–256.
Cruickshank, D., *Competition in UK Banking* (London: The Stationery Office, 2000).
Curran, J., *'A Response to the DTI Consultancy Paper on the new Small Business Service*, Unpublished Paper (ISBA Policy Forum, 11 October, 1999).
Curran, J. and R.A. Blackburn, *Researching the Small Enterprise* (London: Sage Publications, 2001).
Curran, J. and R.A. Blackburn, *'A Critical Examination of the Proposed New Small Business Service and Response to the DTI Consultancy Paper'*, Unpublished Paper (ISBA Policy Forum, 11 October, 1999).
Curran, J., R. Blackburn, J. Kitching and J. North, 'Small Firms and Workforce Training: Some Results, Analysis and Policy Implications from a National Survey', in Ram, M. et al. (eds), *Small Firms: Enterprising Futures* (London: Paul Chapman Publishing, 1997) 90–101.
Daily, C.M. and C.R. Dalton, 'Board of directors' leadership and structure: Control and performance implications', *Entrepreneurship Theory and Practice*, 17(3) (1993) 65–81.
Dalley, J. and B. Hamilton, 'Knowledge, Context and Learning in the Small Business', *International Small Business Journal*, 18(3) (2000) 51–59.
Dawson, J., 'Impact of Structural Adjustment on the Small Enterprise Sector: a Comparison of the Ghanaian and Tanzanian Experiences', in Helmsing, A. and T. Kolstee (eds), *Small Enterprises and Changing Policies: Structural Adjustment, Financial Policy and Assistance Programme in Africa* (London: ITDG Publications 1993).
De Beus, J.G., *'Shall We Make the Year 2000?: The Decisive Challenge to Western Civilization'* (London: Sidgwick and Jackson, 1985).
Deirdre, F., 'Emerging Markets' Push for Private Equity', *Institutional Investor*, 29 (October, 1995) 319–320.
Demirguc-Kunt, A. and V. Maksimovic, 'Institutions, Financial Markets, and Firm Debt Maturity', *Journal of Financial Economics*, 54(3) (1999) 295–336.
Demsetz, H., 'The Structure of Ownership and the Theory of the Firm', *Journal of Law and Economics*, 26 (June, 1983) 375–393.
Desai, M., *India and China: An Essay in Comparative Political Economy*, Seminar, November, New Delhi (2003). (www.imf.org/external/np/apd/seminars/2003/newdelhi/desai.pdf).
Deville, P., 'An Overview of Private Equity and Venture Capital in Europe', *Entrepreneurship Education Course*, Module 1 (Zaventum, Belguim: EVCA, 2002).
Diamond, D., 'Debt Maturity Structure and Liquidity Risk', *Quarterly Journal of Economics*, 106 (1991) 1027–1054.
Dixit, A. and R. Pyndick, 'The Options Approach to Capital Investment', *Harvard Business Review*, 73(3) (1995) 105–119.
Dixon, R., 'Venture Capitalists and the Appraisal of Investments', *Omega*, 19(5) (1991) 333–334.
Dominguez, J., *Venture Capital* (London: Lexington Books, 1974).
Dorsey, T., *Operating guidelines for effective venture capital funds management* (Austin, Texas: University of Texas, 1979).

Dossani, R., 'Reforming venture capital in India: creating the enabling environment for information technology', *International Journal of Technology Management*, 25(21/2) (2003) 151–164.
Dossani, R. and M. Kenney, 'Creating an Environment for Venture Capital in India', *World Development*, 30(2) (2002) 227–253.
Dossani, R., and M. Kenney, *'Creating an Environment: Developing Venture Capital in India'*, Working Paper No. 143, Berkeley Roundtable on International Economy (May, 2001) pp.1–40.
Down, S., 'Owner-Manager Learning in Small Firms', *Journal of Small Business and Enterprise Development*, 6(3) (1999) 267–280.
DTI/Aston Business School, *Constraints on the Growth of Small Firms* (London: HMSO, 1991).
Dunning, J.H. (ed.), *Making Globalization Good* (Oxford: Oxford University Press, 2003).
Durant W. and A. Durant, *The Lessons of History* (US, New York: Simon and Schuster, 1968).
Dutt, R. and K.P.M. Sundharam, *Indian Economy* (New Delhi, India: S. Chand, 2000).
Dyer, W.G., *Cultural change in family firms* (San Francisco: Jossey-Bass, 1986).
Economic Development Board, *Annual Report* (Singapore, 1991).
Ehrlich, S.B., A.F. De Noble, T. Moore and R.R. Weaver, 'After The Cash Arrives: A Comparative Study of Venture Capital And Private Investor Involvement in Entrepreneurial Firms', *Journal of Business Venturing*, 9 (1994) 67–82.
Eisenhardt, K.M., 'Agency Theory: An Assessment and Review', *Academy of Management Review*, 14 (1989) 57–74.
Eisenhardt, K.M. and C.B. Schoonhoven, 'Organizational growth: Linking founding teams, strategy, environment and growth among U.S. semiconductor ventures', *Administrative Science Quarterly*, 35 (1990) 504–529.
Elango, B., V.H. Fried, R.D. Hisrich and A. Polonchek, 'How Venture Capital Firms Differ', *Journal of Business Venturing*, 10 (1995) 157–179.
Ernst and Whinney, *'Characteristics of Successful Companies Financed by Canadian Venture Capital Sources'*, for the Association of Canadian Venture Capital Companies (May, 1994).
Fama, E.F., 'Efficient Capital Markets', *Journal of Finance*, 46 (1991) 1575–1618.
Fama, E.F. and M.C. Jensen, 'Separation of Ownership and Control', *Journal of Law and Economics*, 26 (June, 1983) 301–324.
Fassin, Y., 'The Marketing of Venture Capital Funds', *Journal of Professional Service Marketing*, 16(2) (1998) 129–149.
Fassin Y. and C. Lewis, 'IPO Markets in Europe and the United States: Principles and Practice', in Bygrave, W., et al. (ed.), *Realizing Investment Value* (London: Financial Times-Pitman Publishing, 1994).
Fenn, G.W. and N. Liang, 'New Resources and New Ideas: Private Equity for Small Businesses', *Journal of Banking and Finance*, 22 (1998) 1077–1084.
Fenn, G.W., N. Liang and S. Prowse, 'The Private Equity Market: An Overview', *Financial Markets, Institutions, and Instruments*, 6 (1997) 1–106.
Fethi, G., *'Ottoman Companies in the 16th and 17th Centuries'*, The Great Ottoman, Turkish Civilization (Turkey: Ankara, 2000).
Fiet, J.O., 'Fragmentation in the Market for Venture Capital', *Entrepreneurship Theory and Practice*, 21(2) (1996) 5–20.

Fiet, J.O., 'Reliance upon Informants in the Venture Capital Industry', *Journal of Business Venturing*, 10 (1995) 195–223.

Fiet, J.O., 'Risk Avoidance Strategies in Venture Capital Markets', *Journal of Management Studies*, 32(4) (July, 1995) 551–574.

Fiet, J.O. and D. Hellriegel, 'Post-contractual Safeguards Against Venture Capital Risk', *Entrepreneurship, Innovation and Change*, 4(1) (1995) 23–42.

Finkelstein, S. and D.C. Hambrick, *Strategic leadership: Top executives and their effects on organizations* (St Paul, MN: West Publishing, 1996).

Flamholtz, E., 'Toward a holistic model of organizational effectiveness and organizational development at different stages of growth', *Human Resource Development Quarterly*, 1(2) (1990) 109–127.

Foxwell, H.S., 'The Financing of Industry and Trade', *Economic Journal*, 27 (September, 1917) 502–522.

Fredrickson, J.W., D.C. Hambrick and S. Baumrin, 'A model of CEO dismissal', *Academy of Management Review*, 13 (1988) 255–270.

Freear, J. and W.E. Wetzel, 'Who bankrolls high-tech entrepreneurs?', *Journal of Business Venturing*, 5 (1990) 77–89.

Fried, V. and R. Hisrich, 'Towards a Model of Venture Capital Investment Decision Making', *Financial Management*, 23(3) (Autumn, 1994) 28–37.

Fried, V. and A. Polonchek, 'Research Note: Venture Capitalists' Investment Criteria: A Replication', *Journal of Small Business Finance*, 3(1) (1993) 37–42.

Fruhan, W.E. Jr., *Financial Strategy: Studies in the Creation, Transfer, and Destruction of Shareholder Value* (Homewood, IL: Richard D. Irwin Inc., 1979).

Gatson, R.J., *Finding Private Venture Capital for your firm: A Complete Guide* (New York: John Wiley and Sons, 1989).

Ghosh, B.C, S.K. Teo and A.M. Low, 'Factors contributing to the success of SMEs: Evidence from Singapore', *Journal of Small Business and Entrepreneurship*, 10 (April–June) (1993) 33–46.

Gibb, A., 'Small Firms' Training and Competitiveness. Building upon the Small Business as a Learning Organisation', *International Small Business Journal*, 15(3) (1998) 13–29.

Gibson, L.J. and S.G. Blake, 'Venture Capital and Economic Development', *Economic Development Review*, Spring (1992) 41–46.

Goleman, D., *Working with Emotional Intelligence* (US: Bantam Books, 1998).

Gomes-Casseres, B., 'Alliance Strategies of Small Firms', *Small Business Economics*, 9(1) (1997) 33–44.

Gompers, P.A., 'Venture Capital Growing Pains: Should the Market Diet?', *Journal of Banking and Finance*, 22 (1998) 1089–1104.

Gompers, P.A., 'Optimal investment, monitoring, and the staging of venture capitalist', *The Journal of Finance; New York*, 50(5) (Dec 1995) 1462–1490.

Gompers, P.A., '*The Structure of Venture Capital Investing*', Working Paper (Cambridge, MA: Harvard University, 1992).

Gompers, P.A. and J. Lerner, 'The Use of Covenants: An Empirical Analysis of Venture Partnership Agreements', *Journal of Law and Economics*, 39 (1996) 463–498.

Gompers, P.A., J. Lerner, M.M. Blair and T. Hellman, '*What Drives Venture Capital Fund Raising*' (Washington: Brookings Paper on Economic Activity, 1998) 149–204.

Gorman, C. and R. Doran, 'Mission Statements in Small and Medium-sized Businesses', *Journal of Small Business Management*, 37(4) (1999) 5–66.

Gorman, M. and W.A. Sahlman, 'What do Venture Capitalists Do?', *Journal of Business Venturing*, 4 (1989) 231–248.

Gouri, G., 'Privatization and Public Sector Enterprise in India: Analysis of Impact of Non-Policy', *Economic and Political Weekly* (November, 1996) M63–M64.

Government of India, *Economic Survey* (New Delhi: Ministry of Finance, Economic Division, 1999–2000).

Granitsky, J., 'Strategies for innate and adoptive exporters: Lessons from Israel's case', *International Marketing Review*, 6(5) (1989) 50–65.

Greenwald, B., A. Weiss and J.E. Stiglitz, 'Informational Imperfections in Capital Markets and Macro-economic Fluctuations', *American Economic Review*, 74 (1984) 174–200.

Greiner, L.E., 'Evolution and revolution as organisations grow', *Harvard Business Review*, July/August (1972).

Gudmundson, D. and L.S. Hartenian, 'Workforce diversity in small business: An empirical investigation', *Journal of Small Business Management*, 38(3) (July, 2000) 27–36.

Gupta, U., 'Hands-On Venture Capital', *Venture*, New York, 8(1) (Jan 1986) 44–49.

Haar, N.E., J. Starr and I.C. MacMillan, 'Informal Risk Capital investors: investment patterns on the East Coast of the USA', *Journal of Business Venturing*. Vol. 3 (1988) 11–29.

Hall, C., 'Profile of SMEs and SME Issues in East Asia', in Harvie, C. and Lee, B.C. (eds), *The Role of SMEs in National Economies in East Asia* (Cheltenham, UK: Edward Elgar, 2001) Chapter 2, pp.21–49.

Hall, H.J., and C.W. Hofer, 'Venture Capitalists' Decision Criteria in New Venture Evaluation', *Journal of Business Venturing*, 8 (1993) 25–42.

Hall, P., '*Investment Evaluation in UK Venture Capital Funds: The Appraisal of Risk and Return*', Unpublished MBA Dissertation (London: City College, 1998).

Hamidullah, M., *The Muslim Conduct of State* (Pakistan: Lahore, 1973).

Hannan, M.T., M.D. Burton and J.N. Baron, 'Inertia and Change in the Early Years: Employment Relations in Young, High Technology Firms', *Industrial and Corporate Change*, 5 (1996) 503–536.

Harding, R., 'Plugging the knowledge gap: an international comparison of the role for policy in the venture capital market', *Venture Capital*, (1) (2002) 59–76.

Harding, R., 'Venture capital and regional development: towards a venture capital system', *Venture Capital*, 2(4) (2000) 287–311.

Harris, M. and A. Raviv, 'A Sequential Signalling Model of Convertible Debt Call Policy', *Journal of Finance*, 41 (1985) 815–830.

Harrison, P.D. and A. Harrell, 'Impact of "Adverse Selection" On Managers' Project Evaluation Decision', *Academy of Management Journal*, 36(3) (1993) 635–643.

Harvey, M. and R. Lusch, 'Expanding the Nature and Scope of Due Diligence', *Journal of Business Venturing*, 10 (1995) 5–21.

Harvie, C. and Lee, B.C., 'East Asian SMEs: Contemporary Issues and Developments – An Overview', in Harvie, C. and B.C. Lee (eds), *The Role of*

SMEs in National Economies in East Asia (Cheltenham, UK: Edward Elgar, 2001) Chapter 1, 1–20.

HBS – Harvard Business School, *'Private Equity in Developing Countries'*, Current Research Summaries (2000) pp.1–10, downloaded from www.people.hbs.edu/jlerner/develop.html

Hellmann, T., 'The Allocation of Control Rights in Venture Capital Contracts', *The Rand Journal of Economics*, 29(1) (Spring, 1998) 57–76.

Herms, N. and R. Lensink, 'Financial System Development in Transition Economies', *Journal of Banking and Finance*, 4(24) (April, 2000) 507–524.

Hofer, C.W. and W.R. Sandberg, 'Improving New Venture Performance: Some Guidelines for Success', *American Journal of Small Business*, Summer (1987) 12–23.

Hoffman, C.A., *'The Venture Capital Investment Process: A Particular Aspect of Regional Economic Development'*, Unpublished PhD, Department of Economics (US: University of Texas at Austin, 1972).

Hunt, H.D., R.D. Sparkman and J. Wilcox, 'The Pretest in Survey Research: Issues and Preliminary Findings', *Journal of Marketing Research*, May (1982) 269–273.

Huntsman, B., and J.P. Hoban, 'Investment in New Enterprises: Empirical Observations on Risk, Return, and Market Structure', *Financial Management* Summer (1980) 44–51.

Hutchison, P., and G. Ray, 'Surviving the Financial Stress of Small Enterprise Growth', in Stanworth J. and D. Watkins (eds), *The Survival of the Small Firm* (Aldershot, UK: Gower, 1986) 53–71.

Iqbal, M., *Thirty Years of Islamic Banking* (London: Macmillan, 2004).

Iqbal, M. and D. Llewellyn (eds), *Islamic Banking and Finance: New Perspectives in Profit Sharing and Risk* (Cheltenham, UK: Edward Elgar, 2002).

Iqbal, M. and D. Llewellyn (eds), *Islamic Banking and Finance: Current Developments in Theory and Practice* (UK: Edward Elgar, 2001).

Iqbal, M. and P. Molyneux, *Thirty Years of Islamic Banking* (Basingstoke, UK: Palgrave, 2005).

IVCA: *Venture Activity*, (various), Annual Reports (India: IVCA).

Ivy, R., 'Entrepreneurial Strategies and Problems in Post Communist Europe: A Survey of SMEs in Slovakia', *Journal of Small Business Management*, 35(3) (1997) 93–97.

James, D.R. and M. Soref, 'Profit constraints on managerial autonomy: Managerial theory and the unmaking of the corporate president', *American Sociological Review*, 46 (1981) 1–18.

Jeng, L.A. and P.C. Wells, 'The determinants of venture capital funding: evidence across countries', *Journal of Corporate Finance*, 6 (2000) 241–89.

Jensen, M. and W. Meckling, 'Agency Cost and the Theory of the Firm', *Journal of Financial Economics*, 3 (1978) 305–360.

Johanson, J. and L.G. Mattsson, 'Interorganizational relations in industrial systems: a network approach compared with the transaction cost approach', *International Studies of Marketing and Organization*, 17(1) (1987) 34–48.

Johanson, J. and E. Wiedersheim-Paul, 'The internationalisation process of the firm – a model of knowledge development and increasing foreign market commitments', *Journal of International Business Studies*, 8(1) (1978) 23–32.

John, K., and L.M. Senbet, 'Corporate Governance and Board Effectiveness', *Journal of Banking and Finance*, 22 (1998) 371–403.

Kanellos, M., 'Finding Venture Capital is So Easy', *Computer Reseller News*, 702 (1996).

Kanodia, C., R. Bushman and J. Duckhaut, 'Escalation Errors and the Sunk Cost Effect: An Explanation Based on Reputation and Information Asymmetries', *Journal of Accounting Research*, 27 (1989) 59–77.

Karagozoglu, N. and M. Lindell, 'Internationalization of Small and Medium Sized Technology-Based Firms: An Exploratory Study', *Journal of Small Business Management*, 36(1) (1998) 44–59.

Kariuki, N., 'The Effects of Liberalisation on Access to Bank Credit in Kenya', *Small Enterprise Development*, 6(1) (1995) 15–23.

Karsai, J., M. Wright, Z. Dudzinski and J. Morovic, 'Screening and Valuing Venture Capital Investments: Evidence from Hungary, Poland, and Slovakia', *Entrepreneurship Theory and Practice*, 10 (1998) 203–224.

Karsai, J., M. Wright and I. Filatotchev, '*Venture Capital in Transition Economies: The Case of Hungary*', Occasional Paper No. 63, CMBOR (UK: University of Nottingham, 1995) pp.1–23.

Keeton, W.R., '*The Effects of Mergers on Farm and Business Lending at Small Banks: New Evidence from Tenth District States*', Working Paper (US: Federal Reserve Bank of Kansas City, 1997).

Keeton, W.R., 'Do Bank Mergers Reduce Lending to Businesses and Farmers? New Evidence from Tenth District States', *Federal Reserve Bank of Kansas City, Economic Review*, 81(3) (1995) 63–75.

Khan, M.A., *Economic Teachings of Prophet Muhammad* (Islamabad, Pakistan: International Institute of Islamic Economics, 1989).

Khan, T., 'Islamic Quasi Equity (Debt) Instruments and the Challenges of Balance Sheet Hedging: An Exploratory Analysis', *Islamic Economic Studies*, 7(1&2) (1999) 1–34.

Khan, T., 'Demand for and Supply of PLS and Mark-up Funds of Islamic Banks – Some Alternative Explanations', *Islamic Economic Studies*, 3(1) (1995) 39–77.

King, J.L., V. Gurbaxani, K.L. Kraemer, F.W. MacFarlan, K.S. Raman and C.S. Yap, 'The institutional factors in information technology innovation', *Information Systems Research*, 5(2) (1994) 139–169.

Kleiman, B., J.W. Petty and J. Martin, '*Family controlled firms: An assessment of performance*', Proceedings of the second annual conference of the International Family Business Program Association (US: Nashville, July 1995).

Knight, M., 'Developing countries and the Globalisation of Financial Markets', *World Development*, 26(7) (1998) 118–1200.

Koontz, H., *Essentials of Management* (New York: McGraw Hill, 1990).

KPMG, *An Evaluation of the Small Firms Loan Guarantee Scheme* (London: DTI, 1999).

Kunze, R.J., *Nothing Ventured: The Perils and Payoffs of the Great American Venture Capital Game* (New York: Harper Business, 1990).

La Porta, R., F. Lopez-De-Silanes, A. Shleifer and R. Vishny, 'Corporate Ownership Around the World', *Journal of Finance*, 54 (1999) 471–517.

Lam, S., 'Venture Capital Financing: A Conceptual Framework', *Journal of Business Finance & Accounting*, 18(2) (January, 1991) 13–149.

Lansberg, I.S., 'Managing human resources in family firms: The problem of institutional overlap', *Organizational Dynamics*, 12(1) (1983) 39–46.

Lautanen, T., 'Modelling Small Firms' Decisions to Export – Evidence From Manufacturing Firms in Finland, 1995', *Small Business Economics*, 14(2) (2000) 107–124.

Lee, C.Y., 'The applicability of just-in-time manufacturing to small manufacturing firms: An analysis', *International Journal of Management*, 13(2) (1996) 249–258.

Leinbach, T.R., 'Asian Venture Capital: financing risk opportunities in the Pacific Rim', in Green, M. (ed.), *Venture Capital: International Comparisons*, First Edition (London: Routledge, 1991).

Lerner, J., 'When Bureaucrats meet Entrepreneurs: The Design of Effective "Public Venture Capital" Programmes', *Economic Journal*, 112 (February) (2002) F73–84.

Lerner, J., *Venture Capital and Private Equity: A Casebook* (New York: John Wiley, 2000).

Lerner, J., 'The Government as Venture Capitalist: The long-run Impact of the SBIR Program', *Journal of Business*, 72(3) (1999) 285–318.

Lerner, J., *'The Government as Venture Capitalist: An Empirical Analysis of the SBIR Program'*, Working Paper No. 96–038 (Harvard Business School, 1996).

Lerner, J., 'Venture Capitalists and the Oversight of Private Firms', *The Journal of Finance*, March (1) (1995) 301–318.

Lerner, J., 'The syndication of venture capital investments', *Financial Management*, 23(3) (1994) 16–29.

Lerner, J., 'Venture Capitalists and the Decision to Go Public', *Journal of Financial Economics*, 35(3) (1992) 293–316.

Lerner, J. and G. Pacanins, *A Note on Private Equity in Developing Countries* (N9-297-039), (Cambridge, Mass: Harvard Business School, 1997).

Levenson, A.R. and K.L. Willard, 'Do Firms Get the Financing They Want? Measuring Credit Rationing Experienced by Small Businesses in the US', *Small Business Economics*, 14(2) (2000) 83–94.

Levie, J., 'Convincing the cash-conscious banker', in Birley, S. and D.F. Muzyka (eds), *Mastering Entrepreneurship* (London: Prentice Hall, 2000) 99–102.

Levine, R., 'Financial Development and Economic Growth: Views and Agenda', *Journal of Economic Literature*, 35 (1997) 68–726.

Levitsky, J., 'Credit Guarantee Schemes for SMEs: An International Review', *Small Enterprise Development*, 8(2) (1997) 4–17.

Levy, B., 'Obstacles to Developing Indigenous Small and Medium Sized Enterprises: an Empirical Assessment', *The World Bank Economic Review*, 7(1) (1993) 65–83.

Lewis, M.K., *Models of Corporate Governance*, Working Paper (University of South Australia, October, 1999).

Lin See Yan, *'The Financing of Small-Scale Enterprises in Malaysia'*, Paper presented at 1st National Conference for SMIs (Malaysian Chinese Association), (Kuala Lumpur, May, 1994).

Llewellyn, T.O., 'Islamic Jurisprudence and Environment', *Journal of Islamic Economics* (Jeddah, Saudi Arabia: King Abdul Aziz University), 1(2) (Winter 1984).

Lockett, A. and M. Wright, 'The Syndication of Private Equity', *Venture Capital*, 1(4) (1999) 303–324.

Lockett, A., G. Murray and M. Wright, 'Do UK venture capitalists *still* have a bias against investment in new technology firms?', *Research Policy*, 31 (2002) 1009–30.

Longenecker, J.G. and C.W. Moore, *Small business management* (Cincinnati: South West Publishing, 1991).

Luce, E., *Financial Times*, 13 July (2004).

Luce, E., *Financial Times*, 9 December (2003).

Luce, E. and K. Merchant, *Financial Times*, 28 January (2004).

Mace, M.L., *Directors: Myth and reality* (Boston, Massachusetts: Harvard University Press, 1971).

MacMillan, I., R. Seigel and P. Narasimha, 'Criteria used by Venture Capitalists to Evaluate New Venture Proposals', *Journal of Business Venturing*, 1(1) (1985) 11–128.

MacMillan, I., C. Zemann and P.N. Subba Narasimha, 'Criteria Distinguishing Successful from Unsuccessful Ventures in the Venture Screening Process', *Journal of Business Venturing*, 2 (1987) 122–137.

MacMillan: Cmnd 3897, *Report of the Committee on Finance and Industry* (London: HMSO, 1931) Ch. 4, Part II, para. 4.

Manigart, S. and H. Sapienza, 'Venture Capital and Growth', in Sexton, D.L. and H. Landstrom (eds), *The Blackwell Handbook of Entrepreneurship* (Oxford, UK: Blackwell Publishers Limited), (2000) 240–258.

Manigart, S., K.D. Waele, M. Wright, K. Robbie, P. Desbrieres, H. Sapienza and M. Beekman, 'Venture Capitalists' Investment Appraisal and Accounting Information: A Comparative Study of The US, UK, France, Belgium and Holland', *European Financial Management*, 6(3) (2000) 389–403.

Manigart, S., M. Wright, K. Robbie, P. Desbrieres and K.D. Waele, 'Venture Capitalists' Appraisal of Investment Projects: An Empirical European Study', *Entrepreneurship Theory and Practice*, Summer (1997) 29–43.

Marlow, S., 'So much opportunity, so little take-up: The case of training in small firms', *Journal of Small Business and Enterprise Development*, 5(1) (1998) 38–47.

Mason, C.M. and R.T. Harrison, 'Is it worth it? The rates of return from informal venture capital investments', *Journal of Business Venturing*, 17 (2002) 211–236.

Mason, C.M. and R.T. Harrison, 'The Size of the Informal Venture Capital Market in the United Kingdom', *Small Business Economics*, 15 (2000) 137–148.

Masood, W.K., *Towards an Interest Free Islamic Economic System: A Theoretical Analysis of Prohibiting Debt Financing* (Leicester, UK: The Islamic Foundation, 1983).

McDougall, P.P. and B.M. Oviatt, 'International Entrepreneurship: The Intersection of Two Research Paths', *Academy of Management Journal*, 43(5) (2000) 902–6.

McDougall, P.P., S. Shane and B.M. Oviatt, 'Explaining the formation of international new ventures: the limits of theories from international business research', *Journal of Business Venturing*, 9(6) (1994) 469–487.

McGregor, J. and C. Gomes, 'Technology uptake in small and medium-sized enterprises: Some evidence from New Zealand', *Journal of Small Business Management*, 37(3) (July, 1999) 94–102.

McMohan, R.G.P., 'Modelling the Extent of Financial Reporting Practices Amongst Australian Manufacturing SMEs', *Small Business Economics*, 13(2) (1999) 8–86.

McNaughton, R.B., 'Venture Capital', in Green, M. (ed.), *Venture Capital: International Comparisons*, First Edition (London: Routledge, 1991).

Mechling, G.W., J.W. Pierce and J.W. Busbin, 'Exploiting AMT in small manufacturing firms for global competitiveness', *International Journal of Operations and Production Management*, 15(2) (1995) 61–76.

Megginson, W.L., M.J. Byrd, C.R. Scott and L.C. Megginson, *Small Business Management* (Burr Ridge: Irwin, 1994).

Megginson, W.L., R.C. Nash and M.V. Randenborgh, 'The Financial and Operating Performance of Newly Privatized Firms', *Journal of Finance*, 49 (1994) 403–452.

Mehta, S.N., 'Enterprise: Worker shortages continue to worry about a quarter of small businesses', *The Wall Street Journal*, 2 June (1996).

Meier, R. and M. Pilgrim, 'Policy-Induced Constraints on Small Enterprise Development in Asian Countries', *Small Enterprise Development*, 5(2) (1994) 32–38.

Mensah, S., 'The Valuation of Government Loan Guarantees: A Theoretical and Empirical Perspective', *Public Finance Quarterly*, 24(2) (1996) 263–81.

Merchant, K., *Financial Times*, 7 September (2004).

Merchant, K., *Financial Times*, 8 June (2004).

Merchant, K., *Financial Times*, 20 February (2004).

Merchant, K., *Financial Times*, 9 December (2003).

Merchant, K., *Financial Times*, 14 August (2003).

Meyer, G.D. and T.J. Dean, 'An upper echelons perspective on transformational leadership problems in high-technology firms', *The Journal of High Technology Management Research*, 1(2) (1990) 223–242.

Michael, S.C. and D.K. Robbins, 'Retrenchment among small manufacturing firms during recession', *Journal of Small Business Management*, 36(3) (July, 1998) 35–45.

Miles, G., S.B. Preece and M.C. Baetz, 'Danger of dependence: The impact of strategic alliance use by small technology-based firms', *Journal of Small Business Management*, 37(2) (April, 1999) 20–29.

Millen, R. and A. Sohal, 'Planning process for advanced manufacturing technology by large American manufacturers', *Technovation*, 18(12) (1998) 741–750.

Mishra, A.K., *Venture Capital Financing in India* (New Delhi, India: Shipra Publications, 1996).

Mitchell, F. and N.G. Terry, 'The Demand for Information by Investors', in Reid, G.C. (ed.), *Venture Capital Investment* (UK: Routledge, 1998).

Mitchell, F., G.C. Reid and N.G. Terry, 'Venture capital supply and accounting information system development', *Entrepreneurship Theory and Practice*, Summer, 21(4) (1997) 45–62.

Mitchell, F., G.C. Reid and N.G. Terry, 'Post investment demand for accounting information by venture capitalists', *Accounting and Business Research, London*, 25(99), Summer (1995) 186–197.

Mitra, D., 'The Venture Capital Industry in India', *Journal of Small Business Management*, 38(2) (April, 2000) 67–80.

Moore, B., *Reflections on the Causes of Human Misery and Certain Proposals to Eliminate them* (US: Beacon Press, 1972).

Mukherji, A. and N.J. Nagarajan, 'Moral Hazard and Contractibility in Investment Decisions', *Journal of Economic Behaviour and Organization*, 26 (1995) 413–430.

Murinde, V., 'Financial Markets and Endogenous Growth: An Econometric Analysis for Pacific Basin Countries', in Herme, N. and R. Lensink (eds), *Financial Development and Economic Growth: Theory and Evidence from Developing Countries* (London: Routledge, 1996) 9–114.

Murray, G., 'The UK Venture Capital Industry', *The Journal of Business Finance & Accounting*, 1(8), December (1995) 1077–1106.

Murray, G., *Change and Maturity in the UK Venture Capital Industry: 1991–1995* (London: British Venture Capital Association, 1991).

Murray, G., 'The Second Equity Gap: Exit Problems for Seed and Early Stage Venture Capitalists and their Investee Companies', *International Small Business Journal*, 12(4) (1994) 59–75.

Murray, G. and J. Lott, 'Have Venture Capitalists a Bias Against Investment in New Technology Firms', *Research Policy*, 24 (1995) 283–299.

Myers, S.C. and N.S. Majluf, 'Corporate Financing and Investment Decisions When Firms Have Information That Investors Do Not Have', *Journal of Financial Economics*, 13 (1984) 187–221.

Naqvi, R., *History of Banking and Islamic Law* (Karachi, Pakistan: Hayat Academy, 1987).

Nasscom, *Enabling a Quantum Leap in Successful Indian Venture Creation* (New Delhi: Nasscom, 2000).

Neher, D.V., 'Staged Financing: An Agency Perspective', *The Review of Economic Studies, Oxford*, 66, (227) (April, 1999) 255–274.

Nelson, B., *1001 ways to reward employees* (New York: Workman Publishing, 1994).

Norman, G.R., *'The Venture Capital Industry in New Zealand: An International Perspective'*, Report Prepared for New Zealand Trade Development Board (May, 1989).

Norton, E., 'Venture Capital as an Alternative Means to Allocate Capital: An Agency-theoretic View', *Entrepreneurship Theory and Practice*, 20(2) (Winter, 1995) 19–29.

Norton, E. and B.H. Tenenbaum, 'The Effects of Venture Capitalists' Characteristics on the Structure of Venture Capital', *Journal of Small Business Management*, 3(4) (October, 1993) 32–42.

Norton, E. and B.H. Tenenbaum, 'Factors Affecting the Structure of US Venture Capital Deals', *Journal of Small Business Management*, 30(3) (July, 1992) 20–27.

Nyborg, K., 'Convertible Debt as Delayed Equity: Forced versus Voluntary Conversion and the Information Role of Call Policy', *Journal of Financial Intermediation*, 4 (1995) 358–395.

O'Farrell, P.N., P.A. Wood and J. Zheng, 'Internationalisation by Business Services SMEs: an inter-industry analysis', *International Small Business Journal*, 16(2) (1998) 12–33.

O'Shea, M., Consultant to the Financial Affairs Division of the OECD. Based on her report, *Financial Market Trends, Paris*, published an article titled 'Venture Capital in OECD countries' (February, 1996) 15–32.

O'Shea, M. and C. Stevens, 'Governments as Venture capitalists', *OECD Observer*, No. 213, August/September (1998) 26–29.

Oviatt, B.M. and P.P. McDougall, 'Challenges for internationalisation process theory: The case of international new ventures', *Management International Review*, 37 (1997) 85–99.

Oviatt, B.M. and P.P. McDougall, 'Towards a Theory of International New Ventures', *Journal of International Business Studies*, First Quarter (1994) 45–64.

Pagano, M., 'Financial Markets and Growth: An Overview', *European Economic Review*, 37 (1993) 613–623.

Pandey, I.M. and A. Jang, 'Venture Capital for Financing Technology in Taiwan', *Technovation*, 16(9) (1996) 499–515.

Pandit, B.L. and N.S. Siddharthan, 'Technological Acquisition and Investment: Lessons from Recent Indian Experience', *Journal of Business Venturing*, 13 (1998) 43–55.

Parker, R., R. Riopelle and W. Steel, *'Small Enterprises Adjusting to Liberalisation in Five African Countries'*, World Bank Discussion Paper No. 271, African Technical Department Series (Washington, DC: The World Bank, 1995).

Patricof, A., 'The Internationalisation of Venture Capital', *Journal of Business Venturing*, 4 (1989) 227–230.

Pech, R. and A. Mathew, 'Critical factors for consulting to small business', *Journal of Management Consulting*, 7(3) (1993) 61–63.

Peek, J. and E.S. Rosengren, 'Bank Consolidation and Small Business Lending: It's not Just Bank Size that Matters', *Journal of Banking and Finance*, 22 (1998) 799–819.

Peng, M.W. and S.V. Shekshnia, 'How entrepreneurs create wealth in transition economies', *Academy of Management Executive*, 15(1) (2001) 95–110.

Persaud, A., 'The Knowledge Gap', *Foreign Affairs*, 80(7) (March/April 2001) 107.

Pfeffer, J., 'Size, composition, and function of hospital boards of directors: A study of organization environment linkage', *Administrative Science Quarterly*, 18 (1973) 349–364.

Pike, R., J. Meerjansen and L. Chadwick, 'The Appraisal of Ordinary Shares by Investment Analysts in the UK and Germany', *Accounting and Business Research*, 23(92) (1993) 489–499.

Ping, L., *'Challenges for China's Banking Sector and policy responses'*, IMF Seminar, New Delhi (November, 2003). (www.imf.org/external/np/apd/seminars/2003/newdelhi/ping.pdf).

Poindexter, E.A., *The efficiency of financial markets: the venture capital case*. Unpublished doctoral dissertation (New York: New York University, 1976).

Porter, M.E., *Competitive Strategy: Techniques for analysing industries and competitors* (New York: The Free Press, 1980).

Pousson, J., 'Corporate failure – the lessons to be learnt', *Credit Management* (1996) 32–34.

Preece, S.B., G. Miles and M.C. Baetz, 'Explaining the International Intensity and Global Diversity of Early-Stage Technology-based Firms', *Journal of Business Venturing*, 14 (1998) 259–281.

Punj, G. and D.W. Stewart, 'Cluster Analysis in Marketing Research: Review and suggestions for Application', *Journal of Marketing Research*, 20 (1983) 134–148.

Qardawi, Y., *'English Translation of 'Fiqh uz Zakat'* (Leicester, UK: The Islamic Foundation, 2003).

Rah, J., K. Jung and J. Lee, 'Validation of Venture Evaluation Model in Korea', *Journal of Business Venturing*, 9 (1994) 509–528.

Rajan, R. and A. Winton, 'Covenants and Collateral as Incentives to Monitor', *The Journal of Finance*, L(4) (September, 1995) 1113–1146.

Ravid, S.A. and M. Spiegel, 'Optimal Financial Contracts for a start-up with unlimited operating discretion', *Journal of Financial and Quantitative Analysis*, 32(3) (September, 1997) 269–286.
Reid, G.C., *Venture Capital Investment: An Agency Analysis of Practice* (London: Routledge, 1998).
Reid, G.C., *Small Business Enterprise: An Economic Analysis* (London: Routledge, 1993).
Reid, S.D., 'Firm Internationalization transaction costs and strategic choice', *International Marketing Review*, 1(2) (1983) 45–55.
Reserve Bank of India (Various) *Annual Reports*, Government of India.
Rho, B.H. and D.C. Whybark, '*Manufacturing practice in Korea*', Discussion Paper No. 43, Indiana Center for Global Business (Bloomington, Indiana: Indiana University, 1990).
Riquelme, H. and J. Watson, 'Do Venture Capitalists' Implicit Theories on New Business Success/Failure have Empirical Validity?' *International Small Business Journal*, 20(4) (2002) 395–420.
Robbie, K., M. Wright and B. Chiplin, 'The Monitoring of Venture Capital Firms', *Entrepreneurship Theory and Practice*, 21(4) (Summer, 1997) 9–28.
Robinson, R.B., 'Emerging strategies in the venture capital industry', *Journal of Business Venturing*, 2(1) (1987), 53–77.
Roman, Z., 'Entrepreneurship and Small Business: The Hungarian Trajectory', *Journal of Business Venturing*, 8(2) (1991) 447–465.
Roper, S., 'Modelling Small Business Growth and Profitability', *Small Business Economics*, 13(3) (1999) 235–252.
Rosentein, J., A.V. Bruno, W.D. Bygrave and N.T. Taylor, 'The CEO, venture capitalists, and the board', *Journal of Business Venturing; New York*, 8(2) (1993) 99–114.
Rosman, A.J. and H.M. O'Neill, 'Comparing the Information Acquisition Strategies of Venture Capital and Commercial Lenders: A Computer-Based Experiment', *Journal of Business Venturing*, 8 (1993) 443–460.
Ruekert, R. and O.C. Walker, 'Marketing interaction with other functional units: A conceptual framework and empirical evidence', *Journal of Marketing*, 5 (January, 1987) 1–19.
Ruhnka, J.C. and J.E. Young, 'Some Hypotheses about Risk in Venture Capital Investing', *Journal of Business Venturing*, 6 (1991) 115–133.
Ryan, N., 'Policy Issues for Government in Developing Australian Venture Capital', *Australian Journal of Public Administration*, 50(1) (March, 1991) 61–73.
Sahlman, W.A., 'The Structure and Governance of Venture Capital Organisations', *Journal of Financial Economics*, 27 (1990) 473–521.
Sahlman, W.A., 'Aspects of Financial Contracting in Venture Capital', *Journal of Applied Corporate Finance*, 4 (1988) 23–36.
Sandberg, W.R., D.M. Schweiger and C.W. Hofer, 'The use of verbal protocols in determining venture capitalists' decision processes', *Entrepreneurship: Theory and Practice*, Winter (1988) 8–20.
Sapienza, H., '*Variations in venture-capitalist-entrepreneur relations: Antecedents and consequences*', unpublished doctoral dissertation (USA: University of Maryland, 1989).
Sapienza, H. and M. Korsgaard, 'Procedural Justice in Entrepreneur-Investor Relations', *Academy of Management Journal*, 39(3) (1996) 544–574.

Sappington, D.E., 'Incentives in principal-agent relationships', *Journal of Economic Perspectives*, 5(2) (1991) 45–66.
Sarika, P., 'Screening and Monitoring Venture Capital in India', Unpublished Thesis for the award of M.A. (UK: Business School, University of Nottingham, 1999).
SBA – *Small business answer card 1998*, Small Business Association (1999), available at www.sba.gov/advo/stats/
Scheela, W.J., 'The Increasing Importance of Venture Capital in Singapore', *Journal of Asian Business*, 10(3) (1994) 73–86.
Scherer, F.M., *Industrial Market Structure and Economic Performance*, 2nd Edition (Boston, Mass.: Houghton Mifflin Company, 1980).
Schleifer, A. and R.W. Vishny, 'A Survey of Corporate Governance', *The Journal of Finance*, LII(2) (June, 1997) 737–783.
Scholtens, B., 'Financial Regulation and Financial System Architecture in Central Europe', *Journal of Banking and Finance*, 24(4) (2000) 525–553.
Schrader, H., *Changing Financial Landscapes in India and Indonesia* (New York: St. Martin's Press, 1997).
Schwartz, L.W., 'Developing Countries Need Venture Capital Strategies', *Foreign Affairs*, 73(6) (December, 1994) 14–18.
Scott, P., B. Jones, A. Bramley and B. Bolton, 'Enhancing Technology and Skills in Small and Medium Sized Manufacturing Firms: Problems and Prospects', *International Small Business Journal*, 14(3) (1996) 85–99.
SEBI: Securities and Exchange Board of India, Report of the K.B. Chandrasehkar Committee on Venture Capital (India: Bombay, 2000).
Sekaran, U., *Research Methods for Business: A Skill Building Approach*, 2nd edition (USA: John Wiley & Sons, 1992).
Shepherd, D.A. and M.A. Shanley, *New Venture Strategy* (London: Sage, 1998).
Shilson, D., 'Venture capital in the United Kingdom', *Bank of England, Quarterly Bulletin*, 24 (1984) 207–211.
Siddiqi, M.N., '*Partnership and Profit-Sharing in Islamic Law*' (Leicestershire, UK: The Islamic Foundation, 1985).
Siegel, R., E. Siegel and I.C. MacMillan, 'Corporate Venture Capitalists: Autonomy, Obstacles & Performance', *Journal of Business Venturing*, 3(3) (1988) 233–247.
Singh, A., 'Financial Liberalisation, Stock Markets and Economic Development', *Economic Journal*, 107 (1997) 771–782.
Singh, A. and B.A. Weisse, 'Emerging Stock Markets, Portfolio Capital Flows and Long-term Economic Growth: Micro and Macro Perspectives', *World Development*, 26(4) (1998) 607–622.
Sinha, D., 'The rise of entrepreneurship in India', in *The Knowledge Economy in India*, (eds) Richter, F.J. and P. Banerjee (Basingstoke, UK: Palgrave Macmillan, 2003) 149–162.
Small Business Service, *Small and Medium Sized Enterprises (SME) Statistics for the UK* (2004), http://www.sbs.gov.uk/statistics
Smallbone, D. and F. Welter, 'The Role of Government in SME Development in Transition Economies', *International Small Business Journal*, 19(4) (2001) 63–78.
Smith, J.A., 'The Behaviour and Performance of Young Micro Firms: Evidence from Businesses in Scotland', *Small Business Economics*, 13(3) (1999) 185–200.
Spier, K.E., 'Incomplete Contracts and Signalling', *RAND Journal of Economics*, 23(3) (1992) 23–36.

Srivastava, S., 'Risk Capital in India' (2002) (www.ficci.com/ficci/media-room/speeches-presentations/2002/Feb)

Stathopoulos, N., *Financial Structure of a Private Equity Investment* (Zaventem, Belgium: Entrepreneurship Education Course, EVCA, 2002).

Steel, W., 'Changing the Institutional and Policy Environment for Small Enterprise Development in Africa', *Small Enterprise Development*, 5(2) (1994) 4–9.

Steier, L. and R. Greenwood, 'Venture Capitalist Relationships in the Deal Structuring and Post-Investment Stages of New Firm Creation', *Journal of Management Studies*, 32(3) (1995) 337–357.

Stein, J., 'Convertible Bonds as Backdoor Equity Financing', *Journal of Financial Economics*, 32 (1992) 3–21.

Stein, J., 'Efficient Capital Markets, Inefficient Firms: A Model of Myopic Behaviour', *Quarterly Journal of Economics*, 104 (1989) 655–669.

Stiglitz, J.E. and A. Weiss, 'Credit Rationing in Markets with Imperfect Information', *American Economic Review*, 71 (1981) 393–410.

Storey, D.J., *Understanding the Small Business Sector* (London: Routledge, 1994).

Storey, D.J. and P. Westhead, 'Management Training in Small Firms – A Case of Market Failure?', *Human Resource Management Journal*, 7(2) (1996) 61–71.

Storey, D., K. Keasey, R. Watson and P. Wynarczyk, *The Performance of Small Firms* (Beckenham, UK: Croom Helm, 1987).

Strahan, P.E. and J. Weston, 'Small Business Lending and the Changing Structure of the Banking Industry', *Journal of Banking and Finance*, 22 (1998) 82–845.

Sweeting, R., 'Early-stage New Technology-based Businesses: Interactions with Venture Capitalists and the Development of Accounting Techniques and Procedures', *British Accounting Review*, 23 (1991) 3–21.

Taylor, B., 'Secrets of the Supergrowth League', in Birley, S. and D.F. Muzyka (eds), *Mastering Entrepreneurship* (London: Prentice Hall, 2000) 280–283.

Terry, N.G. and J.A. Smith, 'Risk Management', in Reid, G. (ed.), *Venture Capital Investment* (UK: Routledge, 1998) 171–184.

Teubal, M., 'The Indian Software Industry from an Israeli Perspective: A Microeconomic and Policy Analysis', *Science, Technology and Society*, 7(1) (2002) 151–186.

Thakor, A., 'Strategic Issues in Financial Contracting: An Overview', *Financial Management*, Summer (1989) 39–58.

The Economist, Quoted in the 'History of Banking II', VIII, 21st October (London: Pickering & Chatto, 1911) 134.

Third All India Census of SSI Units (2002): http://www.smallindustryindia.com/publications/books/census/censusch1.pdf

Thompson S., M. Wright and M. Haynes, '*Sources of Venture Capital Deals: MBOs, IBOs and Corporate Refocusing*', CMBOR, Occasional Paper No. 67, (1997).

Thong, J.Y.L., 'An integrated model of information systems adoption in small businesses', *Journal of Management Information Systems*, 15(4), Spring, (1999) 187–214.

Timmons, J.A., *New Venture Creation*, Fourth edition (Irvin, Illinois: Burr Ridge, 1994).

Timmons, J.A. and W. Bygrave, 'Venture Capital's Role in Financing Innovation for Economic Growth', *Journal of Business Venturing*, 1 (1986) 161–176.

Timmons, J.A., D.F. Muzyka, H.H. Stevenson and W.D. Bygrave, 'Opportunity recognition: the core of entrepreneurship', *Frontiers of Entrepreneurship Research* (1987) 109–123.

Towe, C., 'Overview', in Callen, T., P. Reynolds and C. Towe (eds), *India at the Crossroads* (IMF Publications, 2001).

Trester, J.J., 'Venture Capital Contracting under Asymmetric Information', *Journal of Banking and Finance*, 22 (1998) 675–699.

TSJ Media: www.tsjmedia.com

Tyebjee, T. and A.V. Bruno, 'A model of venture capitalist investment activity', *Management Science*, 30(9) (1984) 1051–1056.

Tyebjee, T. and L. Vickery, 'Venture Capital in Western Europe', *Journal of Business Venturing*, 3(3) (1988) 123–136.

Verma, J.C., *Venture Capital Financing in India* (London: Sage Publications, 1997).

Vickerstaff, S.A., 'The Training Needs of Small Firms', *Human Resource Management Journal*, 2 (1992) 1–15.

Vickerstaff, S.A. and K. Parker, 'Helping Small Firms: The Contribution of TECs and LECs', *International Small Business Journal*, 13(4) (1994) 56–72.

VNO Survey (Amsterdam: The Netherlands, 1994).

Vogel, R.C. and D.W. Adams, 'Costs and Benefits of Loan Guarantee Programmes', *The Financier*, 4(1&2) (1997) 22–29.

Waddell, S.J., 'Emerging Social-economic Institutions in the Venture Capital Industry', *American Journal of Economics and Sociology*, 54(3) (July, 1995) 323–338.

Warren, L. and W.E. Hutchison, 'Success factors for high-technology SMEs: A case study from Australia', *Journal of Small Business Management*, 1(7) (July, 2000).

Webster's Pocket Business Dictionary (New Delhi: CBS Publishers, 2001).

Welch, L.S. and R. Luostarinen, 'Internationalisation: evolution of a concept', *Journal of General Management*, 14(2) (1988) 36–64.

Wells, W.F., *Venture capital decision-making*. Unpublished doctoral dissertation (Pittsburgh: Carnegie-Mellon University, 1974).

Welsch, H.P. and E.C. Young, 'The Information Source Selection Decision: The Role of Entrepreneurial Personality Characteristics', *Journal of Small Business Management*, October (1982) 49–57.

Westhead, P., M. Wright and D. Ucbasaran, 'The Internationalization of New and Small Firms: A Resource-based View', *Journal of Business Venturing*, 16 (2001) 333–358.

Wetzel, W.E., (1982) 'Risk Capital Research', in Kent, C.A., Sexton, D.L. and Vesper, K.H. (eds), *Encyclopaedia of Entrepreneurship* (Englewood Cliffs, New Jersey: Prentice-Hall Inc., 1984).

Wijewardena, H. and G.E. Tibbits, 'Factors contributing to the growth of small manufacturing firms: Data from Australia', *Journal of Small Business Management*, 37(2) (April, 1999) 88–95.

Williamson, O.E., 'Transaction-Cost Economics: The Governance of Contractual Relations', *Journal of Law and Economics*, 22 (1979) 233–261.

Wilson, Cmnd. 7503: *The Financing of Small Firms – Interim Report of the Committee to Review the Functioning of Financial Institutions* (London: HMSO, 1979).

Wilson, Cmnd. 7937: *Report of the Committee to Review the Functioning of Financial Institutions* (HMSO: London, 1980).

Winters, T.E. and D.L. Murfin, 'Venture Capital Investment for Corporate Development Objectives', *Journal of Business Venturing*, 3 (1988) 207–222.

Wolf, M. and Luce, E., *Financial Times*, 4 April (2003).

World Bank, *India: Industrial technology development project*, Staff appraisal project (Washington, DC: World Bank, 1989).

Wren, C. and D.J. Storey, 'Evaluating the Effect of Soft Business Support upon Small Firm Performance', *Oxford Economic Papers*, 54 (2002) 334–365.

Wright, M. and K. Robbie, 'Venture Capital and Private Equity: A Review and Synthesis', *Journal of Business Finance and Accounting*, 25(5/6) (1998) 521–570.

Wright, M. and K. Robbie, '*Venture Capitalists, Unquoted Equity Investment Appraisal and the Role of Accounting Information*', Occasional Paper 57, (CMBOR: University of Nottingham, 1995).

Wright, M., T. Buck and I. Filatotchev, 'Bank and Investment Fund Monitoring of Privatised Firms in Russia', *Economics of Transition*, 6(2) (1998) 361–387.

Wright, M., J. Karsai, Z. Dudzinski and J. Morovic, 'Transition and Venture Capital', *Post-Communist Economies*, 11(1) (1999) 27–46.

Wright, M., A. Lockett and S. Pruthi, 'Internationalization of Western Venture capitalists into Emerging Markets: Risk Assessment and Information in India', *Small Business Economics*, 19(1) (2002) 13–29.

Wright, M., S. Thompson and K. Robbie, 'Venture Capital and Management-Led Leveraged Buy-Outs: A European Perspective', *Journal of Business Venturing*, 7 (1992) 4–71.

Wright, M., S. Thompson and K. Robbie, 'Venture Capital and Management Led Leveraged Buy-outs: A UK Perspective' (University of Nottingham: CMBOR Research Paper, 1991).

www.adb.org

www.artquotient.com

www.evca.com

www.worldbank.org

Yap, C.S., J.Y.L. Thong and K.S. Raman, 'Effect of government incentives on computerization in small business', *European Journal of Information Systems*, 3(3) (1994) 191–206.

Zacharakis, A.L. and G.D. Meyer, 'The potential of actuarial decision models: can they improve the venture capital investment decision?', *Journal of Business Venturing*, 15 (2000) 323–346.

Zacharakis, A.L., G.D. Meyer and J. DeCastro, 'Differing perceptions of new venture failure: A matched exploratory study of venture capitalists and entrepreneurs', *Journal of Small Business Management*, 37(3) (July, 1999) 1–14.

Zahra, S.A. and J.A. Pearce, 'Board of Directors and Corporate Financial Performance: A Review and Integrative Model', *Journal of Management*, 15 (1989) 291–334.

Zarqa, M.A., 'An Islamic Perspective on the Economics of Discounting in Project Evaluation', in Ziauddin, Ahmad et al. (eds), *Fiscal Policy and Resource Allocation in Islam* (Islamabad: Institute of Policy Studies, 1983) 159–215.

Zarqa, M.A., '*Shari'a Compatible Shares: A suggested formula and rationale*', The Third International Conference on Islamic Economics (1992) 21–35.

Zelnio, R.N. and J.P. Gagnon, 'The Construction and Testing of an Image Questionnaire', *Journal of the Academy of Marketing Sciences* (Summer, 1981) 288–299.

Zender, J.F., 'Optimal Financial Instruments', *The Journal of Finance*, XLVI (5) (December, 1991) 1645–1663.

Zider, B., 'How Venture Capital Works', *Harvard Business Review*, 76(6) (December, 1998) 13–139.

Index